Designed by Dianne Schaefer/Designworks
Endleaf map and maps on pages 4 and 49 by d'Art Studio, Inc.

"On the Old Fall River Line" written by William Jerome, Andrew B. Sterling
and Harry Von Tilzer.
Copyright © 1913 Harry Von Tilzer Music Publishing Company.
Copyright Renewed (c/o The Welk Music Group, Santa Monica, California 90401).
International Copyright Secured. All Rights Reserved. Used by Permission.

Library of Congress Cataloging in Publication Data

Robinson, William F., 1946–
  Coastal New England, its life and past.

  Bibliography: p. 205
  Includes index.
  1. New England—History, Local, 2. Coasts—New
England—History. 3. Seafaring life—New England—
History. I. Title.
F4.R62   1983   974'.0094'6   83-13106
ISBN 0-8212-1553-1 (Little, Brown)

New York Graphic Society books are published by Little, Brown and Company.
Published simultaneously in Canada by Little, Brown and Company (Canada) Limited.

Printed in the United States of America

Acknowledgments

I would like to thank the great many people who aided me in my research and travels. I would particularly like to thank Mark Bloomer, Guilford, Connecticut; Eleanor L. Everson, Dresden, Maine; Dorothy Freeman, Salem, Massachusetts; John Gosson, Marine Museum at Fall River, Massachusetts; Russell Handsman, American Indian Archaeological Institute, Washington, Connecticut; Ronald Hansen, Seamen's Bethel, New Bedford; Judith Ingram, Plimoth Plantation; Jack Jackson, Boston Athenaeum; Clifford Kaye, U.S.G.S. Water Resource Service; Nathan Lipfert, Maine Maritime Museum; MMCM Gary R. Morrison, Submarine Force Library and Museum, Groton, Connecticut; Robert Oldale, Woods Hole Oceanographic Institute; Bill Peterson, Mystic Seaport Museum; Sally Pierce, Boston Athenaeum; Sally Richards, Guilford, Connecticut; Les Sirkin, Adelphi University; Harold Tantaquidgeon, Uncasville, Connecticut; and the staffs of the Bronson Museum and Plimoth Plantation.

I would especially like to thank Peter and Rita Coté of Guilford, Connecticut, and Orleans, Massachusetts; my excellent editors, Robin Bledsoe and Terry Hackford, who have been most helpful in the boiling and skimming process. I would also like to give recognition to Dianne Schaefer for her work in designing this book, making a visually beautiful balance of illustrations and text.

Finally I would like to give recognition to the expert suggestions and assistance given me by my father, Cedric L. Robinson, whose vast knowledge of American history has time and again shown me the correct paths in my research for facts.

"Any curious critic that lokkes for exactness
of phrases; or expert seamen that regards
propriety of sea-terms, may be disap-
pointed."—Reverend Francis Higginson, at
the beginning of his narrative of a 1629
voyage to New England

Contents

Samuel McIntire Arch, Salem, Mass. ◁

"Let the most absent-minded of men be plunged into his deepest reveries—stand that man on his own legs, set his feet agoing and he will infallibly lead you to water," wrote Herman Melville in his opening to *Moby Dick.* [1] To stare at the ocean is an aboriginal joy, common to all. We stand before the breaking waves and find renewal in the sea's vast realm. And to live near the shore, knowing that just beyond that line of houses, ridge of dunes, or grove of trees lies the ocean, encompasses the mind in a wordless philosophy in which the cares of man fall away before the wonders of sea and sky.

This book is the history of those New Englanders who have lived under the ocean's sway—in this fabled realm, peopled with witch-hanging Puritans, broad-shouldered whalemen, dignified sea captains, and recalcitrant Down Easters.

It would seem that there is something in the contemplative Yankee character that loves the sea. Since earliest times, the majority of New England people have preferred the seaside, with its easy avenues of nautical trade, over the rough interior landscape, where modest farming communities lay isolated in valleys and on hillsides. Even today, life hugs the shore in New England. The mass of its population lives within twenty miles of salt water, and only a handful of cities are not on harbors, or along rivers navigable to the sea.

Even far inland, many cities owe their original growth to having been on rivers navigable to the ships of past centuries. Communities whose waterfronts today witness only motorboats and an occasional oil barge were once thriving centers of the shipping trade. Hartford, far up the Connecticut River near the northern edge of the state, once gathered the upriver produce and shipped it overseas in as lively a trade as in many a saltwater harbor. Maine's state capitol at Augusta looks down across the river at its beginnings—the site of a Plymouth colony trading post and the remains of a colonial fort, both situated here because it was the farthest point to which vessels could sail up the Kennebec River.

The seemingly modest extent of New England's tidewater region is deceiving. A vessel can navigate along the shore from the Connecticut–New York border to the Canada line in a voyage of roughly 600 miles. Estuaries, navigable rivers and other indentations along the shore, however, give this region over 4,000 miles of tide line. If drawn out to straight beachfront, the shoreline would extend down the Atlantic coast and around into the Gulf of Mexico to New Orleans. With the coastline folded into countless little harbors, it is no wonder that so many New England lives intermingled with the sea.

This extensive amount of shoreline, packed into a small geographical region, combined with the fascinating variety of life that makes its history, has, unfortunately, kept most authors preoccupied with favorite individual subjects—Newport, Cape Cod, whaling, the Pilgrims, the China trade, among many. Virtually none

Introduction

A Long Island oysterman. ◁

have provided a framework within which one can understand the region's history as a chronological whole. Those works that have encompassed a broader view of the region have documented the New Englander's maritime adventures offshore, in foreign lands, and on far oceans. What has been lost in all these books has been the comprehensive feeling for the New England coast itself, and for how it has shaped the lives of those who dwelt along it down through the centuries.

It is the primary intent of this work to provide such an understanding, while still conveying a vivid enjoyment of the diversity of the people and places that form its history. The book focuses on specific locations at important eras—creating historical sketches to explore local character and events, savor particular sights, sounds, and atmosphere—and to relate these diverse times and places to each other by a narrative that, as it carries the reader down through the centuries, shows how they all have gradually coalesced to produce today's manifold image of the New England shore. Such a work will, of course, take into account the sea yarns, myths, legends, and preoccupations with life at sea; but throughout the book, the emphasis will be how these affected the quality and very nature of the life of the New England seashore dweller.

My life is like a stroll upon the beach,
As near the ocean's edge as I can go;
My tardy steps its waves sometimes
    o'erreach,
Sometimes I stay to let them overflow.

My sole employment 'tis, and scrupulous
    care,
To place my gains beyond the reach of
    tides,
Each smoother pebble, and each shell
    more rare,
Which ocean kindly to my hand confides.

I have but few companions on the shore,
They scorn the strand who sail upon the
    sea;
Yet oft I think the ocean they sailed o'er,
Is deeper known upon the strand to me.

The middle sea contains no crimson dulse,
Its deeper waves cast up no pearls to
    view,
Along the shore my hand is on its pulse,
And I converse with many a shipwrecked
    crew.

             — Henry David Thoreau,
               "The Fisher's Boy"

Coastal New England

"There is no country greater stored of good harbors than in New England."—A True Relation of the Estate of New England as it was presented to his Majesty ca. 1634.

1

The Shape of the Shore

Trees killed by the gradually rising sea level and the accompanying inland penetration of the salt marsh. Great Harbor Marsh, Guilford, Connecticut. ▷

New England meets the sea as rocky headland, sandy dune, and marshy inlet. The classic image of Maine contains granite bluffs, where pine trees root precariously above the crashing surf. On Cape Cod, large rocks are rare; the topography is sand—blown into dunes by the wind, cut into cliffs by breaking waves, or swirled into hazardous shoals by ocean currents. Along the Connecticut shore, salt marshes predominate. Tidal creeks fill and drain this amphibious region, creating one hundred miles of Yankee bayou, interspersed with a few modest headlands and beaches.

Diverse as it appears, this shoreline, from Greenwich, Connecticut, to Eastport, Maine, is unified by its geologic youth. The rocky Maine shore has yet to be undercut by the tide. The headlands still curve gradually into the surf, with few sea cliffs. Ocean forces are still destroying and reshaping Cape Cod's outline. Along the Connecticut shore of Long Island Sound, dirt cliffs overhang the farthest incursion of spring tides.

Nowhere in New England is there a stretch of shoreline older than some 20,000 years, and in many places the present shore is only 3,000 years old. This is a mere instant in the life of an earth which measures its geologic ages in millions of years. The shoreline did not assume its present character until the last Ice Age glacier, which covered all of New England some 22,000 years ago, began to melt and retreat north.

The Ice Age commenced some million years ago; winter snows did not melt and gradually the earth's water remained frozen in the great ice caps covering the cooler parts of the earth. Water that had returned to the sea each spring no longer filled the rivers in freshets, and the oceans gradually became more shallow. By the middle of the Ice Age, the global sea level had dropped 400 feet below its present height.

During the warmer interglacial periods, runoff ran to the sea across the Gulf of Maine, then an expanse of dry land. Not until the streams reached the sloping edge of the continental shelf, some one hundred miles south of present Cape Cod, did they cross the Ice Age beaches to drop into the sea.

Soil bulldozed before the glacial edge, combined with runoff silt, created the nucleus of what would become Long Island, Martha's Vineyard, and Nantucket. Then the glacial front melted back a distance, before again stabilizing, when the southward movement of the mammoth ice cap was offset by melting along its forward edge. This stabilization laid down the debris that would be shaped by ocean currents into Cape Cod.

Ultimately warmer weather gained the upper hand, and by 18,000 years ago, the ice mass was in full and speedy retreat north, across Long Island Sound. The ice front crossed from New England soil into Canada 12,000 years ago.

New England and the Gulf of Maine lay beneath a deep blanket of ice. With much of the world's water then locked up in the great ice cap, the oceans were lower. New England's shoreline lay far to the south at the edge of the Continental Shelf.

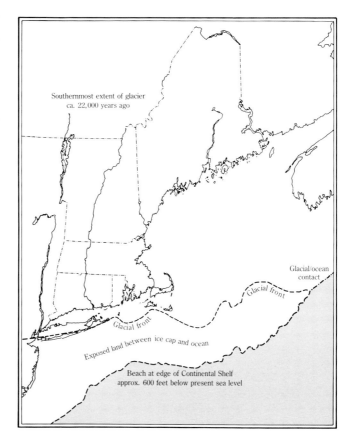

Southernmost extent of glacier
ca. 22,000 years ago

Glacial/ocean
contact

Glacial front

Glacial front

Exposed land between ice cap and ocean

Beach at edge of Continental Shelf
approx. 600 feet below present sea level

A gradually warming climate melted the ice back into Canada by this time, uncovering all of New England. Much ice was still locked up in the world's glaciers, however, and the sea level was lower than today. The southern New England shore still lay far out. Farther north, the refilling ocean flooded inland, as the land had not yet rebounded from being depressed by the ice cap's great weight. Later, the land sprang back faster than the sea filled, pushing the shore out to its present line.

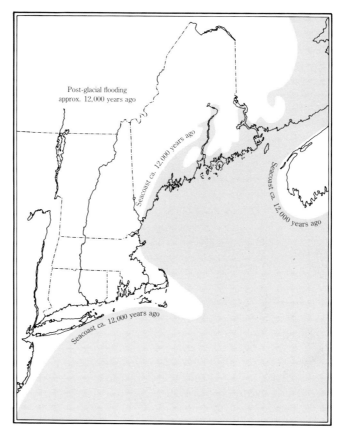

Post-glacial flooding
approx. 12,000 years ago

Seacoast ca. 12,000 years ago

Seacoast ca. 12,000 years ago

Seacoast ca. 12,000 years ago

Much of northern New England had been pushed downward hundreds of feet under the glacier's great weight. Before the land rebounded, melted ice filled the oceans and water crept up through the Gulf of Maine and, by 11,000 years ago, lay over part of the now-dry land. Southern New England, less heavily covered by ice, had been depressed only a few dozen feet, and had consequently little postglacial flooding. In fact, the shore of 11,000 years ago still lay far south of the present coast, about 150 feet below present tideline.

These figures are the findings of glacial geologists, geomorphologists (who study shorelines), and oceanographers. This last group has done extensive work aboard research vessels, dragging and dredging along New England's continental shelf. They have located a line of beach sand 100 miles south of Long Island Sound, built up as the outwash of the stabilized glacier met the ancient shoreline. Between this limit and the present shore, researchers have brought up peat from drowned salt marshes, shells of oysters, which can survive only in shallow waters, and even the teeth and bones of mastodons and mammoths. Carbon-14 dating of these items, which range in age from 9,000 to 11,000 years, pinpoints the ancient shoreline locations at specific dates. Archaeological excavations have shown that early Indians roamed New England during this time, but oceanographic research has yet to raise any human artifacts from the sea bottom.

New England today and its Ice Age shoreline. At its greatest advance south, the glacial front ran from Long Island, at left, across Martha's Vineyard and Nantucket, then made two southerly loops, where oceanographic samples of the bottom have contained reworked outwash and till. The shoreline itself lay farther south, at the edge of the Continental Shelf. ◁

Looking east from Mount Desert Island, Maine, across Frenchman Bay toward the Schoodic Peninsula. The lighthouse sits on Egg Rock, the peak of a drowned ridgeline.

Within a few thousand years the surface of northern New England began to rebound and, when the rate of land rise became faster than the filling of the seas, the coastline pushed south to reclaim flooded lands. Today 50 miles inland one can find gravel deposits that mark the old beach lines.

Finally, 3,000 years ago, the land stabilized. A cooling trend slowed the rate of ice-cap melt, and from 3,000 years ago to about 300 years ago, the seas rose only a few feet. During the last 300 years, the sea level has held steady, although there have been local rises and sinkings of coastline.

From north to south, the New England shore can be divided into six main regions.

The Upper Maine Coast.   New England's most northerly shoreline is a continuation of the rocky headlands—hills partially drowned by the postglacial sea-rise—that stretch down from the Canadian Maritimes and end near Portland. This eastern third is made up of small islands and modest inlets. The middle part forms a wide triangular indentation, whose apex is the Penobscot River. This triangle, Penobscot Bay and adjoining waters, is a maze of islands and peninsulas, which at first glance is hard to recognize as a geographical unit. Southwest of this is a region of alternating ridges and valleys that run down into the sea. As they approach tidewater, the river valleys become long deep estuaries and the ridges become peninsulas. Finally, the ridge itself dips below the water's edge and only the higher elevations of these drowned hills push out of the ocean as island chains.

The intricacy of this coastal outline, in addition to the tidal fluctuations of from ten to 30 feet, tempers the waves' attack upon the shore. Fine abrasive sand, usually common along a shore, had been washed hundreds of miles south by the glaciers. These factors have contributed to keeping the Maine coast uneroded. The result is a spectacular region. Standing upon mountains that rise from the sea—Cadillac Mountain in Acadia National Park, or the Camden Hills along Penobscot Bay—one can look down on water dotted with dark green islands. Nowhere else along America's Atlantic coastline are there views that take such sweeps of rugged grandeur.

The Coastal Plain.   South of Portland the shore flattens into sandy beaches, which continue for some 75 miles along the short New Hampshire coast and end just above Cape Ann, Massachusetts. Unlike the rest of New England's coast, flooded to its present outline by a rising sea level, this region became a flat shore plain with beautiful shallow beaches when a local uplift turned sea bottom into dry land. This plain, which extends at most only ten miles inland before ending at the rocky hills of the old postglacial shore, contains virtually all of Maine's wide, sandy beaches.

The Boston Basin.   Below the rocky peninsula of Cape Ann, the shore curves inward to form Massachusetts Bay, an ancient lowland flooded by the sea. Here drumlins, hilly deposits of ice-carried soil, begin to dot the area. Boston's harbor islands, and even the hills of the city itself, are glacial deposits. Within the history of the European settlers' occupation of Boston, dozens of these islands have been leveled by the flowing tides.

Cape Cod and the Islands.   Leaving Boston and moving farther down along the Massachusetts shore, one encounters a sandy countryside near Plymouth. Here, at the northwest corner of Cape Cod Bay, begins what the colonists called "the region of sea sand." The sand came not from the sea, but from glacial runoff, which formed these deposits, called moraines, shaping the Plymouth shore, Cape

Hurricanes

The New England shore's most dreaded foe is the hurricane. Most of these tempests spinning up from the tropics track far offshore. However, if the storm hugs the Atlantic coastline, it can smash across Long Island and into New England with the full fury of its winds. The effect is most terrible to the east of its "eye," where the northerly blow of its counterclockwise winds is augmented by the speed of the hurricane system. Here, storm waves, the wind-generated equivalent of a seismic tidal wave, smash barriers protecting marshland or pile tide upon tide in the long deep estuaries such as Narragansett Bay and Buzzards Bay. When this happens, whole cities drown.

The first hurricane recorded in New England's written history came on August 14 and 15, 1635. Sudden and violent, it arrived just before dawn, blew the roofs off houses, sank ships at sea, uprooted thousands of trees, and left those still standing with their branches so intertwined as to appear braided. The storm rushed up through Buzzards Bay, raising the sea by about 20 feet and drowning a number of Indians who had taken refuge

in trees. Farther north, the waters washed away fishermen's huts on the Isles of Shoals. One hut was later found on a Cape Cod beach.

Luckily for the early colonists, only two other hurricanes, in 1675 and 1683, came near the magnitude of the 1635 storm. During the eighteenth century 15 violent storms swept across New England, but all of them paled before the destruction wrought by the furious "Great September Gale of 1815."

This hurricane swept across the Connecticut shore at nine in the morning of September 23, 1815, with its eye centered at Old Lyme. By noon it had done its destruction and was breaking up in the Maine–New Hampshire wilderness. Worst hit was Providence, lying along the path of the storm's dreaded "eastern quarter." The winds had stalled the ebbing of high tide, and over these waters came the storm tide, building higher as it pushed up the ever-narrowing funnel of Narragansett Bay toward the apex at the little cove that formed the nucleus of waterfront Providence. First the winds hit:

The vessels there were driven from their moorings in the stream and fastenings at

The "Great Storm of 1815" at Providence. Wood engraving from a contemporary painting.

the wharves, with terrible impetuosity, toward the great bridge that connected the two parts of the town. The gigantic structure was swept away without giving a moment's check to the vessels' progress, and they passed to the head of the basin, not halting until they were high up on the bank. . . .[a]

Then came the storm wave.

Stores, dwelling houses, were seen to reel and totter for a few moments, and then plunge into the deluge. A moment later their fragments were blended with the wrecks of vessels, some of which were on their sides, that passed with great rapidity and irresistible impetuosity on the current to the head of the cove, to join the wrecks already on the land.[b]

For all its horror, only two lives were lost.

Cod, Martha's Vineyard, Nantucket, the lesser islands, and the surrounding shoal waters. Over the last few millennia, wind, currents, and tide have swept the moraines into the familiar right-arm configuration of Cape Cod. Less apparent to the modern traveler is the ancient fertility of this region. Rocks rich in minerals and nutrients were picked up by the glaciers, ground to the consistency of a fine flour, and washed out with this runoff soil. The Cape and islands all had a fine growth of vegetation until the European settlers' agriculture exposed the underlying sand.

The Banks.   Out beyond the Nantucket Shoals lies another gift of the Ice Age. When the sea level fell, runoff streams eroded much of the continental slope and the Gulf of Maine, leaving a number of plateaus, which were later submerged. These "cuestas" are better known as "The Banks": Grand, Georges, Stellwagen, Browns, and others. Here the nourishing waters of the Arctic current meet the animal life of the Gulf Stream and are sufficiently close to the sunlit surface for photosynthesis to occur. The Banks are rich in plankton and abound in fish; today they are still the world's greatest source of seafood. In colonial days they greatly influenced Europeans to settle New England. The Banks begin east of Cape Cod, extend south to the latitude of New York City and north throughout the Gulf of Maine and across Canada's Maritime Province waters, where they culminate beyond Newfoundland in the Grand Banks.

The "Province Lands," a complex of sand dunes at the tip of Cape Cod. In the distance rises the Pilgrim Memorial Monument at Provincetown.

Long Island Sound. Passing west from the Cape region, beyond the ancient lowland of Narragansett Bay, the shore now enters the protected reach of Long Island Sound. These brackish waters are lined on the south by the sandy moraines of Long Island. The northern, Connecticut, side is younger land. The glacier itself had left this northern shore scoured to bedrock. Then the rising of the postglacial sea had developed it into salt marshes and mucky clam flats. Tidal currents moving in and out of the Sound built up bars and spits across inlet mouths. The action of the small waves in the enclosed Sound had little power to break down these fragile barriers. As the glacial melt began to slacken, salt marshes formed behind the barriers. By catching, among their grass blades, mud brought in on the spring tides, and reseeding themselves on this new base, the marshes were able to rise with the increasing sea level. As the sea pushed farther inland, the marshes spread with it, covering freshwater bogs, inlets, ponds, and low-lying forest. Today, Connecticut's oldest salt marshes go down 20 feet, and extend miles inland from the present shore.

This divisional breakdown simplifies the New England shore's characteristics. In reality, salt marshes are not uncommon in Maine, and Connecticut has rocky pockets like those of Maine. Perhaps the most interesting combination of individual types of shore is found along the coast at Ipswich, Massachusetts. Here, adjoining the granite peninsula of Cape Ann, one moves toward the sea through salt marshes and sluice creeks, past drumlins rising out of the bog, to meet a shore barrier of high shifting sand dunes, beyond which is a gently sloping beach. The gradual rise of the sea floor here has created shallows where currents can easily deposit sand to form new land. A lighthouse erected 80 feet from the sea in 1840, lay by 1890 a thousand feet farther inland.

Horse Island tombolo at low tide, Guilford, Connecticut. The variety of bars, spits, and shoals that fill the shoreline give evidence of the shore's youth. Tides and currents swirl the unconsolidated shoreline drift around the many islands and headlands not yet eroded by the sea's pounding. Waves passing by an island often refract and push up a bar, connecting the island's inland side to the mainland and creating what is known as a tombolo. Some are large beaches, quite high out of the water; others, as here, are little causeways that appear only at low tide.

Marshfield Meadows, *Martin Johnson
Heade, 1878. Heade (1819–1904) devoted
much of his skill to capturing the light of
these "prairies by the sea" all along the Atlantic coast of America.*

Spectral Lights

Decaying vegetable matter buried in the salt marshes often produces methane and other gases. Under certain atmospheric conditions the gases ignite just above the ground, producing a light variously called will-o'-the-wisp, fox fire, or ignis fatuus. This phenomenon is sometimes seen along the New England shore, especially in early spring as the ground first thaws or before storms, when the barometric pressure drops. The light is sometimes a flame, ball, or cloudy blanket; the color is red or greenish-white.

The Indians often powwowed in marshes where these lights appeared, performing ceremonies in worship of these magical apparitions.

About 1690 . . . [the local Indian tribe] convened to perform . . . [the powwow] on Stratford Point, near the town. During the nocturnal ceremony, the English saw, or imagined they saw, devils rise out of the sea, wrapped in sheets of flame, and flying round the Indian camp, while the Indians were screaming, cutting, and prostrating themselves before their fiery gods.[c]

More rarely, the gas emerges out of the water, from a mud flat or ancient salt marsh drowned beneath. This might account for the report of John Winthrop, governor of the Massachusetts Bay Colony, about three men, who, while rowing across Boston Harbor one night in 1643,

saw two lights arise out of the water near the north point of the town cove, in form like a man, and went at a small distance to the town, and so to the south point, and there vanished away. They saw them about a quarter of an hour. . . . The like was seen by many a week after, arising about Castle Island.[d]

In the early nineteenth century, such lights commonly were seen off the northern point of Block Island. They appeared from half a mile to seven miles offshore, above a submerged marsh. An 1810 account gave the following description:

Its appearance is nothing different from a blaze of fire. . . . Sometimes it is small, resembling the light through a distant window, at other times expanding to the highness of a ship with all her canvas spread. When large it displays a pyramid form with three constant streams. . . . It is seen at all seasons of the year, and for the most part in the calm weather which preceeds an easterly or southerly storm.[e]

The Block Island phenomenon became known as the Palatine Light, haunting those who were said to have lured a ship of that name ashore to be wrecked (in truth, the *Palatine* dropped a number of sick passengers on the island, who were nursed to health by Block Island families). Sightings such as these were spun into rhyme by Whittier and other poets.

". . . In truth one often finds in these savages natural and political merits, which put to blush whoever is not shameless, when, in comparison, he looks at a goodly share of the Frenchmen who come into these parts."
—Père Pierre Biard, S.J., ca. 1611-1613

2
Red Men on the Ocean

The first humans to make their appearance on the North American continent crossed over from Asia about 26,000 years ago in a lull between glacial advances. Only with the final retreat of the glacial front about 10,000 years ago did they enter the New England region. These first inhabitants were migratory hunters, who followed the herds grazing on the rich tundra just beyond the glacial front.

About 8,000 years ago solitary woodland hunters, today called "Archaic" Indians, arrived. They stalked their prey in forest and at sea with flint-tipped spears, and foraged for ground nuts, roots, and berries.

The Archaics left few artifacts. One curious remnant are their many "banner stones": rocks shaped to resemble birds, seals, whales, and other animals; it remains uncertain whether their purpose was utilitarian or decorative.

When the season did not favor hunting and foraging inland, the Archaics camped along the shoreline, setting out, in boats constructed of hollowed-out logs, to hunt for seals and the smaller whales. They also caught fish in weirs—mazes of poles driven upright and interlaced with brush, into which fish swam at high tide and found themselves enmeshed when the tide fell. Unfortunately the rising sea level has drowned many of the Archaics' shore encampments. Others lie buried under many feet of salt marsh.

Not all the sites have disappeared, however. In 1913, Boston subway excavators, building a new line down Boylston Street in the Back Bay (a great mud flat that had been filled in and transformed into a fashionable neighborhood in the late nineteenth century) began to uncover decayed wooden stakes, some four to six feet high, which had apparently been driven into a layer of clay—once the surface of the flats, but now buried 16 feet below sea level.

Further excavations during the 1930s determined that the weir had extended over a two-acre area and contained an estimated 65,000 poles. Such a project must have required a large population to keep the poles and brush in repair. Tests show the weir is some 4,500 years old. Evidence of repeated attempts to keep it from being silted over by the muck suspended in the rising level of the tidewater reveal that it must have served for a long time.

Around the time of Christ, a more sophisticated culture entered the New England region from the Midwest. The Algonquians introduced pottery-making, the birchbark canoe, the bow and arrow, and crop cultivation. They soon dominated the Atlantic seaboard from the Maritime Provinces to the Carolinas. It was their descendants, by then separated into numerous tribes, that the European explorers described as "of good invention, quick understanding, and ready capacity . . . of tall stature, broad and grim visage."[1]

Much of what we know about the Algonquians, aside from archaeological evidence, has been sifted from the accounts of early European explorers and settlers.

Indian effigies of marine mammals. The smaller sculpture measures 5½ inches long and is almost surely a harbor porpoise. The large rounded forehead on the other sculpture suggests that it might represent a pilot whale, often called a blackfish. These artifacts were excavated from digs in eastern Massachusetts. ▷

A mid-nineteenth-century lithograph of Dighton Rock, which originally lay along the tidal Taunton River near Fall River. The petroglyphs have been variously credited to Portuguese, Viking, and other pre-Pilgrim explorers. Much, if not all, of the inscription is probably of Indian origin. The stone now rests in a museum at Dighton Rock State Park. ▽

This, unfortunately, has made the Indians' history a tale told by their enemies. We see them only in terms of the biases, expectations, and personal involvements of those who came to displace them. Understandably, the image given is hardly a coherent one, with Indian weaknesses and strengths variously reviled or extolled.

Even estimates of Indian population vary greatly from one colonial chronicler to another. If the colonists were touting their prowess at exterminating the native Americans, the numbers ran high; if they were seeking to entice others to cross the Atlantic for the new lands, the numbers ran low. Today, scholars feel most comfortable with a projection of from 50,000 to 75,000 Indians in New England just before the Europeans' arrival.

Most of this population was centered in the fertile lower half of New England. A modern authority locates, circa 1600, 62 inland and 10 shore villages in the Maine–New Hampshire–Vermont region, and 146 inland and 100 shore villages in the lower three states.[2]

A village typically lay beside a lake, river, or protected harbor. Along the coast, Indians chose places of good fishing. When the fish ran, many small groups would congregate together in one great encampment, storing up their catch for the leaner months. Often the shore natives had reciprocal agreements with those living in interior hunting grounds. Such annual visitation rights existed, for instance, between the Indians living above present-day Hartford, on the rich lowlands of the Connecticut River, and the coastal settlements some fifty miles to the south, where abundant clam flats lay just offshore in Long Island Sound.

In season these fishing villages of "great resort"[3] typically had a population of a few hundred. The remainder of the year, the Indians divided into small family clusters, living in huts near fields or hunting tracts allotted to them by the tribal leader. The Algonquians lived a semimigratory life, shifting their simple dwellings as season, food supply, death, disease, or enemy dictated.

Their homes, or wigwams, consisted of saplings set into the ground, usually in a circle, then bent over and lashed together to form a dome upon which were laid woven mats, bark, tree boughs, reeds, or other vegetation. Sleeping benches lined the walls within, a few embroidered mats gave decoration, and a smoky fire drove off the insects. Besides this domed style, which was found throughout the region, the long "Quonset hut" shape appeared in southern New England, and the tribes of far eastern Maine tended towards the conical tepee associated later with the nineteenth-century Plains Indians.

The residences of the sachems and sagamores were often stockaded and fortified. Some were relatively small, serving as ceremonial dwellings for the sagamore and his court, while others could shelter hundreds from the onslaught of hostile neighbors. When Miles Standish led a scouting party into the Boston region in 1621 he encountered such forts, then abandoned because of a recent sweeping invasion by Indians from the north. Standish first came upon the residence of a local sagamore:

His house was not like others, but a scaffold was largely built, with poles and planks some six feet from the ground, and the house upon that, being situated at the top of a hill. Not far from hence, in a bottom, we came to a fort built in the manner thus: there were poles some thirty or forty feet long, stuck in the ground as thick as they could be set one by another, and with these they enclosed a ring some forty or fifty feet over. A trench breast high was digged on each side; one way there was to go into it was a bridge. About a mile from hence, we came to such another, but seated on the top of a hill.[4]

Interminable squabbles igniting into intertribal warfare were a fact of life among the Indians. While some attacks, like the invasion referred to by Standish's party,

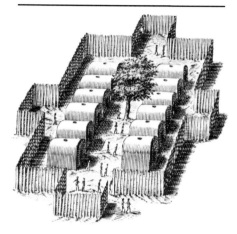

Indian fortresses, from Willem Janszoon Blaeu's map, Nova Belgica et Anglia Nova, *published in Amsterdam, 1635.*

were outright wars of conquest, for the most part, petty hostilities were the order of the day: families attacking each other for wrongs, real or imagined, against themselves or their allotted territory.

Physical hardship, also a part of the Indians' existence, required a stoic outlook. The farther one went north, leaving behind the more fertile lands of southern New England, the harsher life became. Wrote an early English trader along the Maine coast:

Ye shall have them many times take their children and bury them in the snow all but their faces for a time, to make them better endure cold, and when they are not above 2. yeares old, they take them and cast them into the Sea, like a little dogge or Cat, to learne them to swimme.[5]

From European accounts, the belligerence of the New England Indian tribes differed from above to below a line near present-day Portland, Maine, that marked the northern limit at which conditions tolerated the marginal agricultural techniques. South of this point, the Indians worked their fields in the manner described by Samuel de Champlain on a 1605 visit to the tribe at the mouth of the Saco River.

I saw their Indian corn, which they raise in gardens. Planting three or four kernels in one place, they then heap up about it a quantity of earth with shells of the signoc [horseshoe crab; farther south herring was used]. . . . Then three feet distant they plant as much more, and thus in succession. With this corn they put in each hill three or four Brazil [kidney] beans. . . . When they grow up they interlace the corn. . . . They the squaws keep the ground very free from weeds. We saw many squashes, and pumpkins, and tobacco which they likewise cultivate.[6]

Less than 50 miles north of this point, Giovanni da Verrazano, in his 1524 voyage of exploration, noted the shift in Indian aggressiveness:

The people were entirely different from the others we had seen [at a previous landing in Narragansett Bay] whom we found kind and gentle, but these were so rude and barbarous that we were unable by any signs we could make to hold communication with them. . . . They have no pulse [vegetable crops], and we saw no signs of cultivation; the land appears sterile and unfit for growing of fruit and grain of any kind. If we wished at any time to traffick with them, they came to the sea shore and stood upon the rocks, from where they lowered down by a cord to our boats beneath, whatever they had to barter, continually crying to us, not to come nearer, and instantly demanding from us that which was to be given in exchange; they took from us only knives, fish hooks and sharpened steel. No regard was paid to our courtesies; when we had nothing left to exchange with them, the men at our departure made the most brutal signs of disdain and contempt possible.[7]

Yet for all the New England shoreline Indians, both hunters and farmers, the sea played a most important part in survival. Bad weather might ruin the crops, or wolves scatter the game, but the lowly clam and mussel lay in thick beds just below high tide mark. The enduring popularity of this food can be seen from the hundreds of Indian shellheaps located up and down the coast; some, such as the great heap near Damariscotta, Maine, cover many acres to a depth of over 25 feet.

Oysters, too, lay within easy reach. Farther out, men could dive for the quahog, whose dark purple shell found use as one form of wampum. Fish ran along the shore and up the rivers to spawn. By night braves could surprise cormorants and

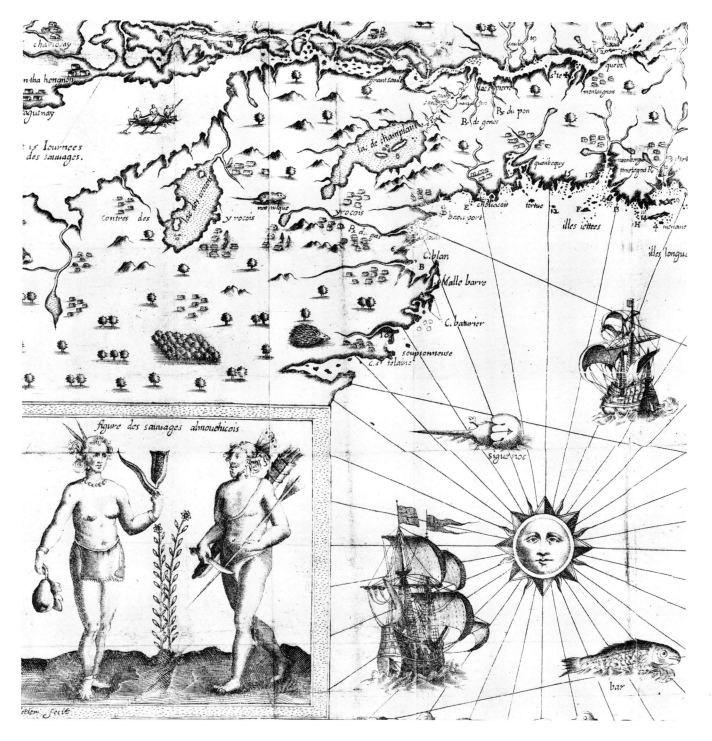

David Pelletier's drawing of "Almouchi-qua" Indians, who lived along the Kennebec River in Maine. The French explorer Champlain found them more sophisticated in language and farming than neighboring tribes. From Champlain's "Map of New France" in his Voyages, *Paris, 1612.*

seals sleeping on offshore rocks. Lobsters of intimidating size frequented the colder-watered shallows. Even the bears lumbered down to wade out for them, flicking them ashore as they did the salmon jumping the falls. Much of the sea's bounty was not eaten on the spot, but dried over smoky fires, to be mixed in a steaming succotash for a winter's meal.

With such abundance, it was only natural that the Indians were as at home upon the waters as in the forest. Adept swimmers, they did not fear paddling miles out to sea when necessary. Their watercraft were the birchbark canoe and the dugout. The former were made from the great paper birches (now decimated by European

Portrait of Ninigret II, Sachem of the Ni-
antics of present Rhode Island. He wears
the tribe's summer costume. The necklace
and headgear are of shell. Painted ca.
1681 by an anonymous American.

blights), into craft measuring up to 20 feet long and 4 feet wide, capable of carrying up to a dozen men. Paper birch did not grow south of Cape Ann, so the southern New England Indians were forced to rely on the dugout. Wrote Champlain of the Indians who inhabited the shores of Boston Harbor in 1605:

The canoes of those who live there are made of a single piece, and are very liable to turn over if one is not skillful in managing them. . . . After cutting down, at a cost of much labor and time, the largest and tallest tree they can find, by means of stone hatchets [at other times they burned the base completely through] . . . they remove the bark, and round off the tree except on one side, where they apply the fire gradually along its entire length; and sometimes they put red-hot pebble-stones on top. When the fire is too fierce, they extinguish it with a little water, not entirely, but so as the edge of the boat may not be burnt. It being hollowed out as much as they wish, they scrape it all over with stones, which they use instead of knives. [8]

Though they sometimes ventured onto the open ocean, the Indians did most of their fishing in protected bays and estuaries. In small coves and river mouths they trapped fish in weirs and hempen nets set permanently in the water, removing the catch by wading out and spearing it. Wrote Roger Williams in 1643:

The Natives take exceeding great paines in their fishing, especially in watching their seasons [seasonal runs] by night; so that frequently they lay their naked bodies many a cold night on the cold shoare about a fire of two or three sticks, and oft in the night search their Nets; and sometimes go and stay longer in frozen water. [9]

They also used hook and line to catch onshore cod. Seal and sturgeon were hunted with spear and harpoon. A few of the bolder Maine coast tribes set out after whales:

They go in company of their King with a multitude of their boats, and strike him with a bone made in fashon of a harping iron [harpoon] fastened to a rope, which they make great and strong of the bark of trees, which they veare [let] out after him; then all their boats come about him, and as he riseth above the water, with their arrow they shoot him to death; when they have killed & dragged him to shore, they call all their chief lords together, & sing a song of joy. [10]

Most tribes, however, simply waited for a benevolent spirit to cast up a disoriented Leviathan upon their shores.

The Indians' dependence on the shore brought them into early contact with European explorers. One story was that the Maine Indians first mistook a ship for a floating island, wrapped together with roots of trees and broken off from the mainland. As the European influx began, the Indians first referred to the men as "the White Foam of the Ocean," imagining they sprang from the sea and came to invade their country because these white-skinned strangers had none of their own. Soon, however, the Indians began to understand European ways, ultimately building primitive sailboats, and occasionally commandeering fishing boats. Before long, the story of the New England shore Indians became the tale of their interrelationship with the European newcomers. Their own heritage, unwritten, faded almost into oblivion. They erected no monuments (save for a few petroglyphs), and their villages were soon effaced by European settlements. Wrote Nathaniel Hawthorne, "when they disappear from the earth, their history will appear a fable, and they—misty phantoms." [11]

3

Explorers and Entrepreneurs, 1500–1620

The identity of the first Europeans to skirt the New England shore and peer from shipboard into the timbered interior will always be shrouded in legend, controversy, and nationalism. Some would have Leif Ericson founding in A.D. 1000 a colony that lasted until A.D. 1350. Others credit the same, dates and all, to Celtic monks (this achievement by a band of celibate brothers can only attest to their miraculous powers). For hundreds of years investigators have found evidence of their own ethnic heritage in glacial scratches (Viking runes) and Indian petroglyphs, lime and charcoal kilns (Celtic monks' cells), lye stones (sacrificial altars), and colonial cellar holes (Viking settlements), and the site of Leif Ericson's Vineland in every bay with a wild grape on its shore. Other theorists conjecture that French and Spanish fishermen were on the Grand Banks off Newfoundland long before Columbus convinced Queen Isabella that Asia lay only a few thousand miles across the western ocean.

The first unchallenged accounts of European contact with North America, however, came from John Cabot, who set out in 1497 with ships fitted out by the merchants of Bristol, England. After touching what is now believed to have been Newfoundland, he returned with news of reaching Asia, and of a sea "covered with fishes. . . . But Master John Cabot has set his mind on something greater; for he expects to go farther on toward . . . where he thinks all the spices of the world, and also the precious stones, originate."[1]

A year later Cabot again sailed west, but one vessel of the fleet soon returned to report that Cabot, and the rest of the fleet, had perished in a storm. It was another century before the European powers realized that Cabot had made the wrong choice to pursue jewels and spices instead of fish.

English ships and those of other nations soon joined in exploring North Atlantic waters but found few marvels, save the great fishing banks where the abundance of cod sometimes stayed the ships' movement. Although official "voyages of discovery" were few during the first quarter of the sixteenth century, their reports always spoke of the large number of English, Spanish, French, and Portuguese boats fishing the waters of Newfoundland's Grand Banks.

Although the Grand Banks lie relatively far from New England shores, the area prompted further explorations, which located good fishing on the lesser banks—Georges, Stellwagen, Browns, and Jeffreys—off Cape Cod and in the Gulf of Maine, and the abundant grounds in the shoal waters off Penobscot Bay. Understandably, the fishermen were reticent about publicizing the source of their wealth, and we see glimpses of them only through an occasional court record of a conflict brought to the home country for resolution.

The first documented visit to the shores of New England was the 1524 journey by Verrazano, sent out with a crew of 50 by the French king François I to discover

a route to "the happy shores of Cathay."[2] Verrazano made his New World landfall near the Carolinas, then sailed north, charting the shore, meeting Indians, and looking for a passage through to Asia. By April 1524, his ship, *La Dauphine,* had rounded the eastern end of Long Island and entered New England waters. Passing Block Island, "having many hills covered with trees, and well peopled, judging from the great number of fires which we saw all around its shores,"[3] they sailed on to the mainland and entered Narragansett Bay,

where we found a very excellent harbor [Newport]. Before entering it, we saw about twenty small boats full of people, who came to our ship, uttering cries of astonishment. . . . By imitating their signs, we inspired them in some measure with confidence, so that they came near enough for us to toss to them some little bells and glasses, and many toys, which they took and looked at, laughing, and then came on board without fear. . . . This is the finest looking tribe, and the handsomest in their costumes, that we have found in our voyage. . . . Their women are of the same form and beauty, very graceful, of fine countenances and pleasing appearance in manners and modesty; they wear no clothing except a deer skin [breechcloth] ornamented. . . . We saw upon them several pieces of wrought copper, which is more esteemed by them than gold . . . yellow being the color especially disliked by them; azure and red are those in highest estimation by them . . . they do not value or care to have silk or gold stuffs, or other kinds of cloth, nor implements of steel or iron. . . . They came off to the ship with a number of their little boats, with their faces painted in diverse colors, showing us real signs of joy, bringing us of their provisions, and signifying to us where we could best ride in safety with our ship, and keeping with us until we cast anchor. We remained among them fifteen days.[4]

Verrazano's party explored much of Narragansett Bay and the surrounding countryside.

Among these islands any fleet, however large, might ride safely, without fear of tempests or other dangers. . . . We often went five or six leagues [15 to 20 miles] into the interior, and found the country as pleasant as it is possible to conceive, adapted to cultivation of every kind, whether of corn, wine or [olive] oil; there are open plains twenty-five or thirty leagues in extent entirely free of trees . . . and of so great fertility, that whatever is sown there will yield an excellent crop. On entering the woods, we observed that they might all be traversed by an army ever so numerous.[5]

The last sentence refers to the lack of underbrush due to the Indians' practice of annually burning the forest undergrowth.

In all, Verrazano painted a glowing account of the Wampanoag Indians and their homeland. "There is no doubt that they would build stately edifices if they had workmen as skillful as ours, for the whole seacoast abounds in shining stones, crystals, and alabaster."[6] Verrazano then continued north, encountering the rude Abnaki and discovering Penobscot Bay before ending the first contact by Europeans with New England soil.

Within a few months after Verrazano's return, the King of Spain also sent a party in quest of the Northwest Passage. Under Esteban Gómez, they crossed to the Canadian Maritimes and sailed south along the Maine coast, across Massachusetts and Cape Cod bays, around Cape Cod, and eventually all the way to Florida. While Gómez's report has been lost, his discoveries are reflected in later maps, and in travel compilations that refer to his voyage along the "Cod Fish Continent."[7]

For the ensuing half-century, New England, like much of the Atlantic coast, received little attention. European interests lay either in the north, for its Grand Banks fishing, St. Lawrence River fur trade, and possible Northwest Passage; or in the south, for its Aztec and Incan treasures. During this lull New England remained a land of legend, the most fantastic, echoed in both seaport tavern and royal court, being that the land held an alabaster-towered golden city called Norumbega.

By the 1580s, such lures to exploration blended with a new interest by the English in colonizing the New World. A lifelong advocate and promoter of exploration, Richard Hakluyt, wrote in 1584:

Through our long peace and seldom sickness [it had been 20 years since a plague had laid waste England's population] . . . we are grown more populous than ever heretofore; so that now there are . . . so many, that they can hardly lie one by the other, nay they are ready to eat up one another; yea many thousands of idle persons are within this realm, which, having no way to be set to work . . . often fall to pilfering and thieving and other lewdness.[8]

Many such could be shipped, willing or not, to the New World. A trade would then arise, "employing them in England in making a thousand trifling things."[9]

Colonizing the Atlantic shore would free England from dependence on trade with all-powerful Catholic Spain, "where our men are driven to fling their [Protestant] bibles and prayer books into the seas, and to forswear and renounce their religion and conscience"[10] each time they traded with the Spanish. Moreover, British colonies would endanger Spanish treasure ships following the Gulf Stream home.

Another promoter, Edward Hayes, called for a colony somewhere between latitudes of 40° and 44° (Philadelphia to Penobscot Bay). Such a northerly location would induce the Grand Banks fishermen to use it as a home port, avoiding the necessity of extra provisions to cross the ocean home. Footholds among the Indians would first be gained by force of arms and then by fortifications, which

Norumbega, detail from Norumbega et Virginia, 1597, *by Corneille Wytfliet. The coastline depicted here runs from the Maine coast at the north, down to a cape which combines Cape Cod with the Entrance to Chesapeake Bay.* ▷

Norumbega: The Crystal-Towered City

According to legend, Norumbega stood near the mouth of a large river and (like El Dorado of South America) held the wealth of a highly civilized Indian race, who grew their own cotton, and whose kingdom, also called Norumbega, stretched the whole length of the Atlantic coast. This capital city was a great metropolis of shining towers, palace domes, and crystal-columned mansions where even the lowliest walked in ermine and gold.

The Norumbega story probably grew from a combination of Verrazano's account of "Refugio," the Narragansett Bay region with its genteel Indians, and the Penobscot Bay region, which appeared prominently on the maps made from the reports of Gómez's 1524 expedition, where even today the Abnaki Indians in Old Town use the word *norumbega* for a stretch of quiet water between rapids.

By the 1540s, virtually every cartographer of the New World depicted in the New England region the shining towers of Norumbega/Aranbega/Arembec/Bega/Oranbega/Anorumbec. Even Mercator, in his great world map, saw fit to include this crystal city.

In 1556 the legend gained more weight when a French expedition reported finding the town of Norumbegue, and, near it, Indians who were richly furred, friendly, and who spoke a language akin to Latin.

The Norumbega legend reached its zenith in the 1568 tale of David Ingram, a British sailor. Ingram had been part of a fleet of "Sea Hawks" defeated by Spanish forces while marauding along the Gulf of Mexico. With Spanish vessels in pursuit, many of their vessels sunken, and supplies woefully inadequate to provide for the survivors, one hundred of the English sailors "elected" to be put ashore. The rest of the decimated fleet limped back to England, leaving the band to face the New World wilderness. Most were never heard of again, although a few survived decades of Spanish enslavement in Mexico. Ingram and two companions headed inland, walking north for three months to reach the St. Lawrence River and the safety of a French trading ship.

Once the travelers were back in England, everyone flocked to hear the account of their travels. Ingram's tale, however, soon merged fact and fancy. He told of wild horses, red sheep, buffalo herds of such size that the earth shook in their passing, and "a beast like unto a horse, saving he had two long tusks,"[a] which Ingram once escaped by climbing a tree (still the accepted procedure for those faced by angry descendants of Ingram's moose). He also reported seeing "in small running brooks diverse pieces of gold, some as big as his finger, others as big as his fist."[b] Had he pocketed a few, he might have been saved from supporting himself by recounting this well-embroidered tale.

The high point of Ingram's chronicle was his visit to the Indian city of "Bega," somewhere along the New England coast. The native inhabitants, he said, were fabulously wealthy. Their city, "a half mile long"[c] (a mile in his later accounts), "hath many streets far broader than any street in London."[d] The citizens decorated themselves with gold, silver, and pearls. Ingram found the king of Bega a likable fellow, who was carried through the streets in a gemstone-encrusted chair of crystal and silver. The city itself was a complex of domed edifices, massively pillared in gold, silver, and crystal.

In an era when the Spanish were carrying home Aztec and Incan treasures by the fleetload, such a tale did not seem as preposterous as it does today.

In 1583, Sir Humphrey Gilbert, nobleman and soldier, set out with five ships "going for the discovery of Norumbega."[e] As one of the party wrote:

We were in number in all about 260 men: among whom we had of every faculty good choices, as Shipwrights, Masons, Carpenters, Smithes, and such like, requisite to such an action: also Minerall men and Refiners. Besides, for solace of our people, and allurement of the Savages, were provided of Music in good variety: not omitting the least toys, as Morris dancers, Hobby horses, and manylike conciets to delight the savage people, whom we intended to win by all fair means possible.[f]

The expedition failed and Gilbert went down in a storm while returning home.

The Norumbega fable soon was laid to rest as explorers like Champlain charted the New England coast. From their unembroidered reports came a true picture of the region's character.

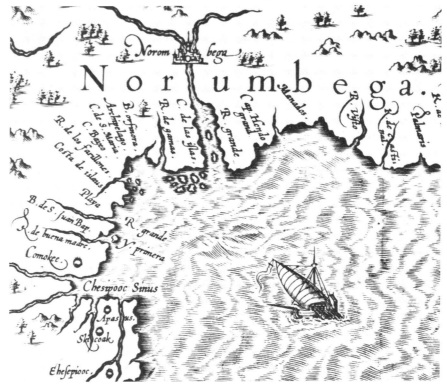

Gosnold at Cuttyhunk, *Albert Bierstadt,*
1858.

"shall keep the natural people of the country in obedience and good order. . . .
We shall purchase our own safety, and make ourselves lords of the whole."[11]

For all the ills besetting late sixteenth-century England—overpopulation, a
stagnant economy, hindrance of overseas trade, Spain's monopoly of New World
treasures, et cetera—"this Norumbega (if it be thought so good) offereth the
remedy."[12]

As it happened, some of England's problems were solved before colonization
took place: in 1588 the Royal Navy defeated the Spanish Armada off the British
Isles. The way now lay clear for England to rise as a sea power and to establish
colonies without maritime interference.

At the same time that scattered attempts at a Virginia colony were being made,
New England was seeing a bustling business in ships of all nations coming along
the coast to trade. In 1602, Bartholomew Gosnold, eight sailors, twelve "adventurers," and twelve intended colonists, arrived off the Maine coast. Here they
were greeted by "a Biscay shallop [a small fishing vessel] with sails and oars,
having eight persons in it, whom we supposed to be Christians distressed. But
approaching us nearer, we perceived them to be savages."[13] The Indians—one of
whom wore a waistcoat, breeches, stockings, shoes, and hat—spoke a smattering
of European words and drew a map of the coast, pointing out the location of the
Newfoundland fisheries.

Gosnold's ship then headed south, rounding a peninsula that the voyagers named
"Cape Cod." In late May they began to set up a fort on Cuttyhunk Island, last of
the chain of islands dividing the waters off Martha's Vineyard from Buzzards Bay.
The site's attraction was its relative remoteness from the Indian-populated mainland and the discovery of an acre-sized island in the middle of a lake not far from
the island's shore: the perfect spot for a fortification.

When Gosnold weighed anchor, his ship filled with sassafras (then considered an excellent remedy for venereal disease), the "planters" declined to be left behind, because of hostile incidents with Indians.

As it turned out, Gosnold had made an illegal voyage. When his glut of sassafras drove down prices in England, Raleigh investigated, found Gosnold had infringed on his patent, and seized the cargo. To recoup his losses and appease Raleigh, Gosnold published an account of his voyage (one wonders how many other New World voyages went undetected and unreported) and gave a glowing picture of the knight's patent:

This main [land] is the goodliest continent that ever we saw, promising more by far than we any way did expect: for it is replenished with fair fields, and in them fragrant flowers, also meadows, and hedged in with stately groves. . . . I am persuaded that in the months of March, April, and May, there is upon the coast better fishing, and in great plenty, as in Newfoundland. [14]

Soon fishermen were added to the traders and explorers off the New England coast.

In 1604, the French came down from their well-established trading locations along the St. Lawrence, and settled on an island in the Saint Croix River, now the international boundary between Maine and New Brunswick. From here reconnaissance parties under Samuel de Champlain sailed as far south as Nantucket Sound, mapping, exploring, and making contact with the Indians. Champlain's efforts produced excellent charts of various harbors, later to become Gloucester, Boston, Plymouth, and Chatham (on Cape Cod). He also investigated the Penobscot region "which many pilots and historians call Norumbegué. . . . I have observed . . . none of the marvels there which some persons have described," [15] only bad weather, a few huts, and natives quite primitive compared to others along the coast. So ended the Norumbega myth.

Over the next fifteen years, the true character of the New England region slowly emerged as explorers like Henry Hudson, Adriaen Block, John Smith, and others with names less familiar to us sailed and mapped the coast.

Champlain's men attacked by Indians, Stage Harbor, Cape Cod. In 1606 the French explored down from Canada as far south as the elbow of Cape Cod. Here at present-day Chatham, they were attacked by Nauset tribesmen when the Indians realized the French were planning a permanent settlement there. A. The Frenchmen are attacked as they bake bread. C. Indians burning the French corpses. P. Cedar Swamp Brook.

Explorers and Entrepreneurs, 1500–1620

During this period two more unsuccessful attempts were made to plant a colony in New England (the French had moved north out of St. Croix after a year of fog and privation). In England, the task of colonization had passed from Raleigh to two groups of "merchant adventurers." In 1607 both groups sent ships to found plantations in America: the London backers chose Jamestown, Virginia, and the Plymouth-Bristol-Exeter backers chose a site on Maine's Kennebec River.

The northern expedition arrived in August 1607, and the hundred men set up a fort atop a hilly peninsula at the river's mouth. The attempt lasted only until the next spring. Everything had gone wrong. The winter was exceptionally cold. The leader, George Popham, had died. The storehouse burned. The expectations of the adventurers and gold seekers who predominated in the group had fallen empty. The group abandoned their fort, with its fifteen homes, church, and burned storehouse, to return home in defeat.

The Popham Colony's failure was a bitter blow in the homeland. Wrote one contemporary, "The arrival of these people in England, was wonderful discouragement to all the first undertakers [original backers] in so much as there was no more speech of settling any other Plantation in those parts for a long time after."[16] The fort lay abandoned, and a visitor in 1660 could find only "Rootes and Garden hearbes and some old walles."[17]

When the French in Canada learned of the English failure, they erected a settlement in 1613 along the deep glacial fjord of Somes Sound, on Mt. Desert Island, in Maine. A few months later, however, an English ship on patrol out of Virginia was greeted by Indians of that area with such embellished flourishes and bows that the sailors immediately recognized their origin in French courtly manners. Duping the well-intentioned Indians to betray the French location, the English quickly put the settlement to flight, thus ending the last attempt at colonizing New England until the arrival of the *Mayflower.*

To restrict the history of New England during this period, 1497–1619, to a chronicle of the failures to establish a permanent European population does not truly reflect the story. Trading posts and fishing stations, though individually short-lived, were a familiar seaboard feature by the start of the seventeenth century. Most of them were scattered along the coast of Maine, where hides were more plentiful inland, and fish offshore, than elsewhere in New England. Ships might pull into any harbor containing an Indian encampment and set up trade for a few weeks. At better locations traders erected stockades for a season.

Fishing stations, with their sleeping huts, warehouses, fish-drying racks, or flakes, and repair yards, appeared on islands and defensible peninsulas. Many such outposts existed well into the colonial period, only to disappear when prosecuted out by those with patents to the land. The best-documented encampments all existed in Maine: on Monhegan Island in 1610, Damariscove (Damariscotta) and Pemaquid Point in 1614, and Winter Harbor and Biddeford Pool in 1616. How permanent they were has always been conjectural. Some were occupied in the warmer months, then abandoned; others may have had a year-round crew to guard the stores and buildings. Merchant adventurers tried sending crews for winter fishing, but were forced to pay the men extreme rates.

John Smith, famed for his leadership of the Jamestown Colony, was also an enthusiastic promoter of New England's commercial promise:

In the month of April, 1614, with two ships from London, of a few merchants, I chanced to arrive in New England, a part of America at the isle of Monhiggan [Monhegan]. . . . Our plot was there to take whales, and make trials of a mine of gold and copper. If those failed, fish and furs were then our refuge, to make ourselves savers howsoever.[18]

Site of St. George's Fort, Popham's Saga-dahoc Colony of 1607.

Flaking fish. The fishermen built seasonal encampments by felling trees for their framework, then making a shelter with the sails brought in from their vessels. They split wide planks, upon which they laid the fish to dry. ▷

NEW ENGLAND

The most remarqueable parts thus named by the high and mighty Prince CHARLES. Prince of great Britaine.

These are the Lines that shew thy Face, but those That shew thy Grace and Glory, brighter bee: Thy Faire-Discoueries and Fowle-Overthrowes Of Salvages, much Civilliz'd by thee Best shew thy Spirit, and to it Glory Wyn. So, thou art Brasse without, but Golde within.

If so; in Brasse (too soft Smiths Acts to beare) I fix thy Fame, to make Brasse Steele out weare. Thine, as thou art Virtues John Davies Heref:

THE PORTRAICTUER OF CAPTAYNE JOHN SMITH · ADMIRALL OF NEW ENGLAND ⋈

A Scale of Leagues

Observed and described by Captayn John Smith 1614

John Smith's map of New England, the first correct map of the shoreline. "I have had six or seven plats of the northern parts, so unlike each to other, and most so differing from any true proportion or resemblence of the country, as they did me no more good than so much waste paper, though they cost me more." *A Description of New England, London, 1616.*

They soon found the whales not to be the kind that yielded oil and bone. The promise of gold prospecting, admits Smith, was simply to attract backers. They turned to fishing, although by June the nets began to come up empty; they had some little success in trading furs, but the competition was rough:

Eastwards our commodities [trade items] were not esteemed, [the Indians] were so near the French [in Canada] who affords them better; and right against us in the main was a ship of Sir Francis Popham's, that had there such acquaintance, having many years only used that port [Pemaquid], that the most part [of the trade] were had by him. And forty leagues westward [Boston Harbor] were two French ships, that had made there a great voyage by trade.[19]

Had Captain Smith looked even farther, that summer of 1614, he would also have discovered, among other activities, Englishmen trading at Damariscove, Maine, an English ship hugging the shore, fishing and kidnapping Indians, another English ship apparently searching for a gold mine on Martha's Vineyard, and Adriaen Block exploring Long Island Sound for the Dutch.

Despite the uncertainties of his own venture, Smith praised this "New England": "of all the four parts of the world I have yet seen, not inhabited, could I have but means to transport a colony, I would rather live here than anywhere."[20] In 1616, he published a *Description of New England,* promoting the colonization scheme put forth by Hakluyt thirty years before, stressing settlement by common working people, in contrast to the current idea of noblemen opening trading outposts.

And here are no hard landlords to rack us with high rents. . . . If he have nothing but his hands, he may set up his trade, and by industry quickly grow rich . . . and fishing before your doors, may every night sleep quietly ashore, with good cheer and what fires you will, or, when you please, with your wives and family.[21]

Smith believed that fishing would be the true support of the settlements, reminding the prospective colonists:

And never could the Spaniard, with all his mines of gold and silver, pay his debts, his friends and army half so truly as the Hollanders still have done by this contemptible trade of fish.[22]

But he differed from earlier visitors in his lack of enthusiasm for the Maine coast:

All this coast to Pennobscot, as far as I could see eastward of it, is nothing but such high craggy, cliffy rocks and stoney isles, that I wondered such great trees could grow on such hard foundations. It is a country [rather] to affright than delight one; and how to describe a more plain spectacle of desolation or more barren, I know not.[23]

Smith's proposal for the colonization of New England did not treat the real question of how to deal with the Indians. Yet even as Englishmen were reading his tract, the Indian problem was resolving itself in a most appalling way.

In 1616, a French trading ship in Boston Harbor was taken by the local Indians, who burned the ship and slaughtered all but five of the crew. These became slaves, distributed to the most important sagamores for sport and menial labor. Although recent historians credit shipborne rats as the cause, tradition names these five captives as carriers of a plague (possibly smallpox), which proved fatal to the Indians. Soon virtually every Indian village within thirty miles of the shoreline from Cape Cod to the Portland region fell to the sickness. Wrote one contemporary, "They died in heaps, as they lay in their houses; and the living that were able to shift for themselves would run away,"[24] leaving the dead unburied. To the Pilgrims, it was "a new found Golgotha."[25] Years later, "Their skulls and bones were found in many places lying still above the ground, where their houses and dwelling had been. A very sad spectacle to behold."[26]

Historians estimate that of the tribes afflicted, only one member in twenty survived. A war among the Maine tribes depopulated that region as well. As the Pilgrims soon to arrive, were to say, God had cleared their path with a "wonderful plague."[27]

4

The Foothold Colony: Plymouth, 1620–1630

"All things to do, as in the beginning of the world"—Cotton Mather, *Magnalia Christi Americana*, 1702

Then came the Pilgrims, about a hundred strong. English religious Separatists and their servants, these "Pilgrims" (the word did not actually come into use until after the American Revolution) deplored Stuart absolutism, decried the "idolatrous" religious conventions of the Church of England, and refused to comply with the rules of conformity dictated by the Church of England. Some had escaped to Holland for a time but now wanted to leave because they saw their children rapidly assuming Dutch ways. As a last resort, they had struck a bargain with some English merchants: in trade for passage to America and regular supplies, these pious shopkeepers would establish a plantation in the New World and repay their debts with fish and beaver pelts.

> *Let Amsterdam send forth her brats,*
> *Her fugitives and renegates . . .*

went a popular ballad,

> *Let all the putrifidean sect,*
> *I mean the counterfeit elect,*
> *All zealous bankrups, punks [whores] devout,*
> *Preachers suspended, rabble rout,*
> *Let them send all, and out of hand*
> *Prepare to go for New England,*
> *To build a new Babel strong and sure*
> *Now called a "Church unspotted pure."*[1]

They made landfall off the sand cliffs of Cape Cod in mid-November 1620. Looking on these heights, then "wooded to the brink of the sea," and not stripped of their thin topsoil as today, they must have ached to stand upon the firm soil after weeks at sea.

Their agreement with the merchant adventurers, however, called for settlement farther south, near the Hudson River, so they set sail in that direction until thwarted by the submerged bars of Nantucket Shoals.

Returning north, they rounded the Cape's tip, taking shelter off present-day Provincetown, then called "Milford Haven" on John Smith's map.

The voyagers could not have dropped anchor off a more inhospitable region of the New England coast. Wide shallows forced those going ashore to wade through icy waters for some distance. The wild and fantastic dunes of the Cape's tip offered neither edibles, water, nor game. Parties scouting south found little save a European fisherman's grave and some stored Indian corn. No promising settlement sites were to be found, "and every day we saw whales playing hard by us, of

The Mayflower II, *docked at Plymouth. A reconstruction of a typical vessel of the original* Mayflower's *design.* ▷

Rainy day at Plimoth Plantation.

which in that place, if we had instruments and means to take them, we might have made a rich return, which to our great grief we wanted."[2]

Demoralized, and beset with racking coughs, the Pilgrims decided to forgo moving farther north (to what would become Ipswich), where fishermen had reported seeing miles and miles of land cleared by the Indians. Instead, they followed the *Mayflower* captain's command to head west across the bay, where a few modest hills broke the monotonous horizon marking the location of a shallow harbor, named "Plymouth" on John Smith's map.

Here they settled, and (as the *Mayflower* wintered in deeper waters over a mile offshore) constructed rude huts, "as full of beds as they could lie by one another."[3] Disease soon claimed half the hundred-odd passengers, enfeebled from malnutrition and depression, sometimes at a rate of two or three a day. Of the survivors, only a half dozen had the strength to bury the victims by night in graves that they camouflaged, lest the Indians realize their helpless condition.

In time, friendly contacts with the Indians gave the Pilgrims the skills to live in a manner which was to become basic to all colonial New England shore dwellers.

If fresh meat be wanting to fill up our dish,
We have carrots and pumpkins and turnips and fish;

Coastal New England

And is there a mind for a delicate dish?
We repair to the clam banks and there we catch fish,
Instead of pottage and puddings and custards and pies,
Our pumpkins and parsnips are common supplies;
We have pumpkins at morning and pumpkins at noon,
If it was not for pumpkins we should be undone[4]

went a song reputedly written by a Pilgrim in those first lean years. Though the Pilgrims never had any success with their attempts at fishing—their hooks being the wrong size, their nets shoddy, their fishing craft having sunk in a storm—the colony did gather much bounty from the sea. They raked the clam flats at low tide and gathered thatch for roofs from the salt marsh; salt hay fed their cattle and sheep, and herring running up the small streams to spawn provided fertilizer for their crops.

This ability to fall back on the resources of the shoreline allowed the Pilgrims time to spend making and gathering supplies for the repayment of their original debt (assumed by a number of colonists in 1626 in trade for tax rights and monopolies on certain exports). They offered payment in furs (obtained from the Indians in exchange for Pilgrim-raised corn), clapboards hewn for a relatively unforested England, and that contemporary wonder drug, sassafras.

Life at Plymouth in those early years must have been a most sad endurance. Frivolity was not a part of the separatists' ethic, and those who tried to liven the dull existence of sun-bleached board, blowing sand, and wood smoke with innocent revels, as did some youths attempting to play ball on a Christmas Day, were quickly rebuked. The little village itself, a huddle of mud-brush-timber dwellings, set on a slope overlooking the sea, must have felt more attachment to the ocean across which its inhabitants once came than to the vast and empty chaos of a continent just over the crest of the hill behind it. At tideline could be found good sustenance and materials for shelter. As the little band went about their daily tasks, they must have gazed longingly across Cape Cod Bay, usually a calm protected flat water, with ever the hope that a sail might suddenly whiten the far blue, bringing news and small luxuries from their old homeland.

Over the next decade, more colonists arrived, some to swell the little colony of Plymouth, still clustered around a single stockaded street; others to move north, toward the fabled richness of Massachusetts Bay. Historians today estimate that by 1630, about 300 Europeans lived along the Massachusetts shore (most by Plymouth), and another 900 could be found along the coasts of what are today New Hampshire and Maine.[5]

The majority of these 900 colonists were not Separatists. Many were adventurers, ready to trade with the Indians for whatever they wanted, including guns, shot, and powder; still others were men of business, overseeing the work of their hired laborers—fishermen, woodchoppers, and traders. Still more were Anglican gentry, hoping to stem a feared Puritan control of New England.

The Anglicans first tried to settle near present-day Weymouth, south of Boston, in 1623, but soon dispersed to set up individual homes among the islands and peninsulas of Boston Harbor. We know little about their style of living, although it is set down that a number lived in homes stockaded like Indian forts, and that William Blaxton or Blackstone, an educated bachelor, brought a copious library to the house he built on the western slope of what would one day become Boston's Beacon Hill. Here he enjoyed his books in a quiet solitude, broken only by the frequent company of visiting Indians. Basic subsistence for these "Old Planters" was most likely easier than for the debt-ridden Pilgrims, as the Massachusetts Bay shores had, before pestilence and invasion, supported great tribes of Indians with crops, shellfish, fish, and game.

In the same year the Reverend John White's party tried to establish a permanent fishing and farming settlement near Gloucester on Cape Ann. Until this time, shore fishing by Europeans had been a seasonal affair, with almost everyone returning to the home country when the holds were filled. A dozen men stayed over at Gloucester with the intention of farming when the fish did not run. The plan soon fell through, for neither farmer nor fisherman understood the other's craft. Wrote White:

First, that no sure fishing place in the land is fit for fishing; at least near the shore; and, secondly, rarely a fisherman will work any land; neither are husbandmen fit for fishermen, but with long use and experience.[6]

However, fishing communities did take hold farther north. The important locations were Portsmouth, Saco, Cape Elizabeth, Pemaquid, Damariscove, and Monhegan Island. All had been long used for fishing stations and flake fields, and, by about 1625, they became all-year communities.

Around 1630, the population of the New England coast changed, virtually overnight. In England, the conflict between the Puritan and the Crown factions in government drove many Puritans overseas seeking a "Bible Commonwealth" in New England. They came in the thousands—city merchants, skilled craftsmen,

Plimoth Plantation and Cape Cod Bay. "The houses are constructed of clapboards, with gardens also enclosed behind and at the sides with clapboards, so that their houses and courtyards are arranged in good order." — Isaack de Rasieres, Dutch trading agent, reporting on his journey from Manhattan to Plymouth in October 1627.

Coastal New England

Interior of a wigwam, reconstruction of the first dwellings (ca. 1630) of the Salem colonists.

and the most lowly indentured servants. Within a decade, some 20,000 people had made the crossing to populate Massachusetts and Connecticut. Although the vanguard who came in 1630 had been caught unprepared for the harsh New England winter—people found shelter in frail tents, wigwams, and even barrels—nevertheless, these first groups fared better than had their Pilgrim predecessors. They quickly learned from the Pilgrims and Old Planters how to get along in this new world. As John Smith once observed, "It is not the work for everyone to plant a Colony; but when a house is built, it is no hard matter to dwell in it."[7]

The newly arrived Puritans soon jostled the Old Planters from the best locations along Massachusetts Bay. The Pilgrims to the south at Plymouth fared better than these latter-day Puritans. The settlers near Massachusetts Bay had money to buy Pilgrim produce. The Pilgrims quickly moved out into remote farms, their "Great Lots," to raise cattle, sheep, and goats, which they then herded north along the sandy coastal path to sell to the Puritans pouring into Boston. At

The Foothold Colony: Plymouth, 1620–1630

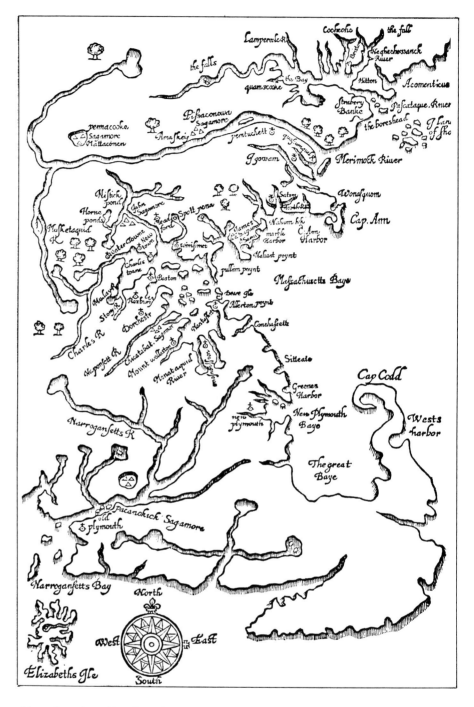

William Wood's map of New England, 1634, showing settlements from Newport to York. Many Viking adherents have seized upon the location of "Old Plymouth" along Narragansett Bay as evidence for a pre-Pilgrim settlement. The reason for the "Old" and "New" locations has never been fully explained.

this point, the old unity of the Plymouth Colony dissolved. Most of those who remained in the village set sail ten years later for the outer Cape lands, which had often shimmered from across Cape Cod like mirages above the horizon. The little Plymouth stockade, symbol of their first ten years of hardship, soon lay almost abandoned.

". . . and join ourselves together in one entire plantation and be helpful each to the other in any common work according to every man's ability."—From the Guilford Covenant of June 1639

5

Deepening Roots: Life in Four Colonial Settlements

Most of the English settlers who began coming to New England in the 1630s arrived with quite specific plans. They had no vague thoughts of adapting to the character of this New World, but instead intended to re-create their Old World existence. Some were farmers, some coastal fishermen, some merchants, and some craftsmen. The stories of four communities—Guilford, Connecticut; Pemaquid, Maine; the Isles of Shoals, New Hampshire; and Marblehead, Massachusetts—epitomize the first part of New England's colonial era and the attempts of the colonists to transform their New World into the Old. The history of these settlements also shows how, with time, these efforts slowly faded in the face of new and exciting lives offered by the unique resources of this "New England."

GUILFORD, CONNECTICUT: A COLONIAL FARMING TOWN

In the fall of 1639 a group of approximately 25 Puritan families and their servants, all from the rural countryside near London, arrived to found the town of Guilford along placid Long Island Sound. The location chosen was a modest inlet at the confluence of some small tidal streams, where marsh-webbed fingers of land extended outward into rocky shallows and mud flats. Like many early settlers, the Guilford planters had no thoughts about making a living from the sea as merchant-sailors or fishermen. Setting up their homes on these peninsular "necks," they re-created the rural life they had left in England. For such farmers the ideal terrain was like that of Ipswich, Massachusetts: connected to the sea by a small river, where marsh-surrounded "islands" rise out of the oozy bogs, "abounding in fish and flesh, meads and marshes, plain ploughing-ground, and no rattlesnakes."[1] Ipswich's fame had reached England long before the *Mayflower* sailed.

For Ipswich, Guilford, and other agrarian communities, settling by a good harbor or the open ocean usually brought more hazards than benefits, exposing their little villages to marauding pirates or enemy warships. On the other hand, a just treaty with the local Indians would protect them from inland threats, enabling them to leave their fortified peninsulas for waterfall mill sites farther up salt rivers where fresh water dropped into brackish tidal meanders. Here they could live relatively safe from sea-borne threats, protected by the shoaling flats offshore.

Guilford's greatest attraction was its "sea-meadows," the marshes, whose black grass (salt hay) could be harvested each year to provide for wintering livestock. These "low meadows" gave as much uncultivated sustenance as did the clam flats lying off the watery edge. Wrote one early chronicler:

The lowest ground be the marshes, over which every full and change [tides at full and new moon] the sea flows. These marshes be rich ground and bring plenty of hay,

of which the cattle feed and like as if they were fed with the best upland hay. . . . I dare not think England can show fairer cattle either in winter or summer than is in those parts . . . that the richest voyagers that shall venture thither [with their herds] need not fear want of fodder.[2]

For the next three hundred years, shore farmers would make their annual mowing of the "medders." In late summer, when the coarse grass became most nutritious, they waited for an exceptionally low tide to drain the marsh and provide good footing (later sluice-gates and low dams were used). Then among ticks, midges, mosquitoes, and blood-letting greenhead flies, the men and boys mowed the grass with scythes. Once cut, the grass was piled onto two-man litters and carried across the spongy surface to waiting wagons. In other locations, where the marshes were extensive, the farmers heaped the hay in mounds on piling "saddles," poles that kept the hay from rotting from contact with high tidewater. Later the hay was removed by unwieldy flat-bottomed scows, called "gundelows" (gondolas), or dragged off by ox teams when winter froze the marshlands.

The marshes also bounded necks of land where cattle could be grazed with the need of a barrier only along the landward side. Such low meadows and necks were a godsend in a wooded wilderness where it was all that a colonist could do to clear land for food crops, let alone pasturage.

As the Guilford planters laid out their houselots, parceling out that portion of the land long ago cleared by the Indians for their corn fields, each family received grants in accordance with its wealth. Every hundred pounds of their estate brought them five acres of upland and six acres of salt meadow; no family was allowed over five hundred pounds' equivalence, or under fifty. For most of the English folk who had risked all on the hard passage to America, land, more than religious liberty, had driven them on. "Wee are all free-holders, the rent day doth not trouble us."[3] Until the last decades of the seventeenth century, Massachusetts and Connecticut were the only British possessions where families of good character would be awarded outright ownership of the land they tilled.

Groups of planters commonly arrived under the supervision of a Puritan "elder," either a minister or nobleman. In recognition of his station, the struggling parishioners constructed his house first, sometimes of local materials, sometimes with prefabricated items brought from England. They themselves made do with tents and wigwams.

The Guilford settlers, being "Gentlemen Husbandmen," and more affluent than most, hired local Indians to haul stones from a nearby outcropping to a small rise, where masons constructed the baronial two-storied edifice of the Reverend Henry Whitfield. As usual, the minister's great house lay just outside the complex of lots that made up the town plat. In the early years, houses such as his served not only as homes for the elders, and meeting places for the congregation, but also as forts in which the settlers might take refuge from the threats of land or sea. Since the local Indians typically had the freedom of the town, the colonists preferred a more remote refuge.

Most towns presented a bleak picture during their formative years. Many of the new arrivals' inflated hopes were dashed as their ships brought them to anchorage off such locations. "I myself heard some say they heard it was a rich land, a brave country, but when they came there they could see nothing but a few canvass booths and old houses, supposing at first to have found walled towns, fortifications, and corn fields."[4] As time went on, the new settlers left their tents and wigwams for roofed-over cellar holes, where they lived while erecting their houses overhead.

Like other villages, Guilford was self-sufficient.

Once or twice each year a coasting vessel might come up on a flood tide to tie

Plank walk through the marshes. Neck River, Madison, Connecticut, which was set off from Guilford in 1826. ◁

Unloading salt hay from a gundelow onto a hay wagon, Nyack, Connecticut, ca. 1920.

The Henry Whitfield House, Guilford, Connecticut. A 1930s reconstruction of the original 1639 structure. In colonial days, the facing would be stuccoed to seal out the dampness.

up at the farmers' or saw-pits' wharves, carrying out corn and flax from the one, planks and barrel staves from the other. For the most part, however, the Guilford farmers lived within the town, seining fish in nets to spread as fertilizer, clamming in the flats (though their own hogs were gradually rooting out the shallow-water shellfish, much to the complaint of the local Indians), or carrying their corn down to the mill, which was set in a sluice where a dam harnessed the great rush of water following the tides in and out of the marshes. Sometimes they rode in small craft down the creeks to visit their more remote neighbors on marsh islands (rocky outcrops rising above the surrounding bog); more often, however, they laid down brush for paths across the spongy lands, using canoe ferries for crossing the mucky tidal streams.

Towns like Guilford did much to remain closed, self-maintaining units. Any land beyond the marsh "low meadows," corn-field "high meadows," or three or four acres of in-town houselots, was held in "commons" for public use. These areas of unsettled forest, field, marsh, stream, and clam flat were regulated by town decree. Millers were told what to charge. Clams and wood could not be sent out of town if doing so raised local prices. Trees could be felled only where the selectmen directed. Everyone could catch the herring on their annual spring runs. In all, the town maintained an effective balance between private property and communal resources.

Once Guilford's original 25 families had settled in, the village, whose early

colonial population never exceeded a few hundred, closed its doors to new arrivals. Any stranger, transient, or prospective landowner was quickly "warned out" by the selectmen if he tarried more than a few days. This closing of the community came from economic necessity. English customs of the day made every towns-person responsible for the welfare of his neighbor, and newcomers who became public charges were often too much for a struggling little town to bear. Notable exceptions might be a midwife, shoemaker, blacksmith, miller, or other prized craftsman. Later, as towns prospered, they often continued the practice of having a constable officially warn out visitors, so if the latter did become destitute, the townspeople would not be legally responsible for their care.

Just as the little settlements let in few, they also let few out. Once settled, a person was expected to live out his life on his allotted land. Sailors of some colonies had to obtain written permission to voyage beyond the colony's jurisdiction. Going among the Indians was expressly forbidden: "Only wild creatures would ordinarily love the liberty of the woods."[5] Among the tidewater settlements along the Connecticut River, the law ordered:

English not to live with Indians
To prevent any of our people going from us and taking up their abode in a prophane course amongst the Indian Natives of this country.
It is ordered by the Authority of this Court; That whatsoever persons that now

Old Homestead by the Sea, *Thomas Worthington Whittredge, 1883. Whittredge (1820–1910) painted a number of similar scenes of house, beach, and marsh, during the time he spent working in the Narragansett Bay area.*

inhabits, or shall hereafter inhabit within this jurisdiction, shall depart from us and settle or joyn with the Indians, they shall suffer one years imprisonment at the least in the House of Correction.[6]

Indians, however, mingled freely with the colonists. Having traded off their best land, they often retired only a short distance away across a bay or river to another migratory village site. The Quinnipiacs of the Guilford region, for example, had been preyed upon by more belligerent tribes and were now quite happy to be near so many European firearms.

In Guilford, as elsewhere, Indians in their little encampment of perhaps a dozen bark wigwams near an offshore clam bed spent much of their time in barter with the villagers. The Indian women caned chairs and wove mats. The men might build stone walls, hunt deer, and exterminate the prowling wolves. Sometimes an elderly Indian couple might accept Christianity and move into a colonist's home as servants. Wrote a Boston woman in 1687 to a friend considering resettlement in America:

The Coasting Trade

From earliest days, the growing colonies relied on small boats that sailed up and down the shore with produce and news to link the scattered settlements. Both they and their owners were called "coasters."

The first recognized coaster was John Oldham, who had arrived in Plymouth in 1623. He soon fell out, first with Pilgrim, and later with Puritan, authorities, who found him "a Man soe affected with his owne opinion, as not to bee removed from it."[a] He kept out of sight of the "Elders" by turning to trade with the Indians and by ferrying goods between the Massachusetts Bay Colony and the settlements in Rhode Island and Connecticut. Ultimately, he was murdered aboard his vessel by Pequots in 1636, precipitating New England's first Indian War.

By the 1650s, little ships scurried up and down virtually all of the seaboard, linking each hamlet with the next community just beyond the headlands, with Bos-

ton, and, indirectly, with England. Some were simply truckers shuffling from their home port to Boston with a steady cargo of firewood. Others became virtual Yankee traders: general stores buzzing here and there in search of bargains to buy and places in which to sell. Some towns, like New London, turned much of their efforts to building and manning these coastal traders. Usually the vessel contained only two people, a man and his son, or perhaps a mate, who was allowed certain cargo space for his own wares.

The coasting system allowed the little settlements to exchange surplus produce for European finished goods. Likewise, Boston acquired both its own necessities and an exportable cargo from the outlying hamlets. Boston harbor was a constant swarm of shallops, pinnaces, and other modest vessels, bringing in beef, pork, and mutton from Plymouth, Rhode Island, and Connecticut; wheat and Indian corn from Connecticut and New York; masts, barrel staves, and clapboards from the Piscataqua River and farther into Maine; tar from Plymouth and the northern settlements; whale oil from Long Island, and cod from the fishing communities.

These small-boat entrepreneurs developed a degree of worldliness that, in the eyes of the more cosmopolitan Bostonians, was a bit humorous. Complained a tongue-in-cheek correspondent to the editor of Boston's *New England Courant* in 1723:

Every Boatman, who commands his Dog and his Boy on board a Wood-Sloop, as arrogantly assumes and receives the title of Captain, *as a Commander of a King's-Ship. What a shame is it, that a Captain should debase his Honourable Shoulders and defile his Hands, by sweating early and late under the Burden of huge Logs of common Fuel. . . . That a Captain should stand in the Hold of a Vessel, up to the Knees in Grain, without Shoes on his Feet or Beaver on his Head, measuring out his Cargo to a Company of Bakers, Carters and Porters? And that he should be so illiterate as to write, . . . instead of* Five Bushels of Barly, *to set down* Five Bushal barely, *as if he design'd to prove himself a Cheat by his own Books? That a Captain should eat Pease with a Wooden Spoon, cut Pork on a Shingle, and pick Bones with his Teeth, (pardon the Expression,) like a Dog under a table?*[b]

The coasters dominated intra-American shipping until the coming of railroads and regularly scheduled steamship lines in the mid-nineteenth century. By this time, coasting had lost all its aura. The more intrepid seamen had put out across the world's oceans all the way to China. Wrote a sailor who spent a short time aboard a New York–to–Boston trader in the 1850s:

You can bring with you hired help in any Vocation whatever. . . . You may also own Negroes and Negresses; . . . there is no Danger that they will leave you, nor Hired help likewise, for the Moment one is missing from the Town you have only to notify the Savages, who, provided you promise them Something, and describe the Man to them, he is right soon found.[7]

One Indian item popular with the settlers was a good canoe or dugout, so common a means of transportation that it was dubbed by the Puritans "water horse." The purchase of this unstable craft must have been an awful test of self-control for the Puritan to retain his sense of divine importance (as well as his black hat), and for an Indian to keep his impassive expression, as the colonist stepped into his newly purchased dugout only to disappear instantaneously over the side in a great splash of water. From colonial records, one also notes that a good sense of balance did not always preclude a wet end to the voyage. In 1645, the New Haven Colony, within which Guilford then lay, declared that for the protection of its citizens, inspectors would test all canoes within its jurisdiction for seaworthi-

The coaster is the drudge among seamen. He shares all the severe toil, and much of the dangers incident to a sailor's life, without any particle of romance to redeem its commonplaceness. With him it is the same old story. New York, Boston, Philadelphia, Norfolk, or whatever may be his trading points, they present no strange scenes, no new life to his view. For a real prosaic, matter of fact, anti-poetic existence, commend me a coaster. One voyage was ever quite sufficient to last me a year.[c]

A View in New Bedford, *by William Allen Wall (1801–1885).*

ness. The Indians, it seems, had discovered a lucrative outlet for their worn-out craft.

As the years went by, Guilford became larger and the Indians became scarcer. Although more ships visited the town docks, the salt-farm economy continued and Guilford, like many other settlements, remained a rural tidewater. Ipswich, above Cape Ann, also populated by affluent gentry, long retained its agricultural character. Many towns along the north shore of inner Cape Cod—such as Wellfleet, Eastham, and Barnstable—literally owe their existence to the salt marshes, as their upland soil regions soon fell barren from the constant plowing of the settlers. In time most of the shore farming towns took to fishing, merchandising, or manufacturing, but the old salt-farming could still be found on isolated marshes well into the twentieth century.

PEMAQUID AND THE MAINE COAST: PATENTS, POLITICS, AND WARS

While Guilford and her sister towns were developing southern New England into the New English Canaan, the lands to the north retained their rugged character. A vessel coasting Maine in the late 1630s reported it "no other than a mere wilderness, here and there by the seaside, a few scattered plantations, with a few houses."[8]

Development of the Maine coast was hampered by its rough and stormy features: high shelving granite that alternated with evergreen forest along tidewater, ten- and twenty-foot tides that receded to drain harbors into expanses of brown mud, fogs that formed wherever tidal rips brought up the deeper cold water, a short growing season, and soil reluctant to the plow.

Yet these natural impediments paled in comparison to the coast's treatment by the grasping, greedy, litigious hand of man. Maine, unlike its southern neighbors, hardly ever had a colonial government in residence. At different times the region was controlled by an overseer and armed men were sent in by various British governing factions, the Massachusetts Puritans, and the Canadian French, with their Indian allies. Today, only the most diehard Down East historian can chronicle these ever-shifting patents and their parade of owners.

Originally the British government intended Maine and New Hampshire to be Royalist domains, divided into feudal baronies and ruled by lords answerable only to the king. Over the decades, these grants changed hands, were divided or duplicated, and sometimes became moot when challenged by Dutch or French warships, or Indian arrows.

During the seventeenth century, shifting intrigues at the English court often left patent holders without royal patronage, and a wilderness planter might find himself turned out from his lands because a now-dishonored name had signed his bill of sale. Many titled landholders found it easiest simply to divide up and sell rights to a disputed region, leaving the buyers to prove the patent's validity in court. These land controversies went on until finally resolved after Maine achieved statehood in 1820.

Curious situations often arose. When John Mason, the proprietor of the Piscataqua settlements along that large inlet on the New Hampshire coast, died in 1636, the "quitrents," indentured servants, and overseers soon divided up the holdings and challenged the heirs in England to litigate with them across the Atlantic. Farther up the coast, at Agamenticus (now York, Maine), the feudal authorities incorporated a city in 1641. It failed, as there were more officials than there were subjects to be ruled.

Maine and New Hampshire's first permanent Europeans were woodchoppers, fishermen, and traders. A few sawmills edged falls along the coast by the 1630s, but most lumber was worked in the ancient sawpits.

Many patent holders first sent over traders, who built little stockades at select sites along the coast, with garrison houses of solid square timbers set within. Proprietors of these so-called "truck houses" invited the local Indians to exchange beaver and other pelts for European cloth, finished goods, and corn raised in the colonial settlements of southern New England. The traders had little affinity with their Puritan neighbors. Plymouth's merchant backers appointed a certain Edward Ashley to barter Pilgrim corn for furs at a trading post set up on Penobscot Bay, at the site of modern Castine. When he arrived in New England in 1629 the Pilgrims were horrified to find him, "a very profane young man; and he had for some time lived among the Indians as a savage, and went naked amongst them, and used their maners (in which time he got their language)."[9] Within a year, the authorities caught Ashley selling munitions to the Indians and sleeping with the native women. They arrested him, broke up his "company of base fellows,"[10] and shipped him back to England.

Ships also put in at the natives' encampments, bartering wherever the Indians had pelts. Some vessels were sent out by patent holders, others were illicit. Often these latter ships, with a half-dozen cannon and fifty men, would beat the natives' into trading, perhaps steal pelts, and sometimes kidnap the populace to sell as slaves in the West Indies. The permanent settlers usually took the brunt of the ensuing retribution.

Rounding out this assortment of strangers, speculators, adventurers, traders, and pirates, were the fishermen. As we know, generations of Spanish, French, Dutch, and English had fished the waters off Maine. By the 1620s certain locations on islands or protected peninsulas had become bases for annual visits from fleets who set out flakes, rested from their sea labors, and made merry.

One such fishing station was Pemaquid, a protected harbor along the lee shore of one of those long Maine peninsulas, where strong tides daily wash the ocean's climate far inland; where the deep estuaries have few freshwater reaches; and where tides alternately fill harbors to the height of the wharves, then drop to leave the small boats marooned in the brown flats, at which time wharf and weir appear contrivances to snare creatures more a-wing than a-fin. The Pemaquid station lay in a tidal river near the peninsula's tip, the anchorage protected at its entrance by a high rock, perfect for a fort. The location had very much the shape of a natural mole and entrance-fortress of some European seaport. The peninsula itself pushes far out into the Gulf of Maine, requiring vessels along the shore to come under the guns of any forces quartered there.

Pemaquid had been long known by the seafaring nations of Europe, and after the Norumbega myth waned, the whole region between Newfoundland and Virginia took its name, until Charles I agreed with John Smith's suggestion to rename the region New England.

For decades before the Pilgrims' arrival, ships fitted out by Bristol merchant-fishmongers had sheltered here to ride out North Atlantic storms. Pine-bough flakes, covered with whitening cod, had lined the shore. "Shoremen" had cleared a bit of the forest back from the sea, split the felled timber, and shaved it into staves for barrels to hold the catch. Indians, too, gathered here for barter. When a fishing vessel entered the harbor, men gathered to pitch the fish into small boats, then rowed to shore and washed the catch at tideline before setting it out to flake. The station was no more than a scattering of humble brown shacks, some wharves and flakes, screaming white gulls, amidst the mingled smells of fish, exposed mudflat, and the smoky green-wood fires.

Time and again, British merchant backers made plans to establish permanent settlements, hoping thereby to save the great expense of sending ships and men back and forth across the Atlantic when the fish ran in spring and early summer. Success finally came in the decade following the founding of Plymouth. By 1630, the Pemaquid peninsula was inhabited by 84 families, in addition to transient

McIntire Garrison House, York, Maine. Built ca. 1640–45 and restored in the early twentieth century (except for the modern windows). Unlike most colonial homes, where clapboards covered wattle (twigs) and daub (a mud/clay plaster), garrison houses were constructed of squared-off timbers, like the log cabins of later eras. This gave protection from Indian arrows and destruction. The house is on the edge of a marshy estuary of the York River.

fishermen. Most lived within sight of a stockaded blockhouse commanding the harbor. This had been built as protection more from pirates and renegades than from the French and Indians (with whom the Pemaquid settlers traded and exchanged intelligence, much to the consternation of colonists to the south). In 1632, one Dixy Bull, who had set out as a privateer with fifteen men to avenge an attack by the French, gave up the mission, and, with the enthusiastic consent of his men, turned pirate. They put in at Pemaquid, walked into the garrison house, beat up the defenders, pillaged the farms, and made their escape.

Pemaquid, along with many of the Maine coast settlements, remained in this vulnerable, disorganized state for almost the entire colonial era.

The population, recruited by titled gentry and the merchants of England's southwestern fishing ports, had neither the dedication nor freedom of the Puritans. Many came from England's West Country, and were Anglicans, who had no quarrel with the Jolly Old Church of England. A relative of one of the "Planters" overseeing a little settlement at Scarborough, just south of Portland, reported that the colonists there "had a custom of taking tobacco, sleeping at noon, sitting long at meals; sometimes four in a day; and now and then drinking a dram of the bottle extraordinarily."[11] In one of these drinking sessions, the visitor was assailed with accounts of sea serpents off Cape Ann, a ship sailed by bewitched women, Tritons in the fishing grounds, and devilish gatherings by night on the beaches.

The laborers sent over to work in this wilderness had little to keep them from fleeing their masters. "If any man's [indentured] servant takes a distaste against his master, away they go to their pleasure," complained one Maine overseer in the 1640s.[12] The proprietors quickly learned to limit their transport of unmarried indentured women: "maids, they are sonne gone in this countrie."[13]

The couples fled north, to less regulated sections of the coast. An official traveling the eastern Maine coast reported it inhabited by

the worst of men. They have hitherto no government and are made up of such as avoid paying debts and being punished have fled thither; for the most part they are fishermen, and share in their wives as they do in their boats.[14]

A landowner's agent in the Portland region lamented that

every man is a law unto himself. It is a bad kind of living to live in a place where there is neither law nor government among people. The people about these parts are very poor, for I cannot conceive what they have out of the country to buy them clothes. The beaver trade doth fail. . . . The wolves do kill their goats and swine. . . . Some Indian corn they sell at harvest time, but are fain to buy again before harvest comes again.[15]

These squatters, runaway indentures, planters preferring Indians to Puritan theocracy, and other refugees congregated around the old fishing stations farther up the coast, like Pemaquid. In time they might have become domesticated and copied the Puritans' success, but this was not encouraged. The patent holders cared more for profits from fish, lumber, and fur than for sharing the Puritan ideal of a New English Canaan.

A fort was erected at Pemaquid in 1677. It served primarily as protection for a dozen stone truck houses built to form a street facing it. Each day the roll of drums "at sun and sun" signaled the start and end of the day's trading with the Indians, which was carried out only in the street or within the houses, all under the protection of the fort's cannons. At night the traders barricaded themselves in the truck houses, and everyone was cleared off the point of land around the

A witch raising a storm at sea.

fort. Fishermen were required to live on land convenient to the fort, or on nearby islands.

The agrarian population did not fare so well. If room for more fish flakes were needed, local authorities, representing the patent holder and the mercantile interests, razed warehouses, saltworks, or farms. The people of Pemaquid had no real title to their land. In 1682 they wrote a letter to the governor of New York, who then had title to Pemaquid, complaining

That, whereas your petitioners have been at great charge in building their habitations, and as yet have noe assurance of their house lots or bounds of our place. . . . And that Pemaquid may still remain the Metropolitan of those parts, because it ever has been so before Boston was settled. Wherefore your honors poor petitioners hereby desire that the Honorable Governor and Council would please take the premises into your pious consideration; to order and confirm the lots, bounds and limits of this place to be laid out, and that we may enjoy the labor of our hands, and have it for our children after us.[16]

The plea fell on deaf ears.

Worse problems plagued the Pemaquid settlers. Sporadic conflicts between the settlers and Indians broke into war in 1675 when the Abnakis and other Maine Indians, emboldened by King Philip's turning the Wampanoags against the lower

Pemaquid Harbor and the reconstructed Fort William Henry, built 1692, destroyed by the French in 1696.

New England colonies, attacked the English settlements in force. For almost one hundred years, Maine became a battleground for the English, who were attempting to regain the territory in the face of constant raids by Indians supplied and encouraged by the French in Canada.

The wars made life in Maine even more tenuous. A father setting out to chop wood or find his wandering cattle might suddenly disappear, having been seized by the Indians and made to "walk the woods" into slavery in Canada. Or he might reappear, brought before some horrified settlers as they peered from the small gun portals of a garrison house. Here, the Indians would tie him to a tree and methodically dismember him, letting his pitiful shrieks be a strong argument for the rest to abandon their humble plantations. By 1690, only four settlements in Maine still had English inhabitants, with fully one quarter of Boston's population impoverished widows and orphans from the frontier settlements.

Peace returned intermittently between the six Indian Wars, and the northern New England towns were periodically repopulated, with the authorities promising better protection. Pemaquid emerged as a fortified location, with a series of ever larger forts being built on the rock overlooking the harbor. By 1701, fifteen families had returned, but they left soon after the third war began in 1703. The final struggle, the French and Indian War, ended with the English victory over the French at Quebec in 1759.

As settlers slowly returned to Maine, they worked the fishing grounds offshore

New England Shore Settlements 1629–1713, after L. K. Mathews, The Expansion of New England *(Boston, 1909). Until 1660, the colonists spread out in little villages up and down the coast. Indian wars after this time forced the abandonment of many frontier settlements, especially in Narragansett Bay and on the Maine coast.*

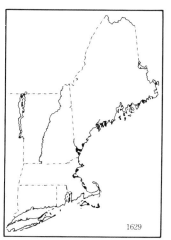

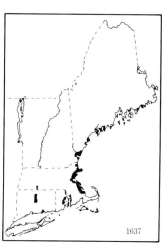

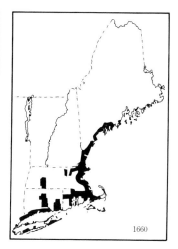

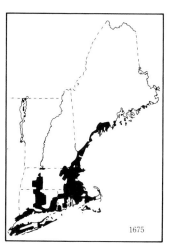

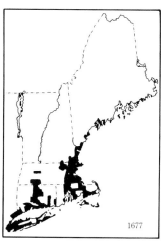

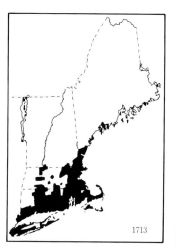

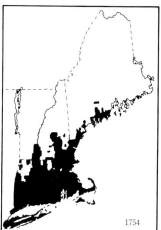

Deepening Roots: Life in Four Colonial Settlements

less, and turned more to chopping wood for warming the hearths of timber-depleted southern New England. Pemaquid, "The Metropolitan of those parts," faded to obscurity as a little fishing hamlet. The fort, once the greatest in New England, the bastion to halt the French tide, stood deserted by the time of the Revolution. The community had moved to "New Harbor" on the other side of the peninsula. When news of the battles of Lexington and Concord reached the peninsula, the townspeople gathered and trekked across to the fort. Knowing they had not the force of arms to man the fortress, and fearing the English might use it as a base, they dismantled the old stone walls, block by block, ignominiously ending the era of Pemaquid. Today only walled cellar-holes remain.

THE ISLES OF SHOALS AND MARBLEHEAD: COLONIAL FISHING

Indian hostilities that began in the 1670s eventually forced the Maine fishermen to move south and take up abode among the Puritans, a difficult situation for both sides. The average Puritan, usually a farmer from England's east who knew little of the sea save the horrors of a transatlantic crossing, shunned these transients from England's western shores who arrived each spring to set up their camps and flakes. The Puritan authorities, however, despite a distaste for the fishermen's un-Puritan character, quickly recognized the potential for financial gain and prohibited interference with fishing boats at sea or the flakes on land.

The fishermen chose good anchorages near fishing grounds where poor terrain kept Puritan settlements at a distance: locations such as the Isles of Shoals in New Hampshire and Marblehead, Nantasket, or Provincetown in Massachusetts.

To entice fishermen closer to their villages, many Puritan towns, Ipswich and Salem among them, enacted attractive laws granting land and pasturage. England's West Country merchants fostered settlements by encouraging their crews to ignore the law that bound them to return to England at the end of each fishing season. Those who jumped ship saved the outfitters the cost of return passage. Ultimately this practice worked against the English, as it allowed colonial entrepreneurs to deal directly with the permanent fishing population.

Boston, Salem, and other growing mercantile ports sent out ships to roam the shore and purchase the catch of the scattered fishermen. According to contemporary sources, the Boston wholesalers sailed "with a walking tavern, a bark laden with the Legitimate bloud of the rich grape."[17] By dint of alcohol, high-priced supplies, and easy credit, they soon foreclosed on the fishermen's homes, farms, and boats.

Through such exploitation, there soon evolved in Boston a "codfish aristocracy," grown rich through the export of fish to West Indies plantations and Europe's Catholic nations. By the end of the seventeenth century, this merchant population, not the Puritan theocracy, ruled the colony. The theologians went down fighting. Their spokesman, Cotton Mather, railed from his pulpit against "Estates Raised by a Cruel Scruing upon Poor Fisher-Men."

Our Fisher-men make a very numerous Tribe in Our Israel. . . . Tis a demand I make on their behalf; That you do not use any Unfair Oppression or Extortion upon them; That you do not improve the Opportunities which their Necessities and Entanglements may give you to Exact Severely upon them.[18]

But for all his disdain for the profit motive, Mather shared the typical Puritan disgust for the fishermen, berating them for their superstitions, intemperance, and profanity: "Broad, Bold *Swearing* is rarely heard among ours; yet they have their *Clipt Oathes* . . . and a Sinful *Discontent* with [their] own *Low, & Small,* and *Hard* Circumstances in the World."[19]

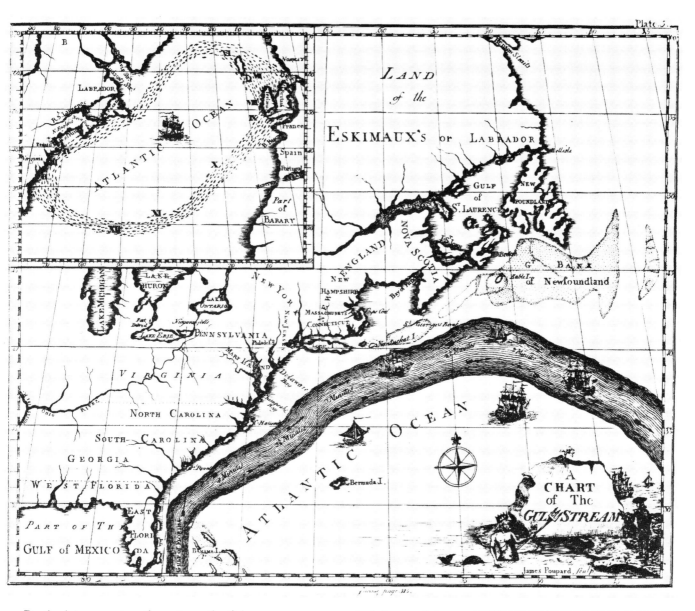

Plate 5.

By the late seventeenth century, the fishermen were concentrated around the Isles of Shoals and Marblehead.

The Isles of Shoals, perhaps originally Shoal (that is, throng) of Isles, is a group of barren rocks about nine miles off New Hampshire's coast. Seven are large enough to be called islands—the largest contains 400 acres. The surrounding shallows teem with fish. Here, remote from Indian threat and Puritan government, lived a riotous collection of fishermen. In the early 1620s, a transient population of about 300 men used the isles in common, setting up their sails for shelter, drying fish upon the bare rocks, and obtaining fresh water from a spring on the largest island. By the 1640s, the isles population had doubled; some were now permanent, but most still transient. They sent their catch to England stowed on ships that moored in the isles and took aboard catches from the many small coastal fishing outposts.

As people from the mainland came over to set up homes and farms, problems soon developed. In 1647 the fishermen petitioned for the farms' removal to the Massachusetts Courts, which ruled that pigs (which despoiled the drying fish) had to go, but that wives and farms could stay.

Benjamin Franklin's Map of the Gulf Stream, 1786, showing the fishing banks. Franklin drew this map from information obtained from his Nantucket uncle, Timothy Folger. The inset map shows the migratory path of the North Atlantic herring.

Deepening Roots: Life in Four Colonial Settlements

Isles of Shoals, *by Childe Hassam, 1901.*

Over the next fifty years, the permanent community grew to about 180 fishermen with wives and families, and another 100 single men. With wood transported from the mainland, they set up homes around the meager anchorages, or wherever a ridge offered a protected lee. These were rude buildings, with little concession to appearance. The population was similarly motley. Oblivious to the transatlantic commerce picking its way in and out of the little harbors, or the importance of the fish he supplied to an overpopulated Europe, the fisherman cared for little save his days at sea and his bottle ashore. Colonial investigations of a number of deaths occurring aboard ship concluded the men were too drunk to cope with ocean conditions.

Domestic harmony lagged on the isles. The women, true pipe-smoking "fishwives," scolded and swore. It was reading the court records of the isles, with their numerous cases of confessed adultery, that gave Nathaniel Hawthorne the idea for *The Scarlet Letter.*

Periodically, Puritan "missionaries" would set up a church on the isles, only to find their flock stretched out napping on the pews during the sermon. Often the clergy sent to attend this flock had histories of failing to inspire mainland congregations. Installation on the Isles of Shoals seems to have been the last rung on the bottom of the clerical ladder.

One such minister farmed out to the isles kept a wonderful journal in which he vented his frustrations and left a unique portrait of his parishioners, as in this passage written after some very un-Puritan Christmas revels in 1746:

Unbelief, Impenitence . . . ye want of love to God, his Sabbath, House, Ordinances, Institutions, & commands . . . yet Great Mispence of Time and Substance . . . ye scoffing at Religion and ye Professors of it . . . ye contention in families and among neighbors; ye Drunkeness and uncleaness; ye Talebearing, Backbiting, Lying & Stealing; ye Deceit; Overreaching, & Defrauding of Persons of their just due. . . . As also the fearful carryings-on yearly on ye 25th of December, in shameful Drunkeness, horrid cursing, swearing, and fighting, bitter exclaiming against such as don't care or dare not to run into the same excess of riot with themselves; firing of guns, singing and dancing, and those things under a pretense of Religion, to honor God, and to give thanks to him for sending his son into the world—which we nowhere read in the Holy Scriptures yt [that] God hath commanded any particular day to be observed in commemoration of ye Lord Jesus, his birth into ye world.[20]

In the eighteenth century, Boston merchants with their own ships forced out the English merchants whose vessels had made the isles their port of call, precipitating the decline of the isles as northern New England's main port of embarkation. Mainland fishing centers like Marblehead, Gloucester, Salem, Chatham, and Ipswich (in order of importance) grew up, drawing the fishermen off the isles to better living conditions. The few remaining families were evacuated during the Revolutionary War, lest they give aid and supplies to the British.

The isles remained deserted for a while, before they were repopulated during the nineteenth century and turned into a resort.

At Marblehead, on the mainland, the fishermen's life also assumed an un-Puritan character. An early court record passed judgment on "George Hardinge of Marblehead, fisherman, for saying that next year he intended to be a [church] member and would then have his dog christened, to pay a fine or be whipped."[21] The town, set off from Salem's jurisdiction in 1648, contained many settlers from Cornwall as well as French-speaking Britons from the Channel Islands. They came to this rocky peninsula and erected homes wherever space could be found among the outcroppings. Marblehead streets resembled twisting alleys as they threaded between the granite and buildings.

From this combination of inhospitable landscape and hardy inhabitants evolved a town that, even in colonial times, had a character not to be matched elsewhere. By 1750, there were about 450 dwellings,

Lee Street, Marblehead.

all wood and clapboarded, the generality miserable buildings, mostly close in with the rocks, with rocky foundations very Cragy and Crasey [i.e., shaky]. The whole town is built upon a rock which is heigh and steep to the water . . . there is a path or way down to the warf, which is but small, and on which there is a large Ware House where they land their fish, etc. . . . The place is noted for Children, and Nouriches [nourishes] the most of any place for its bigness in North America; it's said the chief cause is attributed to the feeding on Cod's heads, etc., which is their Principal Dish. The greatest distaste a person has to this place is the stench of the fish, the whole air seems tainted with it. It may in short be said it's a Dirty Erregular, Stincking place.[22]

While others blamed the local population boom on the annual winter layovers when the fishermen frolicked away the remembrance of their hardships, the real reason was economic. In every fishing town, large or small, the fisher families were controlled by one or two of the affluent merchants. The latter sold the supplies, underwrote the voyages, and bought the catch of the men who risked their lives at sea.

He [the merchant] had all [the fishermen's] earnings in his hands, and paid for them in goods at his own price, and how could he fail to grow rich, or they to remain poor? . . . If a man, with a family, once got into his debt, his only hope was, that when his boys got old enough to have their labor of some value, their wages, added to his own, might enable him to pay off his debt. . . . Hence a father, who had three or four boys, if he can maintain his family by his own earnings, and lay up the wages of his sons from the time they are sixteen till they are twenty-one, amasses enough to buy for himself a snug house and part of a schooner, and then thinks his old age well provided for. Thus a family of sons becomes a fortune to those who are fortunate enough to have them,[23]

Sunset from Crocker Park, Marblehead.

wrote a man who had lived among the New England fishermen some hundred years after Cotton Mather bewailed the "Estates Raised by a Cruel Scruing."

Sunrise over the Atlantic Ocean, as seen from the cliffs of Cape Cod at Nauset Light Beach, Eastham, Massachusetts.

*Outer Cape Cod landscape, near Highland
Light, Truro, Massachusetts.*

Headland and fishing cove, Eastport, Maine.

Dwelling houses and backyard kitchen gardens re-created as they were in 1627, Plimoth Plantation, Plymouth, Massachusetts.

Castle Neck sand dunes, which front the ocean by the Essex River marshes, Crane's Beach State Park, Ipswich, Massachusetts.

West River marshes, Guilford, Connecticut.

Phippsburg, Maine, along the tidewater
reach of the Kennebec River.

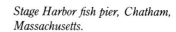

Stage Harbor fish pier, Chatham, Massachusetts.

View from Mason Island, Mystic, Connecticut, looking out past Fishers Island to Block Island Sound.

*Powder House at Manchester, Massachu-
setts, built to store the town's ammunition
during the War of 1812. Most shore towns
had powder houses during this era, in case
of an attack by the Royal Navy. Only about
a half-dozen powder houses remain along
the region's coast today.*

The opulent mansions of the merchants who dominated the little seaport stood out above the general squalor with their wooden exteriors crafted to appear like blocks of granite and marble, their fanlight windows and Georgian porticoes.

Yet the rest of the town, for as long as Marblehead people fished, remained a warren of tumbling houses and twisting streets, its outskirts bounded by acres of gleaming white cod set on the flakes to cure. When George Washington passed through in 1789, nothing had changed in half a century. Marblehead, he put down in his journal, "has the appearance of antiquity; the houses are old; the streets dirty; and the common people not very clean."[24]

During the nineteenth century Marblehead gave up the sea for shoe manufacturing, which in turn died in the early twentieth century. Today, shoemakers and fishermen have been replaced by Boston exurbanites. The winding streets and confusion of house lots remain, but now the homes are brightly painted, in trim repair, and with sloping gardens. Those wishing a feeling for the dark town of old must see it from across the harbor at sunset. At this hour, coming night obscures the many sleek, white-hulled yachts floating at anchor, and only the town's jumble of rooftops can be seen, silhouetted in the afterglow.

For Marblehead, as for Pemaquid, Guilford, and the Isles of Shoals, the rich natural resources of New England ultimately provided a potential development far beyond the visions of the first settlers. Self-contained farming villages like Guilford gave way to the great plantations around Newport, where produce was raised for overseas export. Little fishing hamlets like Marblehead or those on the Isles of Shoals were gradually overshadowed by organized fishing industries, like Nantucket's whaling. Trading and fishing posts, such as Pemaquid, faded to obscurity as Boston and other mercantile cities developed a worldwide shipping fleet.

"The business dealings of ultra-religious people are often peculiar."
—Charles Francis Adams,
The Founding of New England,
Boston, 1921

6
Voyages of Trade and Adventure: The Eighteenth-Century City

BOSTON

When the Puritan planters arrived in 1630 to set up the capital of their Bible Commonwealth, Boston was a hilly, treeless peninsula, covered by blueberry bushes, surrounded by mud flats and shallows, the whole lying virtually hidden from the sea by a maze of islands. Dubbed "Lost Town" by the sailors who threaded their ships through the harbor's many islands, this mean and sad little settlement had few virtues. Its earliest defenses were a few cannon set behind a mud-walled fort. The houses huddled around the small cove were of thatch, beam, brush, and clay. For wood, the colonists had to row over to the islands: they brought hay in on flat scows, cattle and corn were kept on outlying farms. Whenever a ship came up the harbor, rich and poor lined the seaside, ready to barter whatever they had for shipboard provisions. Yet this unlikely settlement soon developed into the commercial center of the Massachusetts Bay Colony; by 1634 a visitor to the town could describe its port as the "fittest for such as can Trade into England, for such commodities as Countrey wants, being the chiefe place for shipping and Merchandize."[1]

During its first decade, Boston supplied the arriving Puritan settlers with the necessities of life in the New World: livestock, seed plants, and other provisions. After 1642, when open hostility in England between Royalist and Puritan factions

stayed the Puritan emigration, the Boston merchants went in search of more remote markets, and for the next fifty years they scoured the world's seaboards for places to trade. In 1642, Boston's first ship, the *Trial,* carrying barrel staves and fish, set sail for Faial in the Azores, where it traded its cargo at a good profit for wine, sugar, and other local products. The next stop was the West Indies, where some of the Faial merchandise was traded for cotton, tobacco, and iron—the last scavenged from local wrecks. The little ship soon returned home with a glorious profit. Boston embraced mercantile commerce, and for centuries prospered on the "triangular trade": buying and selling commodities from a first port

Boston and the Inner Harbor, 1784. From Des Barres's Atlantic Neptune. *Even at the time of the Revolution, Boston still lay along the waterside, and was yet to expand up Beacon Hill.*

Old house at the corner of North and Smith streets, Boston (ca. 1674). From an 1881 painting by S. M. Lane.

for those of a second port, which might ultimately turn a profit in a third (and occasionally into a fourth, fifth, and sixth).

Such ventures did not always meet with success. In 1646, the elders of the New Haven colony bought a ship of somewhat dubious construction (it leaned dangerously in any strong wind or waves), an early effort of the Narragansett Bay shipwrights, and loaded the vessel with 70 young men and the settlement's produce, with the plantation's high hopes of becoming a great mercantile center. The ship sailed off that winter into an icy fog and was never seen again, except, some argue, in the spectral mirage of a storm-battered ship that shimmered over New Haven harbor the following summer.

In Boston, however, shipbuilding was a strongly regulated and inspected activity, and a Boston-made craft, though perhaps not the best in the world, could be expected to hold together for at least a few voyages.

With these ships—loaded with fish, wood, and corn brought to Boston from outlying sea-villages by smaller vessels—the Boston merchants set out on "voyages of adventure," gambling that they could turn a profit somewhere. On their return, they filled the little city with odd cargo, often glutting the market. Someone even brought back a stuffed alligator, which, probably from want of a purchaser, was ceremoniously presented to the governor. The more utilitarian cargo was traded with the coasting captains, who distributed it among their shoreline customers.

In 1663, a traveler through the town could characterize the Puritan mercantile elite as "damnable rich . . . inexplicably covetous and proud."[2]

By 1700, Boston's population of some 7,000-odd souls exceeded that of all but a few of England's largest cities. It had become a "company town," whose income depended almost entirely upon the shrewd shipping ventures of a few Puritan merchants: the codfish aristocracy. Down on the docks, wharfmen unloaded the tar, lumber, corn, cattle, furs, fish, and other raw produce from the many coasters. Nearby, larger ships took aboard these goods for reshipment to England and the West Indies. Warehouses lined the wharves; carters wheeled supplies in through the great street doors, and tackles hoisted barrels up into the upper stories.

Craftsmen converted hides to shoes, pelts to hats, fat to candles, all for shipment aboard vessels bound for places where raw materials and artisans were scarce. Most important of all the crafts was that of shipbuilding.

The shipyards, set up in small fields along the water's edge, were each worked by a master shipwright and his half dozen assistants. Here they collected various sizes and types of wood; then with saw and adze skillfully shaped the timbers that would be put together into a vessel. A shipyard's only structures were simple sheds, serving as office, warehouse, and shelter.

A complex of buildings surrounded the yards, warehouses and work sheds housing the many allied trades. Of these, sailmaking, ropemaking, blockmaking, and ironmaking were the most essential. The more established shipbuilding areas also had carvers, coopers, instrument makers, and specialized gangs who contracted out to set rigging or make masts and spars.

Sails were manufactured in sail lofts, large open buildings or the raftered upper floors of warehouses. Here workers laid out and sewed together pieces of canvas (usually imported). Rope was made in great lengths from hand-spun twine twisted together into thick cables out in the nearby fields. Soon sheds appeared, only a dozen feet wide but hundreds of feet long to accommodate the lengths of rope needed. Blockmakers carved the large wooden pulleys needed for the ship's rigging. Blacksmiths hammered out the anchors, bolts, plates, chains, and other nautical ironwork. By the mid-eighteenth century southeastern Massachusetts had a thriving industry converting bog ore into iron for the shipbuilding industry.

In Boston, as elsewhere, the waterfronts containing these shops, lofts, and yards were rabbit warrens of buildings, their sides open to the carts and wagons constantly trundling the cobbled streets. Here leather-aproned men could be seen working their trades, while children played in the piles of wood shavings. The smell of salt air and hot tar permeated the atmosphere, and ships' masts towered above the roofs.

Unlike most colonial townsmen, the craftsmen lived away from their trades, for Boston's waterfront land was too expensive for homes. At dusk they closed their shops and trudged up the hills to their simple cottages: often one room to a floor—cellar, kitchen, bedroom, and garret. Their neighbors were other craftsmen: candlemakers, shoemakers, cloth dyers, and perhaps a silversmith—for everyone kept his savings in the form of cutlery, plate, and drinking cups. Some, like those catering to the gentry, had separate shops; others simply plied their trade in boxlike lean-tos against an outer wall.

As one ascended Boston's hills, the houses became more dignified, the fruit trees and gardens larger, until, near the crest one reached the mansions of the codfish aristocracy. These American Medici had, during most of the seventeenth century, been disenfranchised from any positions of government because they were middle-class entrepreneurs who had risen to affluence, and were not of the families of nobility and theologians who had first founded Massachusetts Bay.

These merchants were joined in their slow battle for ascendancy over the "Puritan Select" by French Huguenots who had fled to Boston in the 1690s, and by the ever-growing middle class of craftsmen. By the mid-eighteenth century, the practice of rule by clergy and religious principles had been replaced by rule of the merchants and the profit motive. London fashion, not the Bible, was now the main interest of Boston's elite.

This dominant merchant class formed a self-important society around the royal governor, discussed London gossip, wore the latest styles, rode in coaches to the country estates, gave balls and teas, and regally promenaded each evening on the more fashionable streets.

The old Puritans, with their archaic grammar, crabbed logic, and indecipherable script, were gone, but some of their institutions lived on. A Boston child growing

Colonial Shipbuilding

Colonial New England's merchant ships were prized not so much for their quality as for the cheapness of their construction. Shipwrights used green wood, and at first did not differentiate between the white oak, common in England, and a second, American variety, the red oak. White oak made good ship timbers, but the red quickly decayed in seawater, and "colonial ships unfortunately possessed a bad reputation abroad for poor construction and rapid decay."[a]

These vessels, however, were built at half the cost of those constructed in deforested Europe. For the most part, the shipwrights constructed small trading vessels, which they built on order for West Indies or English merchants or which they loaded with local produce and sailed to a foreign port, where both ship and cargo would be put up for sale.

The land edging Boston Harbor was the early center of New England shipbuilding. The local forests still had good timber, and the coasters provided Boston merchants with ready cargo. Problems of labor and supply drove many shipwrights from England to America, to the extent that the standard handbook of the day, Edmund Bushnell's *Compleat Ship-Wright,* put out a new edition (its eighth) in 1716, specifically addressed to shipbuilders in Virginia and New England. Soon Boston had so many boatyards that vessels were being built on streets running into the tidewater, much to the consternation of the selectman. By 1730, one sixth of the British Empire's merchant fleet was American-built; by the Revolutionary War, one third.

With Boston so crowded, shipyards soon flourished along the Connecticut River, the Connecticut shore, Narragansett Bay, and the North River at Hanover, Massachusetts (between Boston and Plymouth). Other yards were found at Plymouth, in the small towns along Massachusetts Bay, across from Boston along the Mystic River, at Salem, Newburyport,

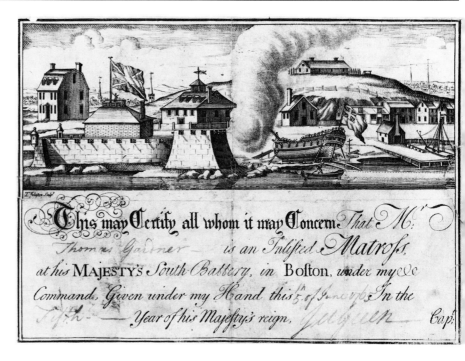

and around the Piscataqua Basin. Many produced ships on a continual basis, launching a vessel every one to three years and sending it off to be sold with the local export aboard.[b] The future of a town often rode with the ship as it set out across the waves. Success meant a profit for all who consigned their produce aboard; a lost ship destroyed years of hopeful labor.

Yet shipbuilding took place simultaneously on a small scale, for fishermen usually built their own vessels. During the season when the fish did not run, a crew, or the fisherman and his sons, would set off into the forest to find a good stand of timber. Here they constructed temporary housing, and soon they were piecing together a vessel. If a curved rib was needed, they simply searched for a limb of the right size and shape. Once finished, the fishermen loaded their small craft on wheels, and carted it to tidewater. If it were large, they dragged it out over winter ice.

As shore timber became scarce, shipwrights often copied the fishermen and headed into the forest. Great ox teams, first used for mast portage, now hauled whole ships over winter snows down to the frozen rivers. Spring thaws and the resulting freshets floated the vessels seaward. The sight of an ox drag attracted

The South Battery, Boston, ca. 1765. To the right a Royal Navy vessel is being repaired in one of the city's shipyards. The main part of the town can be seen at upper right.

the whole region. Once started (a feat in itself), the team, sometimes 200 strong, was virtually unstoppable. Unless expert hands regulated the speed there was constant danger of an ox's strangling if the lines went taut going over a dip in the road and lifted the animal off the ground by his yoke, or of the creature's being crushed from the downward pull on the yoke as he crested a rise in ground. Injured oxen were all removed as the team continued its relentless headway, a most dangerous activity for the handlers. Eight miles to navigable water seems to have been the limit of most of these drags. Larger vessels were sometimes built, then dismantled into quarters for reassembly at tidewater.

up during the Revolutionary era could see Cotton Mather's old adage "Better whipped than damned" still in practice at the pillory:

It was placed in State Street directly below the window of a great writing school which I frequented, and from there the scholars were indulged in the spectacle of all kinds of punishment. . . . Here women were taken in a huge cage in which they were dragged on wheels from prisons, and tied to the post with bare backs on which thirty or forty lashes were bestowed among the screams of the culprit and the uproar of the mob.[3]

Any women involved were most likely prostitutes. In the 1670s, the "Whores of Boston" were known by sailors around the world. No longer could Boston enforce the old practice of "warning out" those it deemed unacceptable. Where once the rejected went north into New Hampshire and Maine, or sought religious liberty to the south on what the Bostonians called "Rogues Island," the Indian massacres forced many to take refuge in Boston. Widows and children filled the town, living off public charity. Misfits took residence among the taverns and dives down near dockside, where "drunkenness, debauchery, and other manners of lewdness" prevailed. To the chagrin of many "Old Saints," the patrons were not just sailors. Cotton Mather confided to his diary, in a passage rivaling Shylock's cry of "My ducats, my daughter!": "A Harlot big with a Bastard Accuses my poor Son Cressy [Increase Mather], and lays her Belly to him. Oh! Dreadful Case . . . what shall I do now for the foolish Youth! . . . oh, ye Humiliations!"[4]

The worse threat to the Bostonians' children was less debauchery than the pernicious lure of the open seas. Young boys grew up as wharf rats, swimming off the docks, watching the ships unload great cargoes, and listening to the sailors' tales of distant lands. As they prowled up the streets each evening and watched their fathers working away their lives in little sheds, many determined to go to sea. The youthful Benjamin Franklin relates how greatly accommodating his father was in finding him an appealing occupation, lest the boy follow in his older brother's footsteps and ship out on one of the vessels exchanging cargo on Long Wharf. As the life of a sailor was hard, and often short, the parents of many a vanished lad simply gave him up for dead, writing the date of his departure in the family Bible: "Gone to Sea, presumed Drowned."

Woodcut from a 1768 broadside of poetry, entitled "South End Forever, North End Forever, Extraordinary Verses on Pope-Night; Or, A Commemoration of the Fifth of November, giving a History of the Attempt, made by the Papishes, to blow up King and Parliment, A.D. 1588. Together with some Account of the Pope himself, and his Wife Joan; with several other Things worthy of Notice, too tedious to mention." Scholars believe that in the year of this broadside, the north and south ends of Boston agreed on a truce and celebrated Guy Fawkes Day peaceably, as opposed to their long tradition of meeting head-on and brawling for each other's effigies.

Newport Harbor today. The city seen from Fort Adams. At right stands "Beacon Rock" built by E. D. Morgan.

Prescott Farm, Middleton, Rhode Island. Mansion and reconstruction of a colonial plantation. Gambrel roofs characterize Newport and South County colonial architecture. ▷

NEWPORT

In the last years of the seventeenth century, while Boston's merchants labored against the Puritan theocracy and places like New Haven kept the old covenant unflinchingly (one wit there observed that everyone over the age of fourteen had been whipped, save the presiding minister and officiating judge); there were other towns along the shore unhampered by such religious preoccupations. The Episcopal gentry of Portsmouth, New Hampshire—old Strawberry Banke—had grown fat on the ship-mast trade, supplying naval stores for the Royal Fleet. Farther south, in towns like Hartford, and Middletown, the "Connecticut River Gods" built ornate homes on profits gained by sending apples, potatoes, hay and livestock to Carolina plantations and "horse jockeys" to the West Indies: small ships with open decks loaded with cattle, mules, and horses; the hold with house frames, and a pandemonium of pigs, sheep, geese, and turkeys. Of all the affluent shore regions however, the most famed, justly, was the lower Narragansett Bay shores and those green islands that dotted its entrance to the Atlantic. Here, on the largest of the islands first settled in 1638, lay Newport.

Not far from the open ocean, approached through easily protected narrows, Newport had perhaps the world's best harbor for sheltering the greatest of colonial fleets. The offshore Gulf Stream tempered the seasonal extremes. Colonial Bostonians were quick to note that Newport was a coat warmer in winter, and thanks to the Gulf Stream, the harbor lay open, no matter how cold. The predominating southwest wind off the waters made it a balmy Mediterranean by summer, bringing brisk sea breezes each afternoon and soft mists each night.

Here flourished a multitude of religious creeds—Quaker, Jew, Baptist, and various splinter Protestant faiths. The Massachusetts Bay Puritans saw it as the sewer into which they emptied their heretics. According to Cotton Mather, if a man were to lose his religion, he could be sure to find it in Rhode Island.

The first settlers hired Indians to kill off all the island's wolves, allowing the settlers to move in and establish large farms of a few hundred acres. At first they raised corn and grain. When the Puritan immigration came to a sudden halt in 1642, depressing cattle prices so quickly that the event became known in New England as the year of the "Fall of Cow," these Rhode Island farmers bought as

much livestock as they could, and turned the island into one vast rolling pasture, filled with herds of cattle, sheep, and horses. At first, they drove their stock overland to the Boston market, but by 1650 (when the island's population was 300) the farmers were shipping them from their own wharves directly to New York or the West Indies.

Coming down from the northern mainland, it was a welcome change from the sand and scrub of southeastern Massachusetts. One ferried over to an island of rolling hills and vales, with a landscape of rising ground, rocks, promontories, and delightful overlooks from which one saw the distant shorelines. The land itself had been well manicured by the 1690s. Wrote a visitor in 1697:

Here are some merchants, and shopkeepers, who live plentifully and easily, the Island affording most excellent provisions of all kind, the people Courteous and obligeing to strangers, the farms for Largeness, and goodness in pasturadge, excelling anything [else] I ever saw in New England, and they produce in each farm wood enough to shelter theyr cattle in the Sumer heates, and warm their chimneies in the winter cold . . . their mutton was pure good—their butter and cheese excellent and their wine, beere and cider very commendable—Exceeding much fish.[5]

The excellence of Rhode Island's assets did not pass unnoticed abroad, and soon Quakers from England and Sephardic Jewish merchant families from Portugal, Holland, and Dutch Curaçao arrived to set up business. Trade with overseas ports in those times depended greatly upon mutual trust between the shipper and receiver. Unlike the Bostonians, who made voyages of adventure, searching for buyers of their cargo each time they sailed, the Jews and Quakers of Newport set up long-term business relations of mutual benefit with their religious brethren in the West Indies. By 1700 Boston, with its 7,000 inhabitants, was a parasite port, buying raw materials from one source, and shipping them out for sale elsewhere; while Newport, with a population of some 2,500, produced its own merchandise in the sure knowledge of a ready market.

In the late 1640s the Newport landowners had begun horse-breeding, producing some strains suited for riding the rough roads of the day and others for endlessly circling the cane crushers of West Indies sugar mills. West Indies planters worked the horses until they dropped dead, thus assuring the Newport breeders a constant market.

The Newport and adjacent "South County" farms along Narragansett Bay's western shore produced more than simply livestock on the hoof. Down in Newport's lower town, the dock laborers filed back and forth across the gangways from wooden wharf buildings, blackened by the salt air, to the awaiting ships. In the holds they rolled casks of butter preserved by heavy salting, cheese, leather, fat for candles, salted beef, and cow horns split and flattened for fashioning into plates and combs.

By the 1720s, Newport had come to symbolize a carefree spontaneous society. "The island is the most delightful spot of ground I have seen in America. I can compare it to nothing but one intire garden. . . . For rural scenes and pritty, frank girls, I found it the most agreeable place," wrote one pleased visitor.[6]

The town began to show its airs. The men dressed in scarlet coats and waistcoats, yellow lace trimming the sleeves. Women copied the latest London fashions. The Quakers kept to their somber garb, but exhibited their material comforts in household furnishings and silver plate. Plantation owners from the West Indies and the Carolinas summered here. Parties of all ages gathered at the seaside to picnic. The more intellectual might indulge in elevated discourse as they walked the long beaches. Bishop Berkeley, the great theologian, who spent time at Newport in the 1720s, describes such a summer ramble:

. . . After breakfast, we went down to a beach, about half-a-mile off, where we walked on the smooth sand, with the ocean on one hand, and on the other hand, wild broken rocks, intermixed with shady trees and springs of water, till the sun began to be uneasy. We then drew into a hollow glade between two rocks. . . . But we had hardly seated ourselves, and looked about us, when we saw a fox running by the foot of our mound, in an adjacent thicket. A few moments after we heard confused noises of the opening of hounds, the winding of horns, and the shouts of the country squires.[7]

Though Newport had its intelligentsia and artists, its intellectual life never equaled Boston's. In 1744, Alexander Hamilton, a Maryland doctor, visited Newport, where he was allowed into the precincts of the "Philosophical Club," Newport's weekly forum. He related:

I was suprized to find that no matters of philosophy were brought upon the carpet. They talked of privateering and building of vessels; then we had the history of some old familys in Scotland. . . . After this history was given, the company fell upon the disputes and controversys of the fanaticks of these parts, their declarations, recantations, letters, advices, remonstrances, and other such damned stuff of so little consequence . . . and therefor disgusted with such a stupid subject of discourse, I left the club and went home.[8]

Trinity Church Burying Ground and houses on Queen Anne Square, Newport.

Even the less appealing aspects of seaport life took on a genteel air in Newport. Boston, to be sure, had its whores, but Newport had mistresses. Dr. Hamilton related a tour of the town given him by a Newport physician:

Dr. Moffat took me out this evening to walk near the town where we had a great many pleasant walks amidst avenues of trees. We viewed Mr. Malbone's house and gardens, and as we returned home met Malbone himself with whom we had some talk about news. We were met by a handsom bona roba in a flaunting dress, who laughed us full in the face. Malbone and I supposed she was a paramour of Moffat's, for none of us knew her. We bantered him upon it and discovered the truth of our conjecture by raising a blush on his face. [9]

The Malbone named in the passage was Godfrey Malbone, perhaps the richest of Newport's merchants. While Dr. Hamilton was taking in Malbone's town house, just outside the community workmen had begun the construction of Malbone's great country mansion, set on a 600-acre farm. Elaborately faced with stone brought in from Connecticut, the house had a circular staircase of mahogany spiraling all the way up to the cupola on the roof. Surrounding it, ten acres of gardens sloped away. Graveled walks led the stroller among trees imported from every port of call. A spring fed a cascade of pools where fish of gold and silver colors swam. The house burned down in 1766.

Yet such largesse did not come from being a simple country gentleman. A trapdoor in Malbone's cellar carried one along a tunnel to a hidden entrance by a secluded cove. Contraband, it seems, ran in the blood of most New England merchants.

Collectors [of Customs duties] and naval officers here are a kind of cyphers [zeros]. They dare not exercize their office for fear of the fury and unruliness of the people, but their places are profitable upon the account of the presents they receive for every cargo of run goods. [10]

Pirates, privateers, and smugglers were all considered "free traders," and part of the "legitimate" intercourse of a New England mercantile port. Though the more notorious or indiscreet might be hanged on some marsh flat below the line of high tide—the limit of Admiralty authority—pirates brought in hard cash when they purchased local homes, and they were known to sell their booty at a fraction of its retail value. King's agents were constantly complaining of "South Sea Men" who had taken up residence in Boston, New London, and other ports where "they are instructed how to govern themselves and live undisturbed." [11] An official of the Crown in 1697 characterized Newport as "a place where pirates are ordinarily too kindly entertained." [12] It would seem that as long as their dark deeds were accomplished beyond the authority of the colonial governments, the pirates were welcome to sell their cargoes, squander their gains, or visit relatives, despite the objections of the King's representatives. James Fenimore Cooper's novel *The Red Rover* revolves around a pirate vessel in pre-Revolutionary Newport, giving the flavor of such activity.

Privateering was essentially authorized piracy: setting out under governmental authority to harass and seize the shipping of enemy nations. Such booty came in without customs charges, and was often auctioned off upon the home-port docks to pay the crew. A prize vessel was a double blessing, providing revenue to the sailors' families and goods at depressed prices to the townspeople. Newport began sending out privateers as soon as it had established itself as a port in the 1650s.

One last maritime activity classified as "free trading" was the slave business. Slave trading began in New England soon after British law opened it to private

Pirates and Other Sea Raiders

Pirates were a constant hazard to towns and shipping during the colonial era. Such raiders came in various forms. One nation's pirate might be another nation's privateer, with legal sanction to raid enemy vessels. New England ports sent out many of their own privateers, happy to receive the silver and booty brought up from raids in the West Indies. Yet, as William Bradford observed of a group that put in at Plymouth in 1646, they usually scattered "more sin than money."[c]

In Lynn, Massachusetts, legend tells of how one pirate took refuge in a cave along the Saugus River in 1658, after authorities seized his three mates. The lone pirate met his fate, the tale goes, when an earthquake tumbled a rock over the entrance, entombing him. This story had such credibility that two hundred years later a man and his son spent most of their lives tunneling some 150 feet through bedrock in search of the fabled cave.

The more realistic stories of New England piracy involve attacks on colonial vessels by Spanish, Dutch, French, and even Indian privateers. The Block Island–New London region was looted repeatedly

Thimble Islands, Branford, Connecticut. A complex of rocks in Long Island Sound just east of New Haven, with some large enough to be termed islands. Legends still persist that Captain Kidd buried yet-to-be-discovered treasure here.

by the French in the 1690s, and an unidentified ship sailing into New London Harbor half a century later still stirred up old fears.

Farther north, raiders commonly attacked the little Maine settlements. In 1724, an Isles of Shoals skipper reported being pursued by a schooner formerly of Marblehead, "full of Indians Extraordinarily well fitted who chased [him] three hours,"[d] preventing the local fishermen from putting to sea.

Once they had their blood up, many New England sailors, originally embarked on a voyage to harass enemy shipping and towns, took a liking to the buccaneer life. Peace might come, but the privateers kept on, sometimes raiding the old enemy, sometimes their own people. Some hung, like bees around a flowerbed, just outside New England harbors, ready to board the slow and defenseless. Most ships prominently displayed what were later called "Quaker guns": wooden mock cannons. Others had painted gunports just above the waterline.

New England waters were never really ideal for pirates. There are tales of Blackbeard's having lived for a time on the Isles of Shoals, but, in truth, New England was simply too well populated for a pirate's liking. Inevitably the news of an incident spread, and then every vessel coasting the region was on watch, ready to pass information to the Admiralty office at Boston, who would quickly dispatch armed vessels. Pirates preferred the uninhabited Carolina bayous, or Florida waters. From these places they could sail out, seize fat

vessels bound for the West Indies, and be quickly home before any reinforcements arrived.

Pirates who were caught received a trial and then usually the noose. Crews were often found not guilty when it became apparent that they had been captured and pressed into joining the pirates under the threat of death.

The guilty, condemned under Admiralty law, were executed where the Admiralty held authority: below the line of high tide.

Ye pirates who against God's laws did fight,
Have all been taken which is right.
Some of them were old and others young,
And on the flats of Boston they were hung[e]

ran a poem about six pirates hanged on a scaffold erected on the mud flats near Boston in 1704.

New England's most famous "pirate" was the Scotsman William Kidd. He had sailed from New York in 1696 with a commission to prey upon the enemy. Three years later he returned to find himself charged with piracy. Kidd deposited some of his booty with the owner of Gardiners Island, at the eastern tip of Long Island. As British law then required all accused pirates to be tried in England, Kidd was taken there. He was found guilty of piracy—for political reasons, according to many, and not from weight of evidence—and of murder. When he was hanged in 1701, the only treasure recovered was what was listed on the witnessed manifest at Gardiners Island.

Many still search and dig for the rest of Kidd's treasure. Some claim it is under the sands of Campobello Island, just across the Canadian boundary. Others interpret cryptic remarks made by Kidd on the gallows to suggest locations in Old Saybrook, Connecticut. For almost a century after his death, virtually every New England shore town had its tales of buried treasure and stories of the pirate's gracious visit among the townspeople. One wry visitor in the mid-eighteenth century observed that anyone wanting to hear a "true story" concerning Captain Kidd, had only to inquire of the oldest lady in the town.

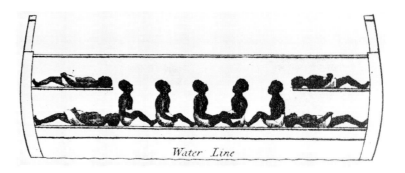

venture in 1698. (Other nations allowed it only under a government-backed monopoly.) Among the American colonies by the mid-eighteenth century, slavers put out from Portsmouth, Salem, Boston, New London and Providence and Bristol, Rhode Island. But a single port dominated all of these—Newport.

At the peak of the trade in the 1760s, Newport had over 180 vessels fitted out as slavers. Unlike the maritime nations of continental Europe, whose ships were great vessels, specially built to carry hundreds of slaves and run by merchants to whom the government gave a monopoly in the business, the Yankee slaver was often a small independent ship. Enterprising captains gathered hardened hands and sailed for the "Slave Coast," where they purchased a few dozen blacks and kept them packed in cramped holds until the ship reached the New World slave markets.

Little of the slave trade's visible brutality reached New England to becloud its starry profits. What human chattels arrived in Boston or the Narragansett Bay communities were small in number, destined for domestic use. There were no wholesale drives, no bodies of the diseased, jettisoned alive lest they prove contagious, floating up on Yankee shores. Only the unmistakable smell of a "slaver" tied up at dock, a stench that even a cargo of heady molasses could not eradicate, bespoke the true misery. Here and there one encountered among the dockside warehouses a little building where "shipments" for local use were herded into the barred upper stories of the cramped edifice. There the slaves would sit behind an iron latticework, which separated them from clerks entering debits and credits at their high desks, and await auction for use as field hands.

In contrast to the graceful town houses, the trees, and the steeples of the upper town were Newport's twenty-two dockside distilleries. Of all the aspects of the slave trade, it was the African dealers' insistence upon rum as payment that most embarrassed the teetotaling Quaker grandees. In a never-ending procession, the great casks of molasses would be rolled off the ships and into the "rummeries." Young boys haunted these docks, scraping off the sweet treacle oozing from between the staves for a sticky treat—simultaneously testing each other's mettle with tales of casks opened to disclose caramelized bodies of slaves who had fallen in. At the height of the slave trade, even the hundred-odd distilleries in New England could not fill the holds of all the vessels making ready to sail for the "Slave Coast."

In 1774 Rhode Island's government moved against its own and abolished slavery in the state. With the onset of war, the British and French alternately blockaded the harbor. The island farms were reduced to a no-man's-land between encamped forces, and Newport's seagoing trade collapsed. Many Quaker and Church of England merchants left the town; so, too, eventually, did many of the Jews.

After the war, the Narragansett shores tried to keep on with hired, rather than slave, labor. This area also declined as the region's main export, a broadbacked horse called the Narragansett pacer—excellent for riding on over rough trails— lost its markets as America began building smooth turnpikes. Soon the old plantations broke up and gradually reverted to wilderness. The swamp and scrub of the Rhode Island shore today make it hard to envision the land as a rolling pasturage, once one of New England's most productive agricultural regions. As for Newport itself, wrote a post-Revolutionary visitor: "The men of wealth live by loaning their money without entering in any great degree into activity, useful business. The poor people catch fish for their sustenance, and lounge and saunter for their pleasure."[13]

A half-century would pass before Newport again emerged into greatness, this time as a resort.

NANTUCKET

Not every location along the shore guaranteed prosperity to the colonists who built their homes and began to plow the fields or cast the net. If the fishing failed, the boatmen, like the city merchants, could keep their homes and simply set out for new waters. If the land failed, however, the farmer had either to begin again elsewhere or change occupations.

Many fields, which yielded under the simple methods of the Indians, were soon exhausted by the colonists' intensive planting. "We found after five or six years that it grows barren beyond belief"[14] was a common complaint. Around Boston, the settlers had other trades to fall back on. At Plymouth, the Pilgrims had no choice but to scatter their population. In the 1640s, fully half their number sailed for the outer arm of Cape Cod, which then had a fertile covering of forest and produced for the Indians a great storehouse of corn.

The dense vegetation protected and contributed to a "black mold," rich humus that covered the forest floor. Below the loam lay the sandy underbase. No laborious spring plowing was needed to break up the hardpan, no glacial boulders pushed their way to the surface from the winter's freeze. Instead, "a plow passes through speedily, and after the corn has come up, a small Cape horse, somewhat larger than a goat, will, with the assistance of two boys, easily hoe three or four acres in a day."[15]

Ultimately, intensive farming also brought an end to the agricultural richness of this "region of sea sand," these peninsulas and islands thrown up by the last glaciers: such as the Plymouth lands, Cape Cod, Nantucket, Martha's Vineyard, the Elizabeth Islands, and Block Island.

As the forest was cleared, the dank humus, once exposed to the drying sun, often powdered and blew away. The erosion occurred at different times in different locations, with the same end result: the underlying glacial sand broke through in a flood, engulfing farms, then towns, and finally the whole Cape. Here, as on the nearby islands, the forest, once gone, would never return. Only scrub pine, bush, and wild rose remain to anchor the sandy, windswept landscape.

As the soil was depleted, many island and Cape farmers gave up and migrated elsewhere. The Maritimes and the Maine coast, once the Indian hostilities had ceased, received many Capelanders in the later decades of the colonial era. Those who stayed behind turned more and more to the bounty of the sea. Of them, none are so famous as the whalers of Nantucket.

The island of Nantucket is a sandy eminence some ten miles at its longest; a hillock of glacial rubble shaped into spits, headlands, and curving shore by storm waves and tidal rips. It lies just over the horizon from Cape Cod's elbow, amid a submerged tableland of shoal waters, long avoided by mariners. The climate alternates between North Atlantic cold and Gulf Stream warmth. Winters can bring pack ice to block the harbor for weeks on end, or such deceptive mildness that flowers sense a false spring, and bloom in December.

As late as the first part of the nineteenth century, Nantucket was still a secluded

isle, fabled for whales and Quakers, though Nantucket town itself was by then the fourth largest community in Massachusetts. When Daniel Webster sailed out to argue a case there in 1835, he summed up the port of some 8,000 inhabitants by calling it "the unknown city in the ocean."

The first settlers, of around 1660, found a large Indian population and a land already barren of almost all forest. Disenchanted colonists from the New Hampshire coast and Merrimack Valley, they had originally emigrated from England's West Country, with the hope of practicing their Baptist and Presbyterian faiths, but soon chafed under the strict regimen of the Puritan authorities.

And every Northwest wind that blew, they crept into some odd chimney-corner or other, to discourse of the diversity of Climates in the Southerne parts, but chiefly of a thing very sweet to the palate of the flesh, called liberty, which they supposed might be very easily attain'd, could they but once come into a place where all men were chosen to the office of a Magistrate, and all were preachers of the Word, and no hearers, then it would be all Summer and no Winter[16]

went a theocrat's 1654 complaint of such dissidents. At this time, Nantucket lay beyond the authority of Massachusetts, and was controlled instead by the New York Royalists.

The newcomers bought half the island from the Indians, and, with beams and boards cut in Merrimack Valley sawmills, constructed their homes. Undeterred by the island's lack of timber, they felt that the rolling hills and thick scrub would provide excellent wintering for sheep and cattle, and they soon settled down into the life of shepherd and husbandman.

Nantucket's population, predominantly rural, grew slowly in the next half-century. A 1693 count put the population at some 300 Europeans and 800 Indians.

But then life began to change, as Nantucket men of both races set out in six-man boats to chase the whales milling offshore. Apparently a Cape Codder had brought the practice over to the Island. By 1700 Nantucketers were gathering on the headlands to watch their men pursue Leviathan, and to cheer the telltale bloody mist from the blowhole of a mortally struck whale.

Today, Nantucket's history has been so embroidered in mystique that it would seem the island invented whaling. In actuality, the first European accounts of whaling go back to the ninth century, and by the 1600s all of Europe's maritime nations had whalers working Arctic waters or the Gulf of St. Lawrence. Even the

A Nantucket lane and the 1746 windmill. From a late-nineteenth-century photograph. ◁

An early lookout tower for shore whaling.

captain of the *Mayflower* remarked that he would be back to hunt the whales surrounding the ship as she lay at anchor in Provincetown harbor. We know that in Maine, the more intrepid Indian tribes often set out in canoes for whales. While the Indians used the catch for food, the Europeans prized its bright burning oil for illumination.

While perhaps lacking the seamanship for offshore whaling, the seventeenth-century New England shore folk (as well as colonists as far south as New Jersey) were quite familiar with "Drift Whales": pilot whales or "blackfish," some 20 feet in length, that for still unknown reasons often push themselves ashore along sandy beaches in schools of various sizes (the highest recorded number was some 2,000 near Provincetown in 1884). Since the whales frequented New England waters from fall to early spring, colonial farmers soon began to alternate their summer planting with winter walks along the shore.

According to British maritime law, which then extended its authority to all activity below the high water line, taking the blackfish was illegal: "The King shall have wreck of the sea whales and great sturgeons taken in the sea and elsewhere throughout the whole realm, except in places privileged by the King."[17] Few colonists complied with such legal niceties.

The next development was for men to set out in boats after unbeached whales, spearing a few or herding the whole pod ashore. This required a constant lookout for whales "struck in" along the shallows. On Nantucket in the 1670s the first lookouts set up position at a headland on the Atlantic that later developed into a little fishing village called Siasconset. The Nantucketers soon parceled the shore into individual whaling territories. Each six-man crew's beachfront had a small thatched warming hut and a lookout post. This latter was a mast or timber tripod, which was set with wooden climbing pegs and crowned with a basketlike seat. Each man spent the winter months taking turns at watch atop this shivering perch. Below in the hut, his mates fared slightly better, warming themselves away from the ocean's windy damp.

Until European diseases virtually decimated the Nantucket Indians in mid-eighteenth century, the braves rowed alongside the colonists. Once a whale lay dead on the beach, the squaws joined their mates in the greasy task of setting up cauldrons on tripods ("trypots") beside the carcass, cutting out the blubber and reducing it to whale oil.

Shore whaling continued virtually unchanged to the end of the nineteenth century. Wrote a visitor to a Blackfish drive on Cape Cod around 1875:

When the school were discovered near the shore, the fishermen, getting outside of them in their dories, by hallooing, sounding of horns, and other noises, drove them, like frightened sheep, toward the beach. As soon as the hunters were in shoal water they left their boats, and jumped overboard, urging the silly fish on by outcries, splashing the water, and blows. Men, and even boys, waded boldly up to a fish, and led him ashore by a fin; or, if inclined to show a fight, put their knives into him. They cuffed them, pricked them onward, filling the air with shouts, or with peals of laughter, as some pursuer, more eager than prudent, lost his footing, and became for the moment a fish. All this time the blackfish were nearing the shore, uttering sounds closely resembling groanings and lamentations. The calves kept close to the old ones, "squealing," as one of the captors told me, like young pigs. It was great sport, not wholly free from danger, for the fish can strike a powerful blow with its flukes; and the air was filled with jets of water where they had lashed it into foam. At length the whole school were landed, even to the poor calf that had wandered off, and now come back to seek its dam. . . . The blubber, nearly resembling pork-fat, was stripped off and taken in dories to town. I saw the men tossing it with their pitchforks on the shore, whence it was loaded into carts, and carried to the try-house

on one of the wharves. Here it was heaped in a palpitating and by no means savory mass. Men were busily engaged in trimming off the superfluous flesh, or in slicing it with great knives resembling shingle-froes, into pieces suitable for the try-pot; and still others were tossing it into the smoking cauldron.[18]

As whaling began to dominate the Nantucket economy in the early eighteenth century, it was soon joined by another important influence, Quakerism.

Quakerism as practiced on Nantucket was very much a revival of the seventeenth-century Puritanism, with a bit of brotherly love added. Though ostensibly without a guiding clergy, the "Meeting" was controlled by the island's leading burghers and, interestingly enough, burgheresses. They adopted drab gray and brown garb, cut in an outmoded fashion—a reaction to finery and ostentation that soon developed into an active cult of plainness. Those who showed too much spontaneity, intellectual curiosity, ornateness in dress, or love of song and dance were expelled from the Meeting. As with the Puritans, the slack of human frailty was taken up by public confession and recantation.

On the mainland, such a group could not have lasted more than a few generations before being undermined by outside influences. On physically isolated Nantucket, Quakerism flourished uncontested.

The Nantucket Quaker soon became a religiously self-assured, geographically chauvinistic businessman. (All non-Nantucketers were called "Coufs," a word of contempt variously ascribed to Old Scotch for "simpleton" or Nantucket Indian for "off-islander.") By the 1750s Nantucket was supreme in America's whaling industry, ahead of the Cape Cod ports of Truro, Wellfleet, and Provincetown, as well as New London, and the towns on Long Island. Nantucket ships now set out for month-long voyages, at first along the Gulf Stream's edge and soon from Greenland on the north to Brazil to the south. They no longer towed whales to shore, but reduced them to oil on shipboard trypots. Their island home, and its central village, Sherburne (which later was renamed Nantucket), had become like an anthill on a sand plain—and perhaps as drab.

Before the whaling out of Nantucket began to slacken in the 1830s (and the merchants began to put their fortunes into homes rather than more ships), the hillside town was as gray as a Quaker's cloak. During the eighteenth century, it

Looking northwest from North Tower, Nantucket. Late nineteenth-century photograph.

lay in two parts, the dockside area divided by the old "Sheep Meadow" from the residences farther up the slope. Down by the town's five wharves, covered with greasy black casks of whale oil and savannahs of drying baleen, among the cooperages, ropewalks, chandleries, and warehouses, stood the oil factories: the "try works."

Here the crude oil was heated and skimmed, then set to cool into blackish cakes. On a mild winter's day, these were shoveled into bags and squeezed in a great press to produce the clear burning "Winter Strained Sperm Oil," Nantucket's finest product. It brightened houses of the rich, and furnished lighthouses, because it was guaranteed not to congeal even in the coldest weather. Spring Strained Sperm Oil and Summer Oil followed, but they were poorer in quality. In 1772, Nantucket started to produce spermaceti candles from the otherwise useless residue of blackish lump left after pressing. The secret formula for these candles,

A View of SIASCONSET (a Fishing Village on Nantucket

which greatly increased the profits of the whaling merchants, had been brought to the Rhode Island region by the Jews.

The residential section, while uphill away from the docks, was not isolated from their disagreeable smell, which permeated the whole community. The homes, set every which way according to their owners' whims, created a huddled scattering rather than an urban grid:

Such is the simplicity of this primitive place, and so small is the resort of strangers, that the streets . . . have branched out from each other by imperceptible degrees, every man being at liberty to place his house according to his fancy . . . being more naturally disposed to regulate his front by a point of compass, than by the direction of the street.[19]

The "streets" existed only in theory, for all was sand. The houses, of graying cedar shingles, also had little ornament: "They are convenient buildings, but there is not much elegance in their appearance."[20] At the top of the hill stood windmills and the Quakers' barnlike meetinghouse.

The only notable features of Nantucket's architecture were the "widows' walks," platforms atop the roofs upon which more romantic writers have imagined Nantucket's female population spending years watching patiently for their husbands' ships to emerge from the sea haze. In fact, many of these women spent much time handling the family business in the absence of their seagoing mates. Any ennui from this existence was, according to a 1772 visitor, rendered insubstantial by a simple expedient:

Frontispiece to The Laws of Siasconset: A Ballad, *by D. A. Leonard, New Bedford, 1797. A unique contemporary rendering of an eighteenth-century fishing village.*

They have adopted these many years the Asiatic custom of taking a dose of opium every morning; and so deeply rooted is it, that they would be at a loss how to live without this indulgence. . . . This is much more prevailing among the women than the men.[21]

By any standard, Nantucket was a queer place. The town abounded in Old Testament names: Shobals, Obeds, or the feminine Keziahs. Three quarters of the male population was at sea. Save for wool and mutton, virtually nothing originated on the island. Those seamen not out whaling spent their time on coasters, bringing in Kennebec lumber, Connecticut River beef and pork, Philadelphia flour, New York ship fittings, or North Carolina caulking tar. Even the whale ships came from the Buzzards Bay yards on the mainland. Provisions for the long whaling voyages were usually taken on in New York, in Edgartown, on nearby Martha's Vineyard, or later in New Bedford.

The once-pampered herds of sheep were now left to survive the elements on their own. To fertilize the barren soil, farmers rented herds for a night, packed them in a field, then passed among them with glowing coals to make the terrified creatures befoul the ground.

The penny-conscious Quakers transformed barren Nantucket into a wealthy land, but their philosophy produced few notable Nantucket figures in American culture (as opposed to their Quaker brethren on the New England mainland or in Pennsylvania). The Quaker school, the countinghouse, the cooperage shop, and

the whaling ship were the course of education for Nantucket boys. There is record of one lad having gone to Harvard in the 1720s, but he returned home soon after having paraded around Cambridge one Election Day dressed as a woman.[22]

One of the few Nantucketers to achieve national attention was Maria Mitchell (1818–1889), who combined her interests in navigational science and counting-house sums to become a great astronomer, though she was ultimately expelled from the Meeting for unorthodoxy.

Probably the best delineation of the Nantucket character came during the Revolutionary War. The town had at this time some 500 homes and 5,000 people, of which some 2,000 males were at sea on between 150 and 200 whaling ships. The ships wandered the Atlantic, hunting the sperm whale, whose great head cavity held the clear fluid that became the oil for lighting the city streets of England and France. With Nantucket's economy based on predominantly European markets, it should have come as no surprise to the mainlanders that the whaling community reacted with indifference to the American colonies' problems with the Crown. This became quite obvious when Nantucket ships brought into Boston Harbor the cargo of tea that the Sons of Liberty soon spread upon the tide. Hatred of Nantucketers increased when merchant William Rotch showed his pacifism by dumping a load of bayonets at sea rather than turning them over to the Revolutionary Army.

Throughout the war Nantucket attempted to remain neutral, and the inhabitants often dealt directly with the mainland British forces. Compounding all this, the

Dr. Alexander Hamilton Visits New England

In 1744 Alexander Hamilton, a worldly bachelor and Maryland physician, decided to journey up the coast and visit the northern colonies. His somewhat droll account has provided a fascinating insight into the life and times of the areas he visited. The following are excerpts:[f]

Old Lyme, Connecticut *After dinner there came a rabble of clowns who fell to disputing upon points of divinity as learnedly as if they had been professed theologues. 'Tis strange to see how this humor prevails, even among the lower class of the people here. They will talk so pointedly about justification, sanctification, adoption, regeneration, repentance, free grace, reprobation, original sin, and a thousand other such pritty, chimerical knick knacks as if they had done nothing but studied divinity all their life time and perused all the lumber of the scholastic divines, and yet the fellows look as much, or rather more, like clowns than the very riffraff of our Maryland planters.*

Stonington, Connecticut *Here we met one Captain Noise, a dealer in cattle, whose name and character seemed pritty well to agree, for he talked very loud, joaked, and laughed heartily att nothing. The landlady here was a queer old woman, an enormous heap of fat. She had some daughters and maids whom she called by comical names. There was Thankfull, Charity, Patience, Comfort, Hope, etc.*

Southern Rhode Island shore *Upon the road here stands a house belonging to an Indian King named George, commonly called King George's house or palace. He possesses twenty or thirty 1000 acres of very fine levell land round this house, upon which he has many tennants and has, of his own, a good stock of horses and other*

cattle. This King lives after the English mode. His subjects have lost their own government policy and laws and are servants or vassals to the English here. His queen goes in a high modish dress in her silks, hoops, stays, and dresses like an English woman. He educates his children to the belles letters and is himself a very complaisant mannerly man. We pay'd him a visit, and he treated us with a glass of good wine.

Boston *. . . We went to Close Street to visit Mrs. Blackater, where we saw the two young ladys, her daughters. They are both pritty ladys, gay and airy. They appear generally att home in a loose deshabille which, in a manner, half hides and half displays their charms, notwithstanding they are clean and neat. Their fine complexions and shapes are good, but they both squint and look two ways with their eyes. . . . It is not half such a flagrant sin [in New England] to cheat an cozen one's neighbor as it is to ride about for pleasure on the sabbath day or neglect going to church and singing of psalms.*

From William Whitstanley's New Help to Discourse: Or Wit and Mirth Intermixt with More Serious Matters . . . *Boston, 1722. A book of facts and anecdotes for the failing conversationalist.*

island held a good number of royalists, who provided refuge for Loyalists driven from their mainland homes. One well-known figure was businesslady Keziah Coffin (1723–1798), known up and down the Atlantic seaboard as the fair-dealing "Aunt Keziah." During the Revolutionary War she smuggled goods to the British by night and by day loudly proclaimed the futility of the Revolutionary cause.

The island's neutrality did little to protect its ships at sea. British ravages of the lumbering whalers reduced the fleet from over 150 to about a dozen. The men themselves were impressed into the British navy, met lingering death aboard rotting prison ships, or volunteered to become whalers for the King.

According to one Nantucket historian, some 1,600-odd seamen of the town's 2,000-odd lost their lives in one way or another during the Revolution.[23]

By the end of the war, Nantucket was prostrate. She had little left of her fleet, and the British had levied impossible import duties. As the Quaker merchants searched for a solution to their poverty, many favored simply abandoning their island home to resettle wherever international regulations would not impede the whaling. Nantucket, after all, was only a base for an industry that then covered half the globe. Around 1786, William Rotch, of bayonet fame, sailed for England and attempted to negotiate a migration to an English port. He was rebuffed. He then turned to France, where he obtained a treaty allowing the city of Nantucket to move en masse to Dunkirk. The great migration never came; the ensuing horrors of the French Revolution soon ended Dunkirk's appeal.

Instead, the Nantucketers remained on their island and slowly rebuilt the industry—with the help of new whaling grounds that were discovered when they rounded Cape Horn into the Pacific in the 1790s.

It may seem somewhat fanciful that a whole population would leave its birthplace and, with a merchant as its Moses, search out a new Promised Land, but during the Revolution it was common for patriot and loyalist alike to sail out from Cape Cod or island homes under a flag of truce to begin again in neutral territory along the Kennebec or in the Maritimes. The Quakers of Nantucket were, it must be remembered, a pragmatic lot, never letting sentiment interfere with logic. Once, in the late 1780s, Benjamin Franklin met two of the islanders on a Philadelphia street. He said that, extending his hospitality, "I invited the two of them to dine with me. Their answer was, that they would, if they could not do better. I suppose they did better, for I never saw them afterwards."[24]

7

The Revolution to the War of 1812

THE REVOLUTION

The Revolution brought on a period of prolonged agony for the people of the New England shore. Long accustomed to protection by the Royal Navy, they suddenly found themselves under siege by their old defenders. The inland farmer could go off to join the Continentals with the expectation that his house, barns, and field would be there upon his return. Along the shore, however, any night might bring sudden raids, burning, and looting, or any dawn reveal a British frigate, stripping the shore of livestock and vessels.

Historians now estimate that one third of the American population supported revolution, one third was loyal to the Crown, and one third was indifferent. There were many along the coast who felt little allegiance to a group that, in their eyes, had knocked the corner posts from a sheltering roof to let it come down on the heads of Whig and Tory alike.

Even patriot leader Joseph Otis on Cape Cod complained after frequent orders to muster up more locals for the army,

There is scarcely a day that the enemy is not within gun-shot of some part of our coast, and they very often anchor in our harbors. . . . As the enemy are around and threaten danger here, it is like dragging men from home when their house is on fire.[1]

Despite this, much of the New England shore entered into the Revolution with a will, as if to seek a self-immolation with the hope of a phoenixlike rebirth. Afterward some communities, such as Salem, surpassed all their pre-Revolutionary dreams, others, like Newport, remained ashes, and a few, like Nantucket, wanted no part of the conflagration and had to be dragged struggling into the flames.

Many of the coastal cities had risen to prominence because of the "Navigation Acts" of the 1660s, which permitted only British (both home and colonial) ships to trade within the empire. America's equal right to the sea was the spark that ultimately flamed desire for revolution among the merchant traders; their unrest was recognized by some of the British long before 1776. The president of the East India Company warned in 1694:

New England is the most prejudicial plantation to this Kingdom. Of all the American plantations, his Majesty has none so apt for the building of shipping—and, in my poor opinion, there is nothing more prejudicial, and in prospect, more dangerous to any mother kingdom, than the increase in shipping in her Colonies.[2]

By tariff protections and other incentives, the Navigation Acts sought to encourage the colonies' production of certain raw materials for the mother country. America was to send hemp and flax for the English textile industry, timber and iron for shipbuilding, and fish. Unfortunately hemp and flax did not grow well in the settled regions east of the Alleghenies. Shipping timber proved too expensive and American shipbuilding grew to overshadow England's. Despite British prohibition, what iron was produced went into American manufactures. The cod, backbone of New England's maritime economy, never reached the homeland; instead, going, for the most part, south to the plantation colonies, and to Catholic Europe. England saw it only in the competition it provided for the home-shore fishing fleets. Wrote one British economist in 1767: "The greater part of their lands will produce nothing but what Britain itself does, and on which she relys, its corn, cattle and wool; by which means the colony interferes with their Mother Country in agriculture, as well as manufactures."[3] Like it or not, England had devoted over 150 years to building a very model of itself in America.

Many colonists might have been satisfied with the status quo, were it not for one detail: the end profit went to England. Trading within the empire always left

Boston, from the summit of Mount Whoredom (later Mount Vernon), by Lt. Gen. Archibald Robertson of the Royal Engineers, 1776. Drawn by Robertson during the occupation of Boston. John Hancock's mansion sits to the right of Beacon Hill, with the city below. Detail from two sections of a five-part 360-degree panorama.

the colonial producers and shippers with "bills of credit" to be used for goods supplied by English merchants. Manipulation of prices by these merchants left the Americans' income from exported goods just short of the cost for necessities imported from England. An owed debt of one million pounds had accrued by the Revolution. Only in stepping outside the British system, by carrying fish to Spain, bringing molasses out of French and Dutch West Indies, running slaves, smuggling, receiving pirated goods did New England merchants obtain hard cash.

This last practice had started so early and was so common that actual enforcement of the law became noteworthy. In 1759, an officer of the Boston port warned a Salem merchant to spread the word among his fellow merchants not to ship any contraband aboard the vessel of a certain Captain Ober:

I shall not concern my self abt. any other Coaster, let'em bring up what they will, but this Capt. Ober has Cheated me in such a manner (tho to no great Value) that I'm determined to keep a good look out on him . . . & if they will Risque any such Prohibetted Goods on sd. Ober's Vessel, they must not (after such notice of my Design) think hard of me.[4]

To become self-sufficient, America lacked only the technology of turning its raw materials into finished goods. If such a thing should happen,

the supplying of themselves with their own necessaries, independent of Great Britain; and trade in their own manufacture; and the relying upon other powers for the vent of their products, it is to be feared, [would] occasion a breach between them and the Mother Country; unless it [were] to be prevented in time.[5]

It was already too late. England had brought America along as far as she could, and now she impeded further growth. When Parliament began in the 1760s enforcing acts intended to restrict the "free trading" activities of the shore cities, America was not to be herded meekly back into the flock.

In Boston, John Hancock organized the merchants, and John Adams the many like-thinking tradesmen and laborers. They worked together to strip power from those who had remained within the system and who still prospered. It often took drastic measures to silence those who still toasted the King's health. Reported Anne Hulton, sister of the King's customs agent in Boston, of one Tory seized by a patriot mob:

He was stripped stark naked, one of the severest cold nights of this winter, his body covered all with tar, then with feathers, his arm dislocated in tearing off his clothes. He was dragged in a cart, with thousands attending, some beating him with clubs and knocking him out of the cart, then in again. This spectacle of horror and cruelty was exhibited for about five hours. . . . It is the second time he has been tarred and feathered and this is looked upon more to intimidate the judges and others, than a spite to the unhappy victim.[6]

By mid-1774, the Royal Navy had sealed off Boston, allowing in only small coasters with food and fuel. By the next summer the British had crossed the harbor to burn Charlestown and fight the Battle of Bunker Hill. They held Boston for another year, until the cannon smuggled in by the patriots from Ticonderoga made their position indefensible. On March 17, 1776, the fleet evacuated the city and sailed for Halifax, Nova Scotia. By then, Boston had been reduced to a sorry state. A Boston patriot entering the city soon after the British evacuation reported:

It presented an indescribable scene of desolation and gloominess, for notwithstand-

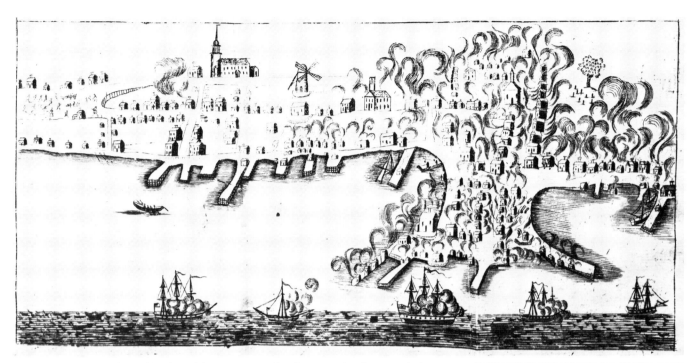

ing the joyous occasion of having driven our enemies from our land, our minds were impressed with an awful sadness at the sight of the ruins of so many houses which had been taken down for fuel—the dirtiness of the streets—the wretched appearance of the very few [nonloyalist] inhabitants who remained during the siege.[7]

The burning of Falmouth (now Portland), Maine, from a 1782 account of the progress of the war.

During its occupation of Boston, the Royal Navy ranged the coast and attacked a number of towns, including Stonington, Connecticut, and Falmouth (now Portland), Maine. In October 1775, a fleet of six British ships, under the command of a Captain Mowatt (who had previously been harassed by local patriots), arrived at Falmouth to announce that, as punishment for aiding the revolutionaries of Boston, the town would be destroyed in two hours. Falmouth quickly fell into pandemonium: "A mingled apparatus of terror and distress!"[8] wrote the local Anglican priest. Some of the cooler heads rowed out to parley with the British, and Mowatt ordered a stay of bombardment till the next day. If by then Falmouth had surrendered its munitions and given hostages for its good behavior, he would consult his superior in Boston for suspension of his orders to burn the town. Though the townsfolk might have agreed to the terms, they were reportedly overruled by an estimated thousand armed revolutionaries from the surrounding countryside, who preferred the town to burn than munitions to be traded for a faint hope. The pastor left this account:

At exactly half an hour after nine, the flag was hoisted to the top of the mast and the cannon began to roar with incessant and tremendous fury. The Commodore, perceiving the streets replete with people, oxen and horses, directed his men to fire over the tops of the houses, but this solemn exhibition struck the multitude into instant alarm . . . some running backwards and forwards with extended arms. Others screaming aloud for assistance. Some were so overcome with the passion of fear as to fall down upon their faces till their companions encouraged them to arise and hasten out of danger. Many affirmed themselves to be killed dead on the spot, but notwithstanding these dismal apprehensions, all escaped unhurt. With the town emptied, the barrage began in earnest. And now a scene inexpressibly grand and terrible was exhibited in the view of thousands of sorrowful spectators. Bombs and

caracasses [mortar shells] armed with destruction and streaming with fire blazed dreadfully through the air and descended with flaming vengence on the defenseless buildings.[9]

Since no wind blew to carry the flames, it took 12 hours of constant firing to destroy the town.

In a word, about three-quarters [400 buildings] of the town was consumed and between two and three hundred families . . . were now in many instances destitute of a hut for themselves and families; and as a tedious winter was approaching, they had before them a most gloomy and depressing prospect.[10]

For the duration of the war, Falmouth lay in ruins, only a few townsfolk returned to the rubble of their homes, and fewer rebuilt, lest they provide a tempting target for a second raid.

In late 1776, Parliament passed a law prohibiting trade with the American Colonies. The Royal Navy returned to New England waters and seized Newport as their blockade base. From here they sent out blockade squadrons to set up pickets along the coast, harassing shore towns, impressing seamen, and confiscating vessels. The fishing fleets were the first casualties, leaving Marblehead, Gloucester, and many Cape Cod towns in economic ruin.

Those American ships still afloat were fair game for the English pickets. One Yankee sailor, Ebenezor Fox, tells how the ship to which he was cabin boy left Santo Domingo headed for Providence, only to make first landfall at Stonington and find that hostilities had broken out. They were determined to make Providence with their cargo.

We left Stonington in the night . . . in the morning found ourselves close by the enemy . . . we bore away and ran our vessel ashore. . . . Our captain [who remained with the ship] having given permission to all . . . the mate and crew jumped overboard and swam for the shore. . . . I plunged into the sea and swam for the shore, where I arrived without injury, but nearly exhausted from fatigue and fear, not a little augmented by the sounds of bullets which whistled around my head while in the water. In dread of pursuit, I ran into a cornfield, and finding my wet clothes an incumbrance, I stripped them off and ran with all speed through the field.[11]

In this "state of nature" Fox soon overtook his shipmates, who gave him clothes and told him that but for his lack of a fig leaf he looked just like Adam hastily exiting from Eden.

Although Britain controlled the seas, its force was far from overwhelming. The blockading fleet had only a few dozen ships of any size with which to patrol the coast from Maine to Florida. Since the close of hostilities with France in the 1760s, the Royal Navy had fallen to slack strength, and the sudden unavailability of New England masts slowed her recovery. Like the British troops advancing in a phalanx, the British Navy could vanquish all that did battle openly with her, but she could not contend with the many seaport towns that sent out ships like snipers to attack whenever her back was turned. The Royal Navy's decision was to follow the colonists' lead, and harass the shore towns, rather than attempt to subdue the whole coast, and for eight years the New England shore population went to bed in fear of nocturnal raids or the arrival of men-of-war with the dawn's light; yet by day they carried on a semblance of normal maritime activity.

Most of the shipbuilding efforts of the Revolutionary era went into fitting out privateers: fast, light boats that avoided formal engagement with the Royal Navy but could lie outside harbors in the British Isles and seize merchant vessels within sight of the land garrisons. During the Revolution, over 1,000 privateers set out from American ports for the high seas, and most sailed from New England.

Privateering was especially popular in wartime for many reasons. Constructing and manning the ships reemployed all the shipwrights and sailors left jobless by the blockade and promised a profit for those able to catch some merchantman on the high seas. Usually the cargo seized was brought home to be auctioned off to the townspeople. Many uncommissioned "privateers" set out on more piratical voyages, plundering Tory refuges and other settlements in the Maritime Provinces.

Probably the worst aspect of the whole eight-year struggle of the Revolution as it affected the New England coast was the constant warring between patriot and loyalist factions. Mob combat plagued life on Cape Cod. Liberty poles went up by day, to be cut down at night. The squadron of British ships at anchor in Provincetown Harbor prevented the patriots from overcoming the loyalists. At Portsmouth, New Hampshire, the revolutionary military commander complained to General Washington:

> That infernal crew of Tories . . . walk the streets here with impunity; and will, with a sneer, tell the people in the streets, that all our liberty-poles will soon be converted into gallows. I must entreat your Excellency to give some directions, what to do with these persons, as I am fully convinced, that if an engagement was to happen, they would, with their own hands, set fire to the town.[12]

Many Tory merchants, with foresight and Royal Navy assistance, antagonized patriots by removing goods they would surely need, and hiding them in loyalist strongholds. The revolutionaries responded to this problem by driving out all who showed loyalist sympathies. Many Tories were physically abused, driven to flee with few possessions, and their estates were confiscated by the colony governments. Those who were able sailed for England or the Maritimes, but many could only hurry to the nearest refuge under British control: first Boston, later Newport, New York, and Long Island. From these bases, many Tories regrouped and undertook missions of revenge against their old persecutors.

The concentration of exiles near New England's southern shore made life there precarious for both sides. Loyalists and patriots alike organized raiding parties, setting out by night in light versions of the many-oared whaleboats to ravage the unprotected settlements of their enemies. These craft became known as "shaving mills," an allusion to the thin corkscrews of wood from a carpenter's plane. In

A British raiding party coming ashore in Connecticut. Contemporary illustration to the mock-epic poem on the Revolution, McFingal, *by John Trumbull.*

The British destroying the American fleet off Castine in 1779. To drive out the British setting up fortifications at Castine, Massachusetts organized its own "state navy." Internal politics among land and sea commands stalled the fleet's assault and they were finally routed by British reinforcements. Retreating up the Penobscot, the revolutionaries scuttled their vessels and escaped overland.

many cases the combat was personal, old scores were settled and vengeances inflicted, particularly by the embittered Tories. The Connecticut shore found itself especially vulnerable to loyalist raiders from the north shore of Long Island.

Revolution-era traffic along the Sound was not entirely warlike, however. A smuggling business flourished. Since the Americans had cut themselves off from English finished goods, and the British forces needed produce, many Connecticut men and dispossessed Long Islanders often slipped nocturnally across the Sound with livestock and corn for New York merchants. For a long time after the Revolution the people of the Connecticut shore towns still described shady businessmen as "Long Island Traders."

At one point the British envisioned turning the eastern half of Maine into "New Ireland." In one stroke this would resettle the displaced Tories, create a buffer between New England and the Canadian Maritimes, and implant a forever hostile refugee population along the Colonies' northern flank. The British sent a small force down in the summer of 1779 to occupy Castine, in Penobscot Bay. Massachusetts sent up a fleet of 20 ships and 2,000 troops to drive them out. The patriots' expedition was a fiasco, and the British commander, who planned to surrender on the first cannon shot, watched the revolutionaries argue among themselves until British reenforcements arrived to rout the "Massachusetts State Navy."

Britain held control of eastern Maine until the war's end, and Massachusetts lost much of the prestige it had gained from firing the first guns of the Revolution. New Ireland, however, never received its expected population, and the many displaced loyalists remained in Nova Scotia or on Long Island.

The last few years of the war also brought formal military engagements to the southern New England shore. After indecisive battles with the Continentals by land and a meeting with the French fleet at sea (which ultimately left both sides battling a hurricane rather than each other), the English departed from Newport in 1779. They burned some 500 houses and left the town destitute. In the same year, Redcoats landed along the Connecticut shore, raiding and razing. Two years later, under Benedict Arnold, they laid waste to New London and nearby Groton.

In 1781 Cornwallis's forces marched out of Yorktown in surrender, with their fifes and drums playing "The World Turned Upside Down." The war, however, had by that time grown beyond an English-American conflict. France, Spain, and

Holland had seized the opportunity to attack their old adversary. America had to wait for the settlement of the European conflict in 1783 before official peace began, and the new nation could sit down and plan its own future.

At first that future looked grim. Depression gripped the land. The old order had gone. Tory merchants, such as those whose pre-Revolution mansions lined Cambridge's "Tory Row," were either impoverished or had emigrated. Those who had remained, in hopes of a British victory or Congressional remuneration for their losses, now gave up the cause and became the band of "United Empire Loyalists," who, 50,000 strong from New York and New England, left to begin again in Canada.

Life in the fishing villages was equally bad. While Britain ceded America the "privilege" of fishing in Canadian waters, she prohibited American ships from selling their catch to their old West Indies customers. America was no longer under the protective trade umbrella of the Crown. She was a foreign competitor and faced a wall of exclusionary import duties. British cannon no longer sheltered Americans on the high seas, and Yankee ships became fair game for such marauders as the Barbary pirates.

Many colonial ports, including Newport, Portsmouth, and Marblehead, fell into an economic malaise from which they never fully recovered.

Elijah Cobb, of Brewster on Cape Cod, told how, after the death of his father at sea, he had been sent to work at the age of six to support his mother and five siblings. Luck evaded the family until, in the midst of the 1783 depression, Cobb, then 14, took his chances in Boston:

The first time I went down the Long Wharf, and stood gazing at a new vessel, wondering, and admiring her monstrous size, her great cables and anchors, etc.— A gentleman stepped from her deck and thus accosted me!
"My lad, do you want a voyage?"
"Yes sir."
"Will you go with me on this vessel?"
"Where are you bound sir?"
"To Surinam."
"I am told sir, that all flesh die that go there."
"Well my boy, to prove that you have not been told the truth, I have been there thirteen voyages, and you see I am alive yet!"[13]

Cobb signed on and helped to collect a crew of hometown friends, bringing financial security to his Cape village.

Desperate voyages such as these became common after the Revolution and they ultimately brought a golden age to those cities that struck out boldly for ports of call in new places—Russia, Scandinavia, South Africa, the islands of the Indian Ocean, and, especially, China. It was a short and glorious period. Lasting some twenty-odd years and cut short by the embargo and War of 1812, it transformed many sleepy old gambrel-roofed towns to vistas of porticoed Federal mansions.

The new prosperity began as the large privateers of the Revolution were converted to armed cargo carriers and sent out to trade with the few non-Empire nations such as China and Russia, unallied with the vast territories held by the English, French, Dutch, and Spanish. Then came Napoleon's rise to power in the 1790s, and Europe was quickly embroiled in war. As these major powers impressed their merchant seamen to stock men-of-war, America was suddenly left alone on the seas. The far-flung ports that had once barred American ships from discharging cargo now clamored for the neutral Americans to bring them supplies.

Old regions again became alive. The Connecticut River "gods" resumed sending their livestock ships to the West Indies. Long lines of ox-drawn sleds made their

Crowninshield's Wharf, *George Ropes,*
1806, Salem.

way by winter's freeze out of interior farms to Portland, Newburyport, Boston,
Providence, and other growing ports.

The profit was not without danger. Each side took a dim view of neutrals trading
with their enemy and lay in wait to attack American ships putting into enemy
ports. No matter; where there was trade, there were New Englanders eager to
take the chance.

Boston led the field. The Yale president, Timothy Dwight, wrote that "their
enterprizes are sudden, bold, and sometimes rash. A general spirit of adventure
prevails here, which in numerous instances has been means of attempts made
with honor and success in cases where many of their commercial neighbors would
have refused to adventure at all."[14]

It was most likely the city's success in the era's most profitable business—the
China trade—that inspired Dwight as he wrote this. The merchants of his native
Connecticut had considered the gamble of sending ships halfway around the world,
but, known for their steady habits, they had refused to undertake the voyage
unless the state legislature promised reimbursement should the venture fail.

Trade with China had been carried on for centuries by Dutch, English, and
Portuguese merchants. In February 1784, only a few months after the British
army's departure from New York, the *Empress of China* left that city's docks for

Coastal New England

a direct run to Canton—China's one port open to the Western world. Other cities quickly sent *their* ships. Canton was controlled by businessmen, or "hongs," who were appointed by the emperor to oversee the exchange of Chinese "gifts" for foreign "tribute." There were no monopolistic agreements with European powers, and the hongs welcomed anyone with a suitable cargo. Even better, these cultivated gentlemen did business amicably, giving the foreigners a fair exchange for their goods, thus encouraging a future supply of attractive imports.

By the early 1790s, both Boston and Salem had a well-established business with the orient. Boston ships setting out for China rounded Cape Horn into the Pacific, then worked their way up the coasts of South and North America to obtain the seal and otter pelts much desired in China. Their rival merchants in Salem started with a series of lesser voyages in smaller vessels, which scoured the Atlantic shores for commodities scarce to the orient; they collected iron, hemp, and canvas duck from the Baltic region, wine and lead from Europe, sugar from the West Indies, and fish, flour, and tobacco from America. Then they consolidated the goods and traveled to China through the other half of the world: down to the Cape of Good Hope, across the Indian Ocean, and up the China Sea. In this way they put into many more African, Indian, and East Indian ports and collected a greater variety of items for the China trade.

Salem had at first shipped over the ginseng root, which grows wild in New England hardwood forests and which was prized as an aphrodisiac by the Chinese, but found the market overrated (as is the legend concerning Salem's profits from the ginseng trade). They did, however, find that the common Atlantic coast sea cucumber was a Chinese delicacy, and soon they added it to the many goods on the ships' manifests. In exchange, the Salem ships returned with tea, silk, and yellow nankeen (Nanking cotton), as well as other luxuries such as Blue Willow ware, bamboo furniture, and brocade. They also brought back Java coffee, Madagascar copal (a resin), Bombay cotton, Calcutta ginger and rock candy, and Sumatran pepper (which seamen harvested in the wilds to break the Dutch monopoly at Batavia, making Salem the world's pepper capital). A successful voyage could double a merchant's original investment.

Such profits transformed Salem into a city of fabled opulence and grandeur.

As a harbor Salem had little to recommend it. Before the Revolution it was just one of the many secondary triangular trade ports. Even the relatively small ships of the late eighteenth century found the town, as Timothy Dwight put it,

Ill fitted for commercial enterprize. All vessels drawing more than twelve feet of water must unladen at a distance from the town by lighters, and the wharves at low water are left dry. Nor are the encouragements on the land side much greater. The produce of almost all the interior is engrossed by Boston.[15]

Yet this town became such a great mercantile "city-state" that it is said the hongs of Canton believed it to be a vast country in itself (though one must also take into account the diplomatic tact of a hong discussing business over tea with some pride-flushed Salem supercargo). Salem was not very large. As it gained its new sea legs, it had a population in 1783 of 6,665, of which 1,283 were the work force of men between the ages of 16 and 50. The town, though the sixth largest in the colonies, was just one long street, with side lanes running down to tidewater.

Salem had tasted the good life through privateering ventures during the Revolution and saw no reason to return now to carrying cod, lumber, and barrel staves. In any case, the New England fishing industry was then moribund. The neighboring fishing villages of Beverly and Marblehead had lost their vessels in the war, and their fishing grounds in the ensuing peace.

Although its population never more than doubled during its maritime heyday, between the close of the Revolution and the start of the War of 1812, Salem's monetary wealth multiplied by the hundreds.

Now such fortunes were being made, you could not believe your eyes, nor the figures you saw on the custom-house books. . . . Seemingly the wealth of the world was funneled into Salem. Springing up out of it came the great houses, silk gowns, pianos, French perfumes and French hairdressing. Gardens, carriages, imported carriage horses. Servants (not old-fashioned "help"), silver, gold, diamonds. And ladies could afford to have the vapors, and gentlemen gout, valets, mistresses.[16]

Salem, by the start of the nineteenth century, was heady with its profits. People talked trade everywhere: on the docks, under the skylights of the counting rooms, within the high lofted warehouses, at the men's clubs, over ladies' teas, and in the dignified libraries of the merchant mansions.

The moneyed people of Salem practiced diversity in their investments. Ships were owned by from 2 to 15 persons, and the cargoes themselves were divided up into shares, purchased by any number of the town's 225 or so mercantile investors. For those townspeople with insufficient funds to purchase shares in the main cargo of a voyage, the "venture" system was developed. Sailors were each

Newburyport and Its Timothy Dexter

In the northeast corner of Massachusetts, just up from the mouth of the Merrimac River, lies Newburyport. Its streets and homes have changed little since its days of Federalist glory. From the end of the Revolution to the start of the 1812 embargo, the town grew in shipping, beautiful homes, and culture, and it enjoyed the rosiest of outlooks until the waterfront district went up in a fire in 1812. By the time Europe was at peace again, the larger ships had too deep a draft to cross the bar at the river mouth. Newburyport became, in the phrase of John P. Marquand, a "Federalist Pompeii."

Part of the town's fame, however, lies in the most bizarre, and consequently most beloved, of all the bold entrepreneurs of the Federalist era, "Lord" Timothy Dexter.

Dexter, a tanner turned merchant, made a fortune by acting the fool. After the Revolution, he bought up, at reduced face value, promissory notes given to soldiers by the government in place of pay. At the time, the notes seemed likely to remain worthless. But when the government later redeemed them at full value, Dexter was on his way to fortune. With this money, he cornered the whalebone

market. As he related in his uproarious autobiography, *A Pickle for the Knowing Ones* (1802):

> *bort all in Boston salum and all in Noue york under Cover oppenly told them for my ships [that he was buying the whalebone for ships' ribs] they all laffed so I had my oan pris [own price] I had four Counning men for Rounners they found the hourne as I told them to act the fool I was full of Cash. . . . all the time the Creaters more or less laffing it spread very fast here is the Rub—in fifty days they smelt a Rat—found where it was gone to Nouebry Port—spekkelaters swarming like hell houns—to be short with it I made seventy five per cent profit.*[a]

Dexter put this money into warming pans, which he sold in the West Indies to plantation owners. They made perfect ladles, with the tops as skimmers, for the sugar cane simmering into molasses in the great vats.

Dexter constantly played the part of a fool who blundered his way to fortune. In truth, he was a shrewd Yankee who knew that a reputation for cunning would hinder his bargaining. In the role of simpleton he could buy what others found useless, at low rates, then turn around and retail them in novel ways.

Dexter seems to have lived his whole life as a sham to protect his business im-

Timothy Dexter's mansion, with the collection of life-sized statues of Dexter's favorite heroes. From an 1840 lithograph.

age. He built a mansion in Newburyport. Lifesized statues of all the public figures he admired adorned columns placed in the front yard and made it quite the local attraction. Wrote a visitor in 1804:

> *His house may be denominated a palace, although the most absurd taste has been employed to render it ridiculous. . . . He showed us his tomb in the garden . . . where he had his coffin ready made, and painted, like his house, white, with green edges. . . . We were shown into the principal apartments, and even into the chambers of the house; the plate was exhibited. . . . In some of the elegant chambers, potatoes were spread over the floor; and in some, nuts and dried herbs; and in others, old barrels and various sorts of refuse articles.*[b]

Here he lived with his much-abused wife and halfwit son.

allowed to take along some 800 pounds weight in personal cargo. They also took on small "ventures" from local folk—money to buy certain foreign items, or a sack of corn, or an ornate highboy to trade. The town's leading merchants benefited greatly from this practice, which they refined into a town institution, choosing their own supercargos from youths weaned on the venture system.

Everyone shared the prosperity with the merchants and private venturers. Everything related to the ships became an important event. People of Salem had a sense of their place in history, as a new city-state in a new nation.

The influence of the sea trade permeated even to the secluded parlors of the town's belles. One minister quit Salem in horror after discovering that the maiden of his desires had, in private teas with other young ladies of quality, actually bantered phrases fit only for shipboard sailors. This is not to suggest that Salem's Puritan heritage was altogether buried. When the town built a new market building in the 1790s, the manager of a Boston theater proposed to rent the market's upper floor and bring the stage to Salem. The town fathers responded gravely in the negative, adding that they would sooner set the place afire.

What most struck the visitor to Salem was not so much the homes, public buildings, or vessels, as it was the incredible variety of merchandise, curios, souvenirs, and other wonders of far-off lands that filled the town's many little shops and knickknack shelves. From live elephants to the jaw-breaking rock candies called "Gibralters," they all first came to America by way of Salem.

Gingham, crepe de chine, and nankeen were all introduced to America from oriental looms. The last material, sturdy and brownish-yellow, was often made into trousers that Salem businessmen wore as a virtual badge of office. The trousers were sometimes topped by a mandarin coat and an East Indian handkerchief for a necktie. This same Indian bandanna also served common duty about town as a carrying bag, enclosing within its knotted corners everything from groceries to weighty tomes. In bad weather, almost everyone clumped about in the latest boots, of imported gum rubber.

In Salem, the old families clung to their export porcelain and bamboo furniture, or its "Sheraton Bamboo" hardwood imitations, long after the styles had waned elsewhere. Besides fine domestic articles, many people, rich and poor, young and old, collected Chinese coins, called "cash." These were hoarded and exchanged with all the enthusiasm given our modern baseball cards.

Sometimes silk-robed or beturbaned orientals themselves would be making the return voyages: young men of families counterparts to the Salem merchants', paying reciprocal visits and observing business techniques. Though rich in the material wealth of the far east, Salem, like all New England ports trading around the world, was little affected by the intellectual heritage of the lands it contacted. It would take a few more generations before Thoreau, Emerson, and other Transcendentalists would delve into Buddhism or Hinduism, and begin translating such thought into passages of New England idiom. Only the patriarchal and orderly maxims of Confucius made any intellectual headway among foursquare Yankees raised on the sayings of Ben Franklin's *Poor Richard's Almanac.*

With such an influx of the strange and exotic, Salem, like most shipping cities of the age, had a public institution wherein one found a "cabinet of natural and artificial curiosities": a glass-fronted case filled with silkworm cocoons, Indonesian masks, native islanders' weapons, and other items picked up by the Yankee sailors. Less well known, but probably more heavily frequented, was a similar collection of items, fit only for adult males, which invariably was housed in a back room of the local barber shop. Here were the shrunken heads and other grim relics of island cannibals. Likewise one could view the export products created by oriental craftsmen for the Yankee sailors, among them beautiful black lacquered folding screens with highly stylized figures on them. They depicted, however, not weeping

willows, pagodas, or arching foot bridges, but characters in quite bizarre and hilariously erotic positions.

Salem's more genteel collections eventually became housed in the rooms of the East India Marine Society, a select group organized in 1799 and limited to Salem captains and supercargos who had ventured into Pacific or Indian Ocean waters. This elite founded a repository of travel and trade reports so that future voyagers could profit from past experiences. They also began a collection of Oceanic curiosities, which each member, in subsequent voyages, tried to outdo: a pregnant queen ant, an African elephant's tail, a flying dragon, four young catfish, Java lava, a hairball from the stomach of a Madagascar cow, a two-headed dogfish, the embalmed head of a New Zealand chief, and so on until there were another 5,000 items by the 1830s. Known today as the Peabody Museum and open to all, it is an ethnologist's paradise, housing perhaps the world's most complete collection of South Sea artifacts. Even more than the streets of tree-shaded mansions, this assortment of the world's most heterogeneous items reflects the true personality of old Salem.

EASTPORT

The first few decades after the Revolution produced an era of optimism among the mercantile towns up and down the New England coast. Wealth seemed to materialize for all who pursued it, from merchant to mechanic to sailor. There were jobs and good pay for all.

The embargo and War of 1812 dramatically interrupted this prosperous moment. Much of the era's profits had come from letting the European nations fight among themselves and remaining neutral, carrying the goods of all. While each side gladly accepted trade with American ships, the antagonists in the Napoleonic conflicts began, as we have seen, to look with disfavor on trade with their enemies.

Unfortunately there was little America could do. The Revolutionary War navy had been given to France as war payment. The Royal Navy and the French fleet were so formidable that no one dreamed that America might build a navy to match them. Contempt for the new nation ran so strong that France went so far as to offer to take Newport as its North American naval base, arguing that it could protect America's shores in war and prove a ready market for Yankee foodstuff in peace. America declined the offer. The Jeffersonian Democrats of the agrarian south envisioned defending our shores with land-based forts and floating batteries that could be shuffled up and down the coast wherever needed. The northern Federalists favored privateering. Neither political party, one isolationist, the other profit-oriented, seemed to address the question of shouldering America to a position of respect among nations by a show of might.

In the face of continued harassment, President Jefferson passed an act that cut off American foreign trade: the Embargo Act.

Salem

The Indies Trade:

We had on a mixed cargo, and we might be going to trade at eastern ports on the way out. Nobody knew what market we should find in Calcutta. It was pure adventure, and a calculation of chances, and it was a great school of character. It was a trade that made men as well as fortunes; it took thought and forethought. The owners planned their ventures like generals planning a campaign. They were not going to see us again for a year; they were not going to hear of us till we signaled outside the harbor on our return. When we sailed it was an event, a ceremony, a solemnity, and we celebrated it from all the tarry throats on board. Yes, the men used to sing as we dropped down the bay.

—William Dean Howells, *A Woman's Reason*

The Custom House:

On some such morning, when three or four vessels happen to have arrived at once,—usually from Africa or South America,—or to be on the verge of their departure thitherward, there is a sound of frequent feet, passing briskly up and down the granite steps. Here, before his own wife has greeted him, you may greet the sea-flushed

shipmaster, just in port, with his vessel's papers under his arm, in a tarnished tin box. Here, too, comes his owner, cheerful or sombre, gracious or in the sulks, accordingly as his scheme of the now accomplished voyage has been realized in merchandise that will readily be turned to gold, or has buried him under a bulk of incommodities, such as nobody will care to rid him of.

Chestnut Street, Salem.

Here, likewise,—the germ of the wrinkle-browed, grizzly-bearded, careworn merchant,—we have the smart young clerk, who gets the taste of traffic as a wolf-cub does of blood, and already sends adventures in his master's ships, when he had better be sailing mimic-boats upon a mill-pond. Another figure in the scene is the outward-bound sailor, in quest of a protection; or the recently arrived one, pale and feeble, seeking a passport to the hospital.

—Nathaniel Hawthorne, "The Custom House," introduction to *The Scarlet Letter*

Our ships all in motion, Once whiten'd the ocean,
They sail'd and return'd with their cargo;
Now doom'd to decay, they have fallen a prey
To Jefferson, Worms, and Embargo

went part of a poem that reflected the mercantile reaction.

By withholding raw materials, the embargo of 1807, later modified to apply only to those nations engaged in the Napoleonic Wars, was intended to injure Europe more than America. Be that as it may, it brought New England's shore towns to their knees. Ships lay rotting and worm-eaten at dockside. The wharves turned green with grass and weeds. Sailors trudged out to the tide flats with the rest of the town to dig clams. The inverted tar barrels protecting the sail-less mast-tops were called "Jefferson nightcaps."

New England did not lie passive. For as long as President Jefferson had been in office, the politicians and merchants of New England had been hatching highly radical plots. A leader of the Essex Junto, an old political alliance based in Essex

---

A visit to the Elias Hasket Derby Mansion:

The evening was calm and delightful, and the moon shone in its greatest splendor. We entered the house, and the door opened into a spacious entry; on each side were large white marble images. We passed on by doors on each side opening into the drawing room, dining room, parlor, etc. etc., and at the farther part of the entry a door opened into a large magnificent oval room. . . . The large marble vases, the images, the mirrors to correspond with the windows, gave it so uniform and finished an appearance, that I could not think it possible I viewed objects that were real. . . . You can scarcely conceive anything more superb. We descended into the garden, which is laid out with exquisite taste, and airy irregularity seems to characterize the whole. At the foot of the garden there was a summer house, and a row of tall poplar trees which hid everything beyond from sight, and formed a kind of walk. I arrived there and to my astonishment found thro' the opening of the trees that there was a beautiful terrace the whole width of the garden; 'twas twenty feet up from the street, and graveled on the top with a white balustrade round; 'twas almost level, and the poplar trees so close that we could only occasionally catch a glimpse of the house. The moon shone full upon it. . . . A large dome

swells quite up to the chamber windows and is railed round on top and forms a delightful walk.

—Eliza Southgate Bowne, *A Girl's Life Eighty Years Ago*

The reconstructed Samuel McIntire Arch. A modern copy of one erected around 1810, when old Salem Common was cleaned up and rededicated as Washington Square. Facing the arch is the Andrew-Safford House, built in 1818. This mansion was the final swan song of Salem's era of great homes.

The children:

One thing of which we never tired was a pair of Chinese picturebooks, with paintings on rice paper in clear and brilliant colors. There was, of course, no attempt at perspective, and we were much entertained by the little mandarins walking calmly about in the sky, quite over the heads of the jugglers with their yellow balls and the women under flat-topped umbrellas. A pair of carved ivory chopsticks also appeared during the display of Chinese curiosities, and Miss Eliza-Ann, from her corner, fed in a few darkly learned remarks concerning Confucius, to which we listened with respect and vacuity. Miss Eliza-Ann was always ready enough to give us useful information, and she was generally called upon to tell us about a curious Japanese bonze in painted clay, with naked chest and stomach. It had an ugly, wrinkled face, and was squatted on its feet. Miss Eliza-Ann explained all about it in very long words, but we only gathered that the bonze was a holy man or priest, and we secretly thought it a pity that while his robes were otherwise so voluminous, so much of his person should be exposed to the inclemency of the weather.

—Eleanor Putnam, *Old Salem*

Windmill at Eastport, Maine.

County, Massachusetts (Newburyport, Salem, and Gloucester), wrote to a Boston merchant:

> *I do not believe in the practicality of a long-continued union [of the United States]. A northern confederacy would unite congenial characters, and present a fairer prospect of public happiness; while the southern states, having similar habits, might be left "to manage their own affairs in their own way." If a separation were to take place, our mutual wants would render a friendly and commercial intercourse inevitable.*[17]

The New England shore would form the nucleus of this new nation.

This northern secession never came. While honest merchants were ruined, others simply evaded the embargo by smuggling. There are those who point out the wharfside decay of the shipping towns, but an equal number of historians point out the incredible rise in goods being shipped to the border towns adjoining Canada and Spanish-owned Florida. In 1807, Boston Harbor recorded some 150 movements—arrivals or departures—of vessels trading along the upper Maine coast. In 1808, with the embargo in force, some 600 coasters departed with supplies for that region,[18] which, it seemed, suddenly acquired an incredible appetite for flour, barreled beef, and the raw cotton previously shipped to English mills.

The center of this activity was Eastport, set on a modest island nestled in Passamaquoddy Bay between the Canadian Campobello Island and the American mainland.

Incorporated as a town in 1798, it was first settled by Massachusetts Bay and Cape Ann fishermen around the time of the Revolution. By 1790 the village had some 80 people, making up about 22 families. On the landward side, there had been little development. The cultivation of Down East Maine was still at a rudimentary stage. Settlers faced long winters and a soil "reluctant to the plow." They had strung their houses out along the seashore. There were no roads, only connecting paths between homesteads. Anything too big to be carried under the arm went by boat. Life was so amphibious that one Eastport citizen later reminisced about "the surprise, curiosity, and even fear excited by a horse that was brought to the island in 1804."[19]

Nor were conditions to seaward ideal. A 15-foot tide drained miles of mud flats, and then sent citizens scurrying to shore, away from their crabbing and clamming, over rock, muck, and seaweed, accompanied by a menagerie of stray dogs, chickens, and hogs, as the waters returned in a rushing tidal bore. Even in deeper waters, the currents through the islands and bays set up whirlpools to trap the unwary navigator. Finally, the fogs that pervade the region are such that even if blue skies cover land and sea, obscurity still settles in at river mouths and over tidal rips between mainland and island. Here strong currents from the tidal fluctuations bring up cooler deep water to meet the warmer air. If there is no wind, knots of fog hang here like ghosts.

In all, Eastport was a smuggler's paradise. As the embargo went into effect, the town began receiving up to 75,000 barrels of provisions a month. Every little cove, every place where the tall evergreens overhung the rocky shore, quite literally every place with room just above tideline—all were stacked high with Canada-bound goods. A Boston newspaper reported how the people of the Eastport region had grown rich guarding landed provisions for two dollars a day, while in every fog they loaded the contraband in small boats and rowed madly for the Canadian shore.[20]

Speed was not essential, though. Customs agents, those who actually tried to do their job, standing guard on headlands (during one point in time they were stationed at twenty-rod intervals along the shore), were hard pressed to make out the sounds of oars against the soft irregular lapping of water against stony beaches. A few agents did their best, but most were either sympathetic to, related to, or in the pay of, their counterparts skulking about the rocks.

When the embargo on all imports was modified to a ban on English and French merchandise, Eastport, with its some 1,500 citizens, began a service of bringing in British cargoes (landed on nearby Campobello and Indian islands), which by dint

Smuggling. From The Book of Commerce.

A Submarine Fights the British at New London in the War of 1812?

In the midst of the rumors and hysteria, a cryptic article appeared in a number of national newspapers, among them Baltimore's *Niles' Weekly Register* of July 17, 1813, describing an incident during the blockade of New London. It reported that

. . . a gentleman at Norwich has invented a diving boat, which by means of paddles he can propel under water at the rate of three miles an hour, and ascend and descend at pleasure. He has made a number of experiments, and been three times under the [British flagship] Ramilies, off New London. In the first attempt after remaining under some time, he came to the top of the water like the Porpoise for air, and as luck would have it, came up but a few feet from the stern of the Ramilies, and was observed by the centinels, on deck, who sung out—"Boat Ahoy"—immediately upon hearing which, the boat descended without making a reply. Seeing this an alarm gun was fired on board the ship and all hands called to quarters—the cable cut and the ship got under way with all possible dispatch, expecting every moment to be blown up by a torpedo. In the third attempt he came up directly under the Ramilies, and fastened himself and his boat to her keel, where he remained half an hour, and succeeded in perforating a hole through her copper, and while engaged in screwing a torpedo to her bottom, the screw broke, and defeated his object for that time. So great is the alarm and fear aboard the Ramilies of some such strategem being played off upon them, that com. [Commodore] Hardy has withdrawn his force from before New London, and keeps his ship under way all the time, instead of lying at anchor as formerly.[c]

Historians have little comment on this report. One book on United States naval history suggests that some credit a Mr. Mix, while Sir Thomas Hardy himself suspected Robert Fulton, who had built his submarine *Nautilus* in 1801.

The story itself could have been a planted fabrication to scare off the British. Torpedoes, then simply waterproof bombs, attached to rowboats, did damage to the British off New London. What gives the account an air of credibility, however, is the submarine's similarity to the submarine *Turtle* of the Revolution.

The *Turtle* was built by its inventor, David Bushnell, in Old Saybrook, not far from New London. She was transported to New York, where she made her famous attempts on the British ships in the harbor. The *Turtle* was later lost when the ship carrying her up the Hudson sank. After the end of the Revolution, Bushnell spent some years in Norwich, just up the Thames estuary from New London. During the War of 1812 he was reportedly in France. Could the "gentleman at Norwich" have been someone with whom Bushnell had worked and who possessed

The Turtle II, *a Bicentennial reconstruction of Bushnell's* Turtle. *In front of the viewing port is the propeller for rising, and the drill to attach the powder keg (at right) to a ship's hull. A snorkel system is just behind the combined hatch and viewing port. The reconstruction is now displayed at the Connecticut River Foundation, Essex, Connecticut.*

the plans of the *Turtle*? Did Bushnell himself try to construct a second *Turtle* in Norwich after the Revolution? Given the pro-British sentiment of a good part of the local population, it is no surprise that such secrecy surrounded even the question of whether the event had actually occurred.

of paperwork became neutral Scandinavian goods. Every rowboat now sported Swedish registry, though all spent their whole time shuffling back and forth between Eastport docks and nearby Canadian waters.

The Nonintercourse Acts tottered on ineffectually until the Anglo-American conflict finally broke into a declaration of war by Congress in June 1812. Despite the outcries of the mercantile northeast, the declaration was pushed through by the "War Hawks," representatives from frontier states that had been under constant harassment by Indians who were armed by the British in Canada. Although many reasoned that Great Britain, still enmeshed with Napoleon, would avoid additional conflict and quickly settle its differences with America, she chose instead to rally against her former colonies.

The antiwar sentiment of the New Englanders did not go unnoticed, however; when the British fleet moved in along the Atlantic coastline in early 1813 and set up a blockade from New York City south, they left New England unmolested. British frigates patroled Yankee waters, but more to protect smugglers from privateers and American warships than to blockade the coast. Off Cape Cod, ships of the Royal Navy escorted British merchant ships that received cargo from Yankee fishing boats turned contraband runners. American naval vessels frequented the same waters, but often proved ineffectual at stopping either Briton or smuggler.

One British-American sea duel took place off Portland in September 1813. A Yankee ship, under "Swedish" registry, had hired the Royal Navy brig *Boxer* to escort her along the Maine coast from Canada, protecting her from American privateers commissioned to seize the vessel of any fellow countryman trading with the British. After she reached Bath (at one point having been towed through fog by the *Boxer*), the American ship ran ashore as the *Boxer* fired blank cannon, making it seem that the British were giving chase. The cannon echoes were heard by the crew of the USS *Enterprise* and they gave challenge. The bloody American victory that followed gave the new nation a name to be immortalized over the centuries in a long line of battleships, aircraft carriers, and space shuttles.

Victories such as this were few. The British raided communities south of New York at will, even burning Washington, and, as the war progressed, the blockade gradually worked its way up the New England coast. In the summer of 1813, the American fleet at New York attempted to escape the British pickets off Sandy Hook by sailing up Long Island Sound. They put in at New London and made ready to slip past the awaiting enemy under cover of dark. On the night when they got under way, blue lights suddenly shone out from shore. Tory sympathizers in the area had been spying on the American fleet and had alerted the British. There was a national uproar over this Yankee treachery, but the American fleet spent the rest of the war bottled up in the Thames River estuary.

By 1814, the British had sailed into Provincetown Harbor, set up a base, and dispatched picket ships to close off the New England shore. In Maine, their forces moved in from the Maritimes and annexed one third of Maine to New Brunswick.

The blockade brought fears of a renewal of razed towns, midnight attacks, looting by deserters, and other horrors unforgotten since the Revolution. Along most of the New England coast, however, these things never happened. Defenseless locations, such as Block Island, were declared neutral and left to their daily existence. When the British troops, some thousand strong, came down with their wives, children, and camp followers into Eastport, the town turned from smuggling to supplying the invaders. Eastport lay under martial law, but, by all accounts, justice was as fair as it was swift. The soldiers set up a racetrack and wagered on races between British thoroughbreds and Yankee "nags." Whenever the commander of the occupation forces arrived at his box in the newly built opera house, the mixed audience rose as the band played "God Save the King," followed by "Yankee Doodle."

Farther south, life was less peaceful. The British, although they mounted no invasions, searched the Connecticut shore for privateering vessels, sailing up every little tidal stream to destroy anything afloat. Elsewhere, ships rotted as they lay hidden in creeks and small coves.

The blockade had a mixed effect on the smuggling trade. On the one hand, it forced smugglers to carry their contraband overland; on the other, it meant that they had only to reach Castine to exchange their goods with the enemy. "Mud clippers," drawn by horse and oxen, filled the post roads leading into Maine. Many newspapers replaced the columns once devoted to listing ship movements with a "Horse Marine List." From the *Kennebunk Weekly Visiter* of 1814:

Arrived: November 6th, at noon, two horse-cutters "Timothy Pickering" and "Quincy Cannon Ball." Commander Delande from Portland to Boston spoke on her passing sixteen ox-schooners from Bath to Portland, cargo, tin plate, all well. Also saw on the Scarborough Turnpike a suspicious looking cutter which he escaped by superior sailing.[21]

In other papers such reports came under "Terrapin Ship News," and "Jeffersonian Commerce." Customs agents sent out to slow such commerce quickly found that the state of their health was inversely related to their diligence in pursuit of their duties.

As a body, the New England shore people felt they had been greatly betrayed by a central government that had declared a war in their front yards and then had left them completely defenseless against the enemy. Some believed they had been purposely left to be destroyed. This antipathy came to a head in 1814 at the Hartford Convention. Delegates from the New England region met to discuss—and they almost voted for—the Essex Junto's plan to secede and make a separate peace with England. Moderates were able to defuse the meeting, and the matter was dropped as the war ended in late 1814.

Settled by diplomatic rather than military means, the war was a lesson lost on America. The twin naval policy—the Federalists' privateers and the Jeffersonian Republicans' floating batteries—proved a failure. The collapse of the whole American economy had been prevented only by a timely end to the war. Just a handful of merchants had realized the danger of trusting in smuggling as a substitute for their previous far-flung overseas trade. All this went unrecognized.

The New England shore dwellers looked forward to a return to business as usual. This did not happen. With the ultimate fall of Napoleon in 1815, the European powers were once again at peace. The English, French, Dutch, and others now returned to their shipping worldwide, which during the Napoleonic Wars had fallen by default to the enterprising Yankees. European merchants now sent out their own ships; they no longer needed Yankee sail. The glorious golden age of the New England shore had passed.

"We had a grand smash. We had overdone it. We had warnings enough, but we couldn't realize that our world was coming to an end. It hadn't got so low as telegraphing yet; but it was mere shop even then, compared with the picturesque traffic of our young days."—William Dean Howells, *A Woman's Reason*

8

Seafaring's Indian Summer: Whaling, 1815–1860

Times changed quickly for the seaport towns after the War of 1812. European competition and American intransigence over treaty terms with England slowly dried up the old profits. The size of merchant vessels doubled in a decade, and the new ones could no longer navigate shallow harbors such as those of Nantucket, Newburyport, and the Connecticut River towns. Even Salem began to lose its commerce, and by 1825 most of its merchants had left for Boston; by 1840, New York had cornered the China trade, leaving Boston the scrapings of lesser profits from the Baltic and South America.

In a semifictional romance written at that time, the heroine, on a visit to Salem ("Belem"), has this conversation with her cynical host:

"Is every woman in Belem an heiress?"
"Those we talk about are, and every man is a fortune hunter. Money marries money; those who have none do not marry. Those who wait hope. But the great fortunes of Belem are divided; the race of millionaires is decaying."[1]

Nathaniel Hawthorne characterized the old order as a "worm-eaten aristocracy" which, like potatoes, provided a declining return, "if it be planted and replanted, for too long a series of generations in the same worn out soil."[2]

No longer could these maritime cities afford to keep their eyes on the far horizon, ignoring the continent at their backs—save as a source of corn, beef, and firewood. Canal lines, with their placid ribbons of water, and railroads with their shining rails blessed cities like Boston, Portland, and Providence, allowing inland goods to be unloaded for transfer to waiting ships. The Industrial Revolution changed the measure of a town's success from the safety of its harbor in storms to the convenience of abundant waterpower near navigable tidewater. The day had passed when wealth depended solely upon a good ship and resourceful trading. When Hawthorne became Salem's Surveyor of Customs in 1845, the old wharf before the customhouse lay empty "except, perhaps, a bark or brig, half-way down its melancholy length, discharging hides; or, nearer at hand, a Nova Scotia schooner, pitching out her cargo of firewood."[3] Hawthorne's "charges," an aged crew of Customs Inspectors, passed the days

sitting in old-fashioned chairs, which were tipped on their hind legs back against the wall. Oftentimes they were asleep, but occasionally might be heard talking together, in voices between speech and a snore, and with that lack of energy that distinguishes the occupants of almshouses.[4]

In truth, many of the old towns along the shore faded because they no longer

Boston Harbor from Constitution Wharf, *Robert Salmon, 1833. Salmon's view shows the still active waterfront. His works mark the turning point from stylized paintings of ships to a more realistic portrayal of every-day life and a sensitivity to the atmosphere.*

cared for the old maritime ways. The merchant sons put their money in railroad building or textile manufacture. The farmer sons went west to seek their fortune. This left no ready body of sailors and supercargos to man its ships, only the dregs and a few "born sailors." No longer did the teenaged boy lie in his forecastle bunk studying navigation, dreaming of the day he would take his place in the captain's cabin. By the 1840s, the "better" families of Cambridge were sending their more uncontrollable boys to sea as a punishment/cure.[5] Only in the fishing and coasting trades were maritime traditions handed from father to son.

The shore region did not die altogether. Those locations with shallow harbors, or with inland region untapped by railroads, or without nearby waterfalls were the victims. There was still to come an Indian summer of more whaling and fishing, shipbuilding and town building. The Cape Cod skippers developed trade with Hawaii. Castine cornered the market on imported salt. Boston exported ice. Melville would write of New Bedford, of Ishmael, Queequeg, and Ahab. Houses of the most inspired beauty would appear along the Maine coast, designed by ship-builders and seagoing men who had seen all the architectural wonders of the world. The coming of the steamship would drive shipwrights like Donald MacKay to create fast packets and evolve the clipper: the most classic Yankee embodiment of high art, combining greyhound beauty with utterly utilitarian ends.

The greatest success of the era after the War of 1812 was New Bedford, which around 1820 skyrocketed into becoming the world's greatest whaling port.

New Bedford came into existence in the 1760s, after a Nantucketer obtained a license to import whale oil duty-free into France and England. Casting about for an alternative port to crowded Nantucket, he settled on sloping farmland along

The Ice Trade

In 1805, a Bostonian named Frederic Tudor cut ice from a small pond north of the city, loaded it aboard ship, and sailed with it to the Caribbean port of Martinique, where he sold it to expatriate northerners grateful for a cool drink. At first, people took his idea about as seriously as they had Timothy Dexter's warming pans. Tudor, however, persevered. He surmounted the problems of convincing sailors that the cargo would not sink the ship, of insulation (with sawdust), and of creating a receptive market with lots of advertising and free samples. The effort took about twenty-five years before it made Tudor rich. The docks of Boston, a city slowly turning back into a fishing port and a clearinghouse for merchant carriers, once again bustled with activity.

By 1833, Tudor's ice was being sold in Calcutta, reviving Boston's Federalist-era East Indies trade. Instead of tea from China, it was ice for India. Thoreau, like many, found the whole business intriguing—this export of "Crystal Blocks of Yankee Coldness." Sitting in his cabin by Walden Pond, plumbing the depths of the Bhagavad-Gita and other classics of Indian philosophy, he could look outside to see Irish laborers cutting the pond's ice into blocks that would soon be "mingled with the sacred water of the Ganges."[a]

Mystic thought and monetary profits were, however, not all that Boston received for its ice. As Samuel Eliot Morison wrote:

The homeward voyage from Calcutta was not so pleasant as the cool outward passage. Various forms of insect life came aboard with the jute and gunnies [rough fibers made into cord and sacking in New England mills] and propagated with surprising rapidity. . . . An arrival from Calcutta in Boston (I have been told) was sometimes announced by a pack of terrified dogs running up State Street pursued by an army of Calcutta cockroaches![b]

Ice remained a maritime mainstay for Boston, until Maine successfully took the trade from her after the Civil War. Down Easters had made a few attempts to compete during the first half of the nineteenth century, but Boston had gained firm control over the export market. Other cities, stretching north and west from the southern limit at Philadelphia, supplied America, the center of the domestic trade being the giant icehouses along the Hudson.

In 1870 an unusually warm winter gave Maine its chance. Once Americans tasted ice frozen in virgin watersheds, unpolluted save for a few specks of sawdust picked up as it floated by the sawmills, they quickly made Maine ice their favorite.

The most active region of the Maine ice industry lay along the tidewater of the Kennebec River. By 1880, 36 great icehouses—huge sheds, doubly insulated and painted a gleaming white to reflect the sun's rays—lay along the riverfront. During the winter, farmers came down from their snowbound farms to cut the ice into huge blocks. When the harbor thawed in spring, the ice ships arrived to load their frigid cargo. More than 1,700 shiploads would be carried south during warm weather before winter again locked up the river.

The trade lasted only some fifty years. Mechanical and electric refrigerators replaced iceboxes in the early twentieth century, and the ice harvesters quickly went bankrupt. As the industry died in the 1920s, some tried to convert the giant icehouses into mushroom factories, but these never caught on. A few icehouses lingered on as movie theaters or skating rinks, but ultimately they too were abandoned, finally to collapse under their own weight.

Independent ice houses of the American Ice Company, Pittston, Maine. In the left foreground, horses clear the snow from the ice. In the background, ice is cut, blocked, and sent up the elevator.

the Acushnet River estuary, in the township of Dartmouth, adjoining Buzzards Bay. The village of New Bedford grew slowly at first, just another of the many little whaling ports along the New England and Long Island shores. Like the others, it built its own ships, manned them with local lads, and sent them to roam the oceans. When the ships returned with casks full of raw blubber chunks, they were brought in broadside to the shore with the high tide, and when the ebbing water beached the craft, the casks were rolled off onto carts and drawn by oxen to the try works.

Like Nantucket, New Bedford was a somber, clean, little Quaker community. The sloping land drained well (although the soft, loamy soil made traveling a miry experience in bad weather). Marsh flats farther down the Acushnet provided good cattle fodder, and the rolling hills boasted many productive fields. It was a lush contrast to sand-blown Nantucket.

After the War of 1812, the larger ships could not navigate the sandy bar at the mouth of Nantucket Harbor. As Nantucketers transferred operations to the mainland, they gravitated toward New Bedford. By 1823 New Bedford's fleet equaled Nantucket's in size. For forty years, right up until the Civil War, the town enjoyed virtually continuous growth and prosperity. Twenty years before its peak in 1857, the registered tonnage of ships, including 300 whalers, from the Acushnet River (including those from Fairhaven across the inlet) was already fourth, behind only New York, Boston, and New Orleans.

By the 1840s the community had become a famed "City of Palaces": great Greek Revival mansions, the most opulent examples of antebellum architecture. The streets were laid out with fixed regularity, in contrast to those of most seaports, and visitors were surprised to discover that the streets actually crossed at right angles. The better sections of town had flagstone sidewalks, and barrel-filled carts rumbled and clattered over cobblestoned streets.

The uphill part of town, as in Salem, was all splendid homes, newly built and reflecting the town's increasing wealth. What impressed the traveler most about the residential neighborhoods was the freshness and the unhurried air. One sailor in the 1850s wrote:

For a place in which so large a business is carried on as here, "Bedford" is remarkably still. At the distance of three squares from the water side, one would never guess that he stood within the bounds of a city which ranks in commercial importance the seventh seaport in the Union [although fourth in registered tonnage], and whose ships float upon every ocean. A more quiet and rural looking place than that portion of the city beyond the immediate business limts, it would be difficult to imagine.[6]

Ishmael, in *Moby Dick,* called it "perhaps the dearest place to live in, in all New England."[7]

The local society was gracious and democratic. One Englishman remarked how constant intercourse with the world's great nations had rubbed off "many angles of national prejudice."[8] He found the community surprisingly classless, as the opportunities in the whale fishery allowed men to rise quickly in fortune. This democratic predisposition, coupled with Quaker sobriety, caused the New Bedford gentry to judge each other on moderation, character, and manners. Fine dress, however, was not shunned, as on Quaker Nantucket. "The women of New Bedford, they bloom like their own red roses," wrote Melville.[9] The more successful men appeared as portly nabobs, sporting broadcloth suits, beaver hats, and jeweled watch fobs.

Success blessed not only the whale-oil merchants. The whole town was self-sustaining: the outlying farms, the mechanics' shops, the shipbuilders all worked

at fitting out the whalers for their years-long voyages. Each departing whale ship required from 2,000 to 5,000 barrels to store its catch, and food enough to feed a modest farming village for one year.

Coming ashore in the town, one passed through a double maze of docked whale ships and wharves covered with the great casks of "greasy luck," the whale oil. The whale ships themselves, if not being unloaded, were usually "hove down," or turned on their sides, being refurbished for another voyage.

Here lies a huge hull, careened over on the flat, her exposed side and bottom being resheathed and new coppered, dozens of men crawling all over her vast bilge, sawing, fitting, and hammering. Yonder is an old hulk, whose topsides have been torn away, to make room for new ones, by which means she will become as strong as a new vessel. Here, at the wharf, is a craft in a more forward state; her masts are now being put in, and as we are looking at her, a general shout proclaims that the mainmast has just been stepped. And a little farther on we see a rusty-looking old tub, just being converted into a saucy clipper by the aid of a plentiful application of paint.[10]

Although whaling itself was probably the most romanticized of the nautical trades, it was a brutal, dangerous business. The work repulsed the average merchant marine sailor, who had only contempt for the green hands lured into signing on for a voyage. The cool reception to *Moby Dick* in 1852 came, at least in part, from a general distaste by the public for the subject. Not until the early twentieth century, after the whaling industry had passed into embroidered fable, did critics "discover" Melville's masterpiece.

The Greek Revival front of the William Rodman Mansion, built in 1833 along fashionable County Street, New Bedford. The modern sculpture to the left of the door is an addition by the Swain School of Design, the present tenant.

Seafaring's Indian Summer: Whaling, 1815–1860

"Stove Boat," by the whaling artist Clifford Ashley, from his Yankee Whalers, *1926. The sperm whale, entangled in lines, is chewing up the boat. Shark fins can be seen at right.* ▷

Interior of the Seamen's Bethel, New Bedford, where Melville's Ishmael heard Father Mapple's sermon. Built in 1832, its walls are lined with cenotaphs that date from that time to the present, memorializing New Bedford sons lost to the whales, or, in more modern times, to Atlantic storms. ▽

At sea, men spent weeks on end in maddening idleness, waiting for the sight of a blowing whale. Once they were in pursuit, life became cheap as they rowed in close to give the harpooner a good target. After the kill, the men were driven to exhaustion as they sliced up the carcass to bring it aboard before the circling sharks took too large a share.

The shipowners and captains institutionalized a system for exploiting the common whalemen. The ship worked by "lays": a percentage of the final profit against which a seaman was advanced money for clothes and food. The New Bedford "outfitters" were notorious for gouging prospective whalers, and the captains "often like Ahab, half-crazed with too many years of flat seas and lonely suns,"[11]

Leonard's Oil Works, *William Allen Wall, ca. 1855. Here, the crude whale oil was transformed into spermaceti candles. Samuel Leonard sits atop the barrel.* △

Whaling ships being refitted at New Bedford for another voyage. One is hove down for repairs to its hull. On the wharves are the great casks for whale oil. ◁

were quite happy when a seaman tired of unending brutality and jumped ship, thus forfeiting his end-of-voyage pay.[12]

This oppressive side of the whaling industry originally developed in the years after the War of 1812. Local youths no longer signed aboard to form close-knit crews, and the Indians who had been a significant work force became scarcer because of deaths from European diseases.

As the Indians died out, they were replaced by blacks—escaped slaves, freedmen, and foreign recruits—who emerged as an employable group after the Revolution when each New England state abolished slavery. By 1820 an average whaler put to sea with a crew that was half white, three-eighths black and intermarried Indians, and one eighth pure-blooded Indians. The shipmasters preferred blacks, finding them more apt to obey orders than white sailors, and better able to get along among themselves during the months of inactivity at sea. (They were, according to reports, harder to get back aboard after in-port frolics.) A testament to the character of the black sailor can be found in the old tradition that when a pirate captain buried a crew member so that his ghost might guard a nearby treasure chest, the "honor" often fell to a black "because they were the most honest."[13]

The New Bedford region had a number of black merchants, whose ships were manned entirely by blacks. The town, like many of the era, had its "Angola" or "New Guinea" section. In *Moby Dick,* Ishmael wanders through here one night and, in search of an inn, enters a church:

A hundred black faces turned round in their rows to peer; and beyond, a black Angel of Doom was beating a book in a pulpit. It was a negro church; and the preacher's text was about the blackness of darkness, and the weeping and wailing and teeth-gnashing there.[14]

Many of the blacks were from the Cape Verde Islands off West Africa. This Portuguese possession, as well as Portugal's other Atlantic islands, the Azores, was the homeland of the "Island Portuguese," who were ready candidates for the whaler's life. One whaling hand wrote:

Whaleships rarely leave home fully manned, but make it an object to procure men and boys, which they can do easily and cheaply, at some of the numerous islands in the Atlantic and Pacific Oceans. The government of Portugal requires one-third of

Paul Cuffee greeting John Hancock at Boston's "Equality Ball," December 1792. Massachusetts, especially its Quaker-populated New Bedford region, had a number of affluent black merchants by the end of the eighteenth century. Foremost among them was Paul Cuffee (1759–1817), owner and sometime captain of an entirely black-manned merchant fleet. An active reformer, he forced the Massachusetts government into giving all legal rights and privileges to Blacks by making it impossible to collect property tax on his wealth unless he were declared a free and equal citizen of the Commonwealth. Cuffee married a Pequot and their son gained fame as as harpooner.

all male children in the Azores to join the army. The boys prefer to follow the sea, and their parents generally approve their choice, as those who go to swell the armies of Portugal rarely if ever get back, while those who go to sea commonly return in a few years in comfortable circumstances. Portuguese do not make as thorough-going seamen as Americans, but they are more frugal, and though nourished in a wine-growing country, their habits do not tend to intemperance. [15]

("Thorough-going" or not, it was the Azoreans in their "Faial" sections of Yankee ports who were to take over virtually all of New England fishing in the late nineteenth century.)

Added to the Indians, blacks, Portuguese, and Yankees were various Pacific Islanders, from vegetarians to alleged maneaters, picked up en route to replace the crew members who had jumped ship.

The image of this mixture was vividly painted by Melville:

In New Bedford, actual cannibals stand chatting at street corners; savages outright; many of whom yet carry on their bones unholy flesh. It makes a stranger stare.

But besides the Feegeeans, Tongataboors, Erromanggoans, Panangians, and Brighggians, and, besides the wild specimens of whaling-craft which unheeded reel about the streets, you will see other sights still more curious, certainly more comical. There weekly arrive in this town scores of green Vermonters and New Hampshire men, all athirst for gain and glory in the fishery. . . . Many are as green as the Green Mountains whence they came. . . . Look there! that chap strutting round the corner. He wears a beaver hat and swallow-tailed coat, girdled with a sailor-belt and sheath-knife. [16]

The Yankee recruits for the whale ships were mostly country hayseeds, bored clerks, and criminal riffraff. With such hands, the turnover meant that each vessel departed with at least half a crew of green sailors.

The influx of fresh men, lured by explicit tales of the Pacific Island girls, created a special section in New Bedford—the realm of the "landsharks." First were the "shippers," who brought in prospects, and, for a portion of their lay, found them berths.

Turning down one of the little by-streets which lead from the main street to the water side, I came upon a large building, evidently once used as a factory, which I saw by a conspicuous sign over the principal entrance was a "Shipping Office." Entering, I saw before me, in a very long room, about sixty young men, some lying down upon the bare floor, some lounging upon boxes, and a few, sitting in a corner apart, having a stealthy game of cards. . . . The greater number were whittling pine sticks, and keeping up a running fire of low ribaldry, wherein the most vulgar was evidently the best liked. These were embryo whalemen. . . . There were among them some intelligent faces, and a few, a very few—not more than two or three of the fifty or sixty present—who bore in their countenances and their manners the unmistakable evidences of careful and moral training.

Most of those before me had already made a beginning upon the paths of vice, and for them the sea was pleasant only in so far as they thought to find in a sailor's life a larger license than the laws and customs of the shore permit. [17]

Next came a trip to the "outfitter," who also took a part of a sailor's lay in trade for sea clothes. A good portion of the town worked at producing quality ready-to-wear, but the gullible neophyte often found himself at sea with dog-hair shirts and boots of varnished cardboard.

For those who made the long voyage and were not lost at sea, nor jumped ship

Other Fiddler's Greens

The decline in the nautical trades and in the character of their sailors had a marked effect on the dockside sections of the sea-port cities.

In my day there was no Nahant [excursion] boat about India wharf, I can tell you, nor any other steamboat; nor any dirty shanties ashore. The place was sacred to the shipping of the grandest commerce in the world. There they lay, those beautiful ships, clean as silver, every one of them, and manned by honest Yankee crews. . . . Not by ruffians from every quarter of the globe. There were gentlemen's sons before the mast, with their share in the venture, going out for the excitement of the thing, boys from Harvard, fellows of education and spirit; the forecastle was filled with good Toms and Jims and Joes from the Cape [Cape Cod], chaps whose aunts you knew; good stock through and through, sound to the core.[c]

Thus laments an aged Boston Brahmin in a novel by William Dean Howells.

The old gentleman was probably too dignified to note the growing number of waterfront dives that catered to the new sailor, "a creature in which good and evil are so intimately blended, that it is exceedingly difficult to tell which predominates."[d] A newspaper reporter assigned to the Boston police court in the 1830s wrote,

He bows and swears in the same breath, and celebrates the termination of each successive voyage in a flowing can of grog. . . . He wore a red flannel shirt, a blue jacket, and kept his duck trousers in position by a leathern strap, above his hips, buckled in front; and in navigating the chops and channels of the city, he contrives to occupy both sides of the way, by constantly tacking and running foul of everything he meets or overtakes.[e]

The sailor accepted a hard life of dangerous work in exchange for an existence on the open sea, far from the complexities of a landsman's life. He was simultaneously in contempt of, and intimidated by, landlubbers. Such sentiments boded ill for him between voyages, when he

divided his time between his boarding house, which is often kept by a sharper or pickpocket; a grog shop, and a brothel. He associates with the vilest of the vile, and sacrifices alternately at the shrines of Intemperance and Licentiousness, until the landlord, and other kindred spirits, have possessed themselves of his last dollar, when a ship is provided for him, and with hardly a suit of clothes upon his back—with little in his chest save a bottle of rum, which his compassionate landlord has given him in lieu of a wardrobe and other necessaries—with nerves unstrung, and a frame debilitated with debauchery, he is conveyed in a carriage, or a handcart, unable to

"Improvidence of Sailors," from Sleeper's Tales of the Ocean, 1841. The scenes are of Boston's waterfront.

walk, on board the ship—and not infrequently dragged by violent hands up the gangway.[f]

This passage comes from a description of the most notorious of all the New England waterfronts, Boston's dockside, in the 1830s. Such places could be found wherever there were transient sailors, and were commonly known as *Fiddler's Greens*, like the traditional sailor paradise. Here one found the prostitutes, land sharks, and "crimps"—the last providing new crews to paying captains by putting dents or "crimps" in the skulls of unwary sailors. New Bedford was second to Boston in the infamy of its dives. In Providence, one crimp dealt exclusively with Azoreans, so that he was referred to as the "Portuguese Consul."

to become South Sea Island beachcombers until, usually, venereal disease ended their days, New Bedford had one last offering, its "dives." Competition was stiff, and the most successful "sharks" had the fastest boats in the harbor, enticing the returning whalers even before they made port. By the time a ship was in dock, the sharks had hooked their prey.

Then comes a scene still more lively and unique. A cart rattles by, loaded with recently discharged whalemen—a motley and savage-looking crew, unkempt and unshaven, capped with the head-gear of various foreign climes and peoples—under the friendly guidance of a land shark, hastening to the sign of the "Mermaid," the "Whale," or the "Grampus," where, in drunkenness and debauchery, they may soonest get rid of their hard-earned wages, and in the shortest space of time arrive at that condition of poverty and disgust of shore life that must induce them to ship for another four years cruise.[18]

"Just Landed." Whalers with headgear picked up in various ports are transported in a land shark's cart to a waterfront dive.

New Bedford's whaling prosperity began to decline just before the Civil War, as a result of the successful drilling for oil in Pennsylvania in 1859 and the subsequent popularity of the kerosene lamp. Though sperm oil was still in demand for lubricating precision machinery, the business was all but dead by the close of the war. Shipmasters gladly sold their vessels to the government, which loaded them with stones and sank them in Confederate harbors as barriers to navigation. Others still on the high seas fell prey to Confederate steam-raiders. Two of the few fleets remaining after the war were virtually wiped out when pack ice locked in and slowly crushed them in Arctic waters.

Nantucket's fate, as described in 1860, was all too common:

A few battered and dismantled hulks of whaleships sleep alongside lethargic old wharves; quiet listless seeming people saunter about with an aimless air very uncommon in New England; grass-grown streets and dingy warehouses all combine to complete the picture of departed glory.[19]

New Bedford, too, lost its whaling trade, but survived, for the New Bedford merchants had shrewdly kept a weather eye on the economy, and by the dying days of whaling the town was prospering from its many steam-driven cotton mills.

The days were gone when scrimshaw—those whalebone creations ranging from the most intricately contrived geegaw, to artless scratchings that resemble the furtively sketched imaginings of bored schoolboys—lined the shelves of every home and boardinghouse. No longer could Queequeg, Melville's cannibal harpooner, find the town already overstocked with the shrunken heads he was trying to peddle on the street—in the words of Ishmael's aghast landlord, "four heads strung on a string, for all the earth like a string of inions."[20]

The Saltworks

Salt, the most common preservative (besides smoke) before the age of refrigeration, was an expensive import for the New England fishermen, who required it in bulk to pack with their catch. Over the centuries, people attempting to extract it from seawater have been exceeded in number only by those trying to turn base metal into gold.

In 1624, the Plymouth Colony obtained a "salt maker," who spoke of the great mystery of the process, and gave such complicated directions to his Pilgrim apprentices that it took a while for them to realize "he could not do any thing but boyle salt [-water] in pans."[g] By the next year he had burned holes in most of his boiling pans and set fire to the building where he worked.

Before the Revolution, most salt came from the Caribbean and southern Europe, brought back in the holds of ships delivering New England fish. What little the New Englanders made themselves was produced laboriously by boiling away seawater as the Pilgrims had done. It took a great amount of firewood to produce a small amount of salt.

"A Perspective View of the Salt Works in Salisbury [Massachusetts], New England," ca. 1776. An attempt to combine the old boiling process with evaporation vats. 1. Hook's Rock 2. The Dam 3. The Wharf 4. The Sluice 5. The Reservoir 6. A Refining Cistern 7. A Boiling House 8. The Hot House 9. Another Boiling House 10. Another Refining Cistern 11. A Dwelling House 12. The Store 13. The Salt Boat

The hindrance of trade in the post-Revolutionary years put an end to the easy importation of salt and forced Congress to offer bounties for domestically produced salt. In 1776, a Cape Codder named John Sears had taken the first practical steps in America to develop a technique that was long discussed in scientific circles. He had constructed great shallow troughs, 10 feet by 100 feet, in which seawater was left to evaporate.

After the Revolution, others on the Cape used windmills to pump the water, a series of troughs to obtain progressively stronger salinities, and covers for rainy days. By the first decades of the nineteenth century, the system was perfected. In the 1830s there were 440 separate saltworks in business on the Cape; the only sight more common for Cape visitors was the old fish flakes.

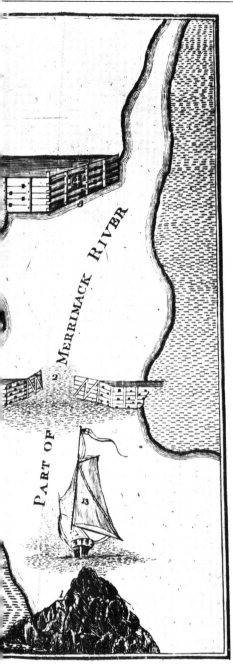

Reconstructed salt works at Aptuxcet Trading Post, Bourne, Massachusetts. Once the Cape landscape was dotted with these evaporation trays with their sliding rain covers. They appeared in the early nineteenth century and were a curious antiquity by the early twentieth.

Many hailed salt production as a low-investment high-profit livelihood for the coastal dwellers. Simply by operating a saltworks, it was asked,

May not multitudes who habitually spend life in casual and parsimonious efforts to acquire a bare subsistence, interluded with long periods of sloth and drunkenness, be-come sober, diligent, and even virtuous, and be formed for usefulness and immortality?[h]

So thought that old Puritan throwback, Timothy Dwight of Yale. Although he predicted that these morally uplifting structures would appear along all the flat shoreline from Maine to Florida, the industry stayed concentrated on Cape Cod and the shores of adjoining Buzzards Bay. It propped up the Cape economy, however, for only a few decades.

The industry began to suffer in the 1850s when railroads brought in trainloads of salt excavated from the salt domes of Louisiana and Texas. It revived temporarily when the southern supply was cut off during the Civil War, but soon the Cape works were abandoned.

Most accounts identify the works at Padanarum (now Padanaram), near New Bedford, to be the last to close. It went out of business in the first years of this century. By that time it had become a quaint landmark, a favorite subject for sketcher, watercolorist, painter, and etcher.

9

Spindles and Ship Hulls: Manufacturing Towns, 1810–1900

*"Did you ever go down to Pawtucket?
Good Lord what a buzzing it makes,
Like fifty live crabs in a bucket,
What a darn sight of cotton it takes!"*
—From an almanac of the 1820s

The success of New Bedford and the whaling towns was an exception along the New England shore in the 1830s. The whaling trade was one of the few maritime industries in which the seagoing part of the business brought in the greatest profit. Elsewhere, manufacturing was bringing new riches to its operators and reducing the mercantile shippers to a fetching-and-carrying vassalage. No longer did families rise to grandeur, as they had in Boston, Newport, and Salem, by searching foreign ports for cargo; the rich families, if they were smart, now funneled their money into textile mills or shoe factories.

Often the old curious cargoes became foundations for new enterprises, like the importing of latex to Bristol, Rhode Island, from South America, which ultimately led to the establishment of the U.S. Rubber Company in this little port town. Hartford bankers, with no voyages to underwrite, turned to insuring buildings against fire, boilers against explosions, and travelers against the perils of their journey. The city is now America's insurance center.

Although hopes for developing America into an economically independent nation after the Revolution had interested many legislators and local mechanics in primitive imitations of the vast textile industry then booming in such English cities as Manchester and Birmingham, the Industrial Revolution at first came slowly to the New England shore.

Timothy Dwight passed through Ipswich, Massachusetts, around 1795, and stopped to talk with the workers at a newly erected mill:

From them we received such accounts of the past and present state of the business as led us to form very faint hopes of its future success, and to pity the undertaker, whose enterprise and public spirit we thought merited a better reward. While population is so thin and labor so high as in this country, there is reason to fear that extensive manufactories will rarely be profitable . . . . On the other hand, there is a class of men, and that not a small one, who regard them with an enthusiasm not unlike a mania. Wisdom probably lies somewhere between these extremes.[1]

Dwight was wrong. Wisdom lay on the side of mania, or at least with those who could combine mania and money.

The first success beyond these early, disorganized attempts was made possible after the English mill-expert Samuel Slater slipped out of England in 1789. With the financial backing of Moses Brown, a merchant of Providence, Slater, assisted by a woodworker, a metalworker, and an aged black man who had long been in Brown's employ and trust, worked for almost a year reconstructing thread-spinning machines from memory. By late December 1790, the men had installed the complex of ropes, belts, rollers, gears, and frames in the dark interior of an old fulling mill along the graceful curve of water at Pawtucket Falls, where the fresh-water Blackstone tumbles into tidewater to become the Seekonk. With Brown looking on, they set the machinery in motion, and America's Industrial Revolution was heralded by Brown's characteristically Quaker words of praise, "Samuel, thee has done well."[2]

At first the Slater Mill and the duplicates that sprang up at every mill site around Providence made only thread, which was distributed to local households for weaving. Providence quickly grew as a port, bringing in raw cotton from the south and shipping out finished, if somewhat coarse, cloth. However, the textile industry soon proliferated along New England's waterways, and ultimately it dominated the region's economy.

The phenomenal success of the merchant cities in the decades after the Revolution had brought a great store of capital to New England. After the embargo and the War of 1812 made investment in seagoing ventures risky, prudent merchants began looking for suitable sites on which to build mills of their own. In New England, they had not far to search. Glacial disruption had pushed the fall line of most rivers to within a dozen miles from the shore, especially in New Hampshire and Maine. The "house high falls," which the colonists from the gentle English countryside had found a barrier to inland settlement and waterborne communication, now proved the motive force for a new age along the seashore.

Cities now rose or fell depending on simple geography: their access to water-power. Newport, with perhaps the world's greatest harbor, was nothing, for it was on an island. Providence, far up Narragansett Bay, became by 1815 Rhode Island's axis, with its 140-odd local mills. Farther west, in Connecticut, ships now

Pawtucket Falls in 1836. Other mills have joined the original Slater Mill at the falls. At right, a vessel takes on cargo.

bypassed the old whaling port of New London as they rode the tide up the Thames River estuary to unload supplies at Norwich, once an unassuming farming town around an old green, now a growing industrial community around nearby falls.

The next development began in Boston during the dark days of the last war with Britain. A group of merchants began operating a mill complex at Waltham, on the Charles River. The mill, unlike the simple thread mills of Rhode Island, turned raw cotton into printed cloth. The venture's success led them to find a site with sufficient waterpower and easy access, then to construct, from scratch, a great manufacturing city. The town, called Lowell, had by 1840 become second only to Boston in size in New England.

Soon investors were scouring the river banks for prime mill locations, where navigable waters lay in close proximity to a waterfall, and finding them in such places as Fall River, Massachusetts; Dover and Somersworth, New Hampshire; Saco, Biddeford, Brunswick, and inland Augusta, Maine.

This movement out of Boston had its detrimental effects on the old city. The financiers remained in the city, but the actual physical activity was moving elsewhere, prompting one writer to characterize mid-nineteenth-century Boston as "the matron of stayed and demure air, a little past her prime, perhaps, yet showing no symptom of decay . . . fat, fair, and forty, a great breeder, but turning her children out of doors, as fast as she produces them."[3]

Extensive development along the streams of lower New England ultimately forced new mills to go up farther inland along falls in the rolling upland. On the Maine coast, however, the greatness of the rivers made it possible for many mills to share the same shoreline falls.

Big-city entrepreneurs now reevaluated villages that for centuries had eked out a living cutting wood and fashioning barrel staves.

They soon found what they searched for, some 10 miles south of Portland. Here along the lower coast of Maine, the Saco River pours out the melted snows of the White Mountain chain into the Gulf of Maine. Only a few miles from its mouth, the river narrows around an island and makes a roaring cataract as it drops over an eight-foot and a thirty-two-foot waterfall, the two only a few hundred yards apart. High banks range the river on either side. In 1699, an English military engineer inspecting a fort there remarked, "The Fall or Cascade makes so great a noise that one can scarce hear ones self speak. This place is not so much a Frontier [against Indians] as a place of defense for the Salmon Fishing."[4]

Sawmills, too, jostled with men catching the spawning salmon along the falls, for trees felled upriver were cut and shipped from the hamlet of Saco. Life until the arrival of the Industrial Revolution was relatively static. Farmers worked the high and low bluffs, with their almost medieval names: Ram Cat Hill and Yoe Cat Gully. Fishermen had established a village in a modest inlet nearby. By 1815 there were a few more mills: eighteen sawmills, three gristmills, one fulling mill, and a nail works. Ships were built along tidewater downriver. The township contained some 2,500 people, all served by "four lawyers, four physicians, and one minister, all liberally educated, except two of the physicians."[5] The author of this report attributed the clergy/parishioner ratio to a great local populace of "nothingarians." He saw great changes in store however:

It is no exaggeration to say, there is probably not a better place in the world for all kinds of mills and factories. Vessels of 100 tons can come up within a few rods of all these mill seats, where there is through the year enough for 2000 mills and factories. This town will, at some future day, be celebrated for its manufactories.[6]

Some ten years after this prophecy, Boston money arrived, and in 1826 the seven-story cotton mill of the Saco Manufacturing Company was erected. Soon

The falls at Saco, Maine, in 1829, just at the time when the location was becoming a textile center. ◁

Factory Island, Saco, in 1840. No longer a rural village, although cows still graze in the shadows of the mill towers at left. ▽

Indian Island, which divided the river at the falls, became known as "Factory Island." To quote a Saco historian: "The spindle had arrived to sustain and to plague the townspeople. . . ."[7]

Saco village, with its sawmills, shops, and homes thinning out to fields and rolling hills, suddenly found a dense knot of humanity dropped in its midst, all jammed in on the newly purchased company land. The mill complex, with factory buildings, power houses, and boardinghouses for some 500 workers, was something new and exotic to the old shore-dwellers. Like a medieval village grown up around a castle, the village's little one-and-a-half-story saltboxes, their gardens and small pastures now formed a modest fringe of domesticity around the central blocks of high tenement row houses.

Spindles and Ship Hulls: Manufacturing Towns, 1810–1900

The people who came to live in Saco and work the looms and spindles were drawn from inland. For the first two generations, about three quarters were young women, from the ages of eighteen to twenty-five, who were amassing dowries or simply escaping the bleakness of an unmarried girl's life on an isolated hill farm. The long hours and the regimented boardinghouse life might seem a horror today, but when compared to longer hours on the farm, for no pay, it is easy to see why many flocked to the mill towns, where an unmarried girl gained real wages and the comradeship of her peers.

Mills brought to the region a new type of man and woman: one who lived completely independent of the tides. For them, the sea held no challenges, no promises, no fears. These inlanders had no relatives or neighbors out on the ocean. Marine trades meant little to them. The color of the sky, the taste and direction of the breezes held no import. Their daily contact with the sea was only quick glances from the mill windows down onto the ships at adjoining wharves.

In their lives, and soon in the lives of the families of the town itself, the mill was everything. Never before in New England had such a crush of humanity responded in unison to the pealing of bells. No Puritan sexton, ringing out his call for Sunday services, commanded such quick response and unwavering allegiance as did the work bell in the square mill-tower.

The Saco mill worked six days a week. The original work schedule called for a twelve-hour day, but the companies soon voluntarily lowered the time to ten hours. In winter, the mill was lit with expensive whale oil. Hundreds of lamps

*Detail from "Saco and Biddeford, Me.,"
1855, by J. B. Bachelder. The Factory Island has now ceded its importance to the
giant mills lining the Biddeford riverbank.
Saco and Biddeford had become prospering
tidewater mill towns.*

Cape Cod homes in the scrub, near
Newcomb Hollow Beach, Wellfleet,
Massachusetts.

Seventeenth-century saltbox houses, Fair Street, Guilford, Connecticut.

Old house on Indian River, Clinton, Connecticut, a tidewater creek connecting Long Island Sound to the village center.

*House on the shore by Singing Beach,
Manchester, Massachusetts.*

Wickford Cove, Wickford, Rhode Island.

*Fog and low tide on Passamaquoddy Bay
near the mouth of the St. Croix River,
North Perry, Maine.*

Wreck at Crane's Beach at the mouth of Plum Island Sound, Ipswich, Massachusetts.

Sunrise from Cadillac Mountain, Mount Desert Island, Maine. Below lies the town of Bar Harbor and the waters of Frenchman Bay. A cruise ship stands just off the harbor.

Nauset Beach Lighthouse at dawn,
Eastham, Massachusetts.

*Evening, looking out toward Marblehead
Harbor, Marblehead, Massachusetts.*

filled the interior with the fragrant yellow light. Before dawn, laborers left their dimly candlelit homes and trudged to work down snowpacked streets. Ahead loomed the high industrial buildings, story above story shining forth in brilliant squares onto the darkened town, filling the streets with strange shapes reflected off the winter white. Compared to the glow of so much whale oil, even the moon had not such beauty. For the townspeople, this liberal use of what was for them a luxury, brought home, more than anything else, the vast chasm that lay between the old fish-and-barrel-stave economy and the awesome profits of the textile industry.

Saco's first textile mill lasted only a few years before burning down. New mills soon replaced it, and by 1840 they employed some thousand people. The boom years came around 1850, when more Boston money arrived to develop the bluffs on the southern, Biddeford, side of the falls (the northern bank and the mill-saturated Factory Island were part of the town of Saco). A new organization, the Pepperell Manufacturing Company, slowly developed into a sixty-odd-acre plant and eventually dominated the Saco-Biddeford mill site. Pepperell's greatest profits came from sheeting and cotton twill, much of which went to oriental markets, where the company's dragon symbol commanded premium prices.

In the years following the Civil War, the influx of native Yankee millhands had waned. They could now find better jobs in the cities. The textile magnates turned instead to imported labor: first English, then Irish, then French Canadians, then Europeans of every variety, and finally anyone they could get—to the point of bringing Chinese halfway around the world to New England mills. In Saco and Biddeford, most of the British and Europeans took temporary lodging in the boardinghouses left vacant by the Yankee farm girls. While there, they brought their own character to the town, but, with no permanent roots, they soon moved on. The French Canadians, however, were more domestic. They brought their families, established new homes, and, despite the language barriers, became well rooted in the community's life. By 1891, 55 percent of the towns' mill force was from Quebec. For the last century this group has stayed on in Maine, giving parts of the state their curious mixture of Down East twang and Québecois.

Saco and Biddeford rode the textile boom into the twentieth century, but, in the end, even their great reservoir of waterpower could not compete with the steam-powered mills that came into widespread use in the decade following the Civil War. Some mills had used steam as early as the 1840s, when Portsmouth, Newburyport, Salem, and other decaying mercantile towns replaced their wharf-side warehouses with coal-fired factories in an attempt to retain their old prosperity. But steam did not really come of age until the 1870s, when it began to usher in a second age of New England industrialization. Industrial cities that had reached the fullest use of their waterpower could now expand farther with steam. Towns with no waterpower had a chance to begin anew.

In the period between 1860 and 1920, two places in southeastern Massachusetts, Fall River and New Bedford, rose to become the premier mill cities of America. Fall River, on tidewater far up the intertwining bays and islands of Narragansett Bay, was an early entry in the textile business, with its first cotton mill in successful operation around 1813. Its rocky hillside was an ideal location for development. From the heights a chain of lakes emptied down a swiftly plunging stream that dropped some 130 feet in its mile-and-a-half course from a plateau to an excellent harbor. By 1860, mills ran the whole length of the river, virtually bisecting the town: they were multistoried structures of granite that had been quarried on the site, the waterwheels and turbines of whhich could be bolted directly to the river's bedrock base.

Unlike investors elsewhere, the moneyed families of Fall River never needed to look away from home when they wanted to build another mill. When steam

Panoramic view of Fall River in 1877. The factories straddle the river that falls from the lakes above the city. (Overleaf) ▷

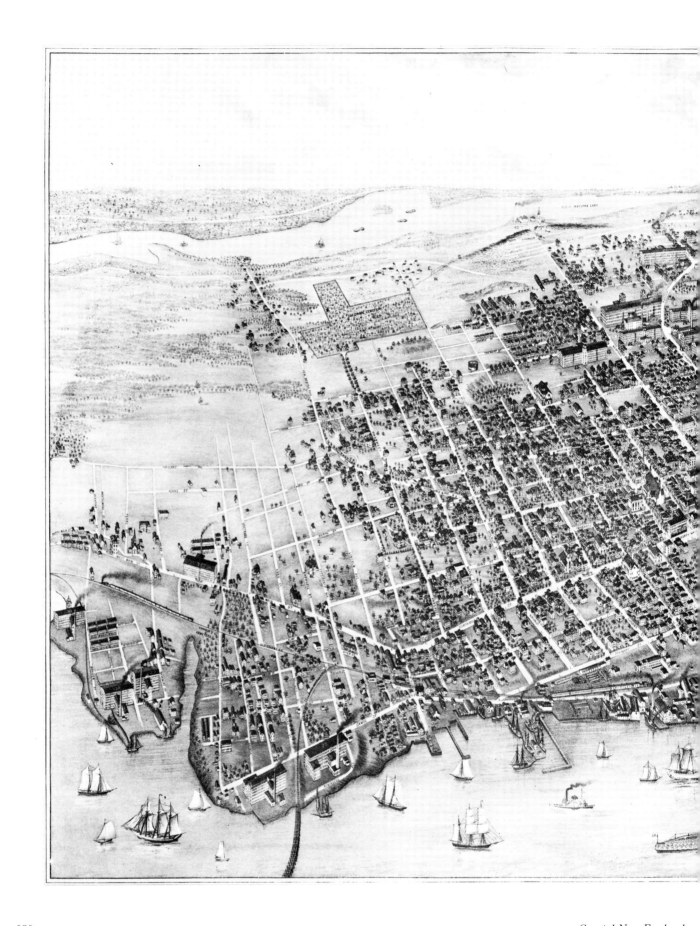

power was perfected after the Civil War, they filled in the salt marshes and built new factories along the shore. Soon the Fall River wharves were a contrast of white bales of southern cotton and the sooty "coal pockets": high bins of Pennsylvania coal, brought up along the coast on schooners and barges. Since the Cape Cod Canal had yet to be built, the price of coal was lower in southern New England than in those locations where vessels had to push out around the treacherous waters off Cape Cod.

Fall River's other advantage over its northern competitors was its "good weaving weather": a soft misty air whose relative humidity averaged 74 percent. The moist air kept down static electricity, allowed high thread tension in the looms, and permitted an even drying of the printed cloth. By the 1880s and 1890s, when southern mills were making coarse grades of cotton cloth, the New England mill owners avoided being undercut by turning to the weaving of light, finely printed cloth. Fall River was just right for such production. By 1900, its 87 mills produced 2 miles of cloth a minute.

The textile industry was the bottom rung of America's ladder of opportunity with a turnover in "operatives" of about 5 percent a week; it relied on a massive influx of newly arrived immigrants to stay in business. Foreigners crowded Fall River's streets: "the Italian woman, her hair surmounted by a huge bundle tied up in a bright shawl; the pretty French girl, who tries to dress stylishly, if cheaply; the Portuguese laborer smoking his cigarette; the long bearded rabbi; the Dominican monk in the garb of his order."[8]

In 1900, the Fall River population count was approximately 30,000 French and French Canadian; 25,000 Irish; 15,000 American-born; 15,000 English; 5,000 Portuguese (most from the Atlantic islands); and another 15,000 of Italian, various other European nationalities and Russian and Armenian. Today Fall River's many cathedral-sized churches raise an Old World skyline above a wide escarpment of factories and homes sloping down to tidewater.

Fall River's leadership in American cotton manufacture passed in 1910 to New Bedford, fifteen miles to the east. New Bedford had entered the textile business quite late. Although its first cotton company, Wamsutta Mills, had been chartered in 1846, it had had to struggle to obtain backing from the leading whaling families. Even after the firm showed a profit, New Bedford's old guard still resisted the spindle. They looked at nearby Fall River and wanted no part of a "dinner pail" economy, with its labor unrest, tenements, massive immigration, and the other horrors of nineteenth-century industrial cities. They preferred reaping the profits of distant whaling grounds.

But, as the case of New Bedford demonstrated, whaling was in its death throes in the 1870s and 1880s. It was at this key moment, as the moneyed whaling families looked to new investments, that the textile manufacturers decided that the shores of Buzzards Bay and Narragansett Bay were climatically most favorable for the manufacture of fine cloth. Once convinced, the New Bedford investors used all their funds and business savoir faire to turn the town into a coal-fired industrial metropolis. Unlike many other seaports, however, that replaced their warehouses, shipyards, chandleries, and lofts with factory buildings, New Bedford people held their old waterfront in reverence. Instead they built along the humid, marshy shoreline just north and south of the old town. One can still walk the old cobblestoned alleys of early nineteenth-century New Bedford, and look up at buildings unchanged since the days of Ishmael, Queequeg, Captain Ahab, and Moby Dick.

The industrial community they built fulfilled the worst fears of the once-hesitant investors. The men of the shipyards, oil works, and wharves had all but disappeared. No longer did the town resound from a medley of hammers, mallets, and sledges, the creaking of wagons, squeaks of hoists, and flapping of sailcloth. Now

Abandoned whale ship Palmetto, *lying der-elict along New Bedford's textile factory wharves, ca. 1910.*

the town echoed with the roaring clatter from hundreds of thousands of spindles and looms, punctuated by the shrilling of the work whistle. Gone were the diversity of craftsmen, the single-family homes, and the variety of sea trades; all New Bedford became regimented.

The mill hands each morning joined in a massed migration, as, lunch pails in hand, they left identical doorsteps to trudge down the hill to the mill yards. Once within the company fence, they left sunlight behind to walk in deep shadows between the closely set mills.

The factories were high boxy structures at the waterside, so tight and near to the tideline that from across the river they seemed more like a fleet of huge, square-ended hulks. As if moored along the shore, their ground floors almost awash, they stretched out to absorb the humid air from the water's surface.

When the natural humidity failed, the manufacturers resorted to artificially created moisture. The shirt cloth sent off by night boat for a morning delivery to New York City's garment district may have been of high quality, but it took a toll on the laborers. A visitor wrote in 1909:

The weaving rooms were very ill ventilated; there appeared to be no fans to introduce a proper supply of fresh air; it was intensely hot, gas-jets were burning in the middle of the room, volumes of steam were spouting up like geysers from the floor, and the condensed moisture was pouring down the closed windows. The faces of the weavers looked pinched and sallow, and the arms of many of them were pitifully thin. I do not care how many dollars a week those people may have been earning: they were badly off.[9]

The laborer could be liberated from such a life in various ways. At one extreme, he could take his family elsewhere, obtaining work at a less oppressive factory, in one of the many other industrialized cities of the region. Seemingly all of Massachusetts Bay around Boston had become lined with steam-powered mills, turning out textiles and leather goods. Come Sunday, wherever they were, the families needed relief, which came most often in the form of excursions to nearby beaches.

The open shore began to represent all that stood opposed to their workaday urban existence. The oceanside picnic was wholesome, healthy, spiritually inspiring. The shore offered beaches for children and rocks upon which adults could sit and gaze out on an empty horizon undefiled by mill towers, factory smoke, cramped streets, and tenements. This new consciousness of the shore marked a subtle but distinct transition from escape to the sea to regeneration from the seashore. Once the open water itself had beckoned others, with promises of distant treasures. Now family folk saw it not as a means of cutting loose from all ties, but as a place to bring their children for pleasure. Here nature, not man, reigned. In time, this desire for relief would transform much of the rural seaside into a flourishing vacation region.

Although the textile cities continued as centers of New England population, the industries themselves waned in the beginning of the twentieth century. Southern mills, imports, and synthetics undercut prices and by the Depression there were few mills left open. The immigrants moved elsewhere, sometimes to the surrounding farm region, others to new industrial areas, and others to embrace old maritime pursuits.

BATH, MAINE: NINETEENTH-CENTURY SHIPBUILDING

As many towns along the shore changed from mercantile city-states into water- and steam-powered mill complexes, many of the old ways, but not shipbuilding, vanished. More and more vessels were needed to meet the factories' ever-increasing demand for materials such as raw silk from China, shoe leather from California and Argentina, and cotton from New Orleans.

Sailing ships were still beautiful, swift, and well designed, but they evoked little of the old adventure. William Dean Howells, the chronicler of Victorian Boston, summed it up in this dialogue among a Boston merchant, his daughter, and an aged sea-captain describing the overseas trading business:

"It was all changed before you were born, Helen," began her father.

"Oh yes, all changed," cried the Captain, taking the words away from him. "The ships had begun, long before that, to stop at East Boston, and we sold the cargoes by sample, instead of handling them in the warehouses, and getting to feel some sort of human interest in them. When it came to that, a mere shopman's speculation, I didn't much care for the New Yorkers getting it." The Captain sat down and smoked in silence.

"How did the New Yorkers get it?" asked Helen, with some stir in her local pride.

"In the natural course of things," said her father. "Just as we got it from Salem. By being bigger and richer."

"Oh, it was all changed anyway," broke in the Captain. "We used to import nearly all the cotton goods used in this country,—fabrics that the natives wove on their little looms at home, and that had the sentiments you girls pretend to find in hand-made

124

Coastal New England

things,—but before we stopped we got to sending our own cotton to India. And then came the telegraph [with the first transatlantic connection in 1865], to put the finishing stroke to romance in the trade. Your father loads now according to the latest despatches from Calcutta. He knows just what his cargo will be worth when it gets there, and he telegraphs his people what to send back."[10]

This steady use of vessels as cargo haulers between fixed ports encouraged further increase in the size of ships, but continued to pull business away from many shallow-water harbors. Many of the old colonial yards in Narragansett Bay, along the tidewater Merrimack, New Hampshire's Piscataqua Basin, and the South Shore between Boston and Plymouth could not accommodate the larger hulls and had fallen silent. Even Boston began channel dredging by the 1850s, in a futile attempt to keep the deep-draft vessels from making New York their home port. Continuing the trend that began after the War of 1812, the inhabitants of many minor ports throughout southern New England turned to new pursuits, or migrated to New York or Boston. Former Salem merchants now operated out of Boston Harbor. Along the Connecticut shore, villages like Old Lyme, which had long since given up fitting out ships from its marshy inlet, sent their sons to work in family businesses with offices and docks in New York City. Merchants and captains later returned to retire in their hometowns, giving a most nautical flavor to hamlets that had not seen a sizable square-rigger for the good part of a century.

Shipbuilding also became consolidated. The industry in New England, by the 1840s, was centered in three locations: the greater Boston area (especially East Boston), the Connecticut shore (the construction being fed by logs driven down from the Connecticut River's upper reaches), and the darkly forested Maine coast.

Merchantmen off Boston Harbor, by Fitz Hugh Lane, 1862. The vessel at left is a lumber ship. Lane (1804–1865) was a Gloucester native. Above all his contemporaries who also depicted the New England shore—Frederic Church, Sanford Gifford, Martin J. Heade, John Kensett, and others—Lane's restrained romanticism and accurate rendition of the shore region's light make him the most honored by those who have experienced the qualities of that light.

Launching of the Marion F. Sprague, *East Boston, November 11, 1889. The three-masted schooner was built at Brooks's shipyard on Barber Street.*

These centers no longer relied on local forests for all their timber, however. The Boston yards kept their lead by sending out agents to scour Carolina forests for live oak and hard pine. Other lumber came from the Canadian Maritimes.

Maine did not come into its own in shipbuilding until the 1840s. In colonial days and post-Revolutionary years, it had supplied the needs of local fishermen and lumber haulers, and it had produced some "fir-built frigates" during the Revolution and the War of 1812—hasty assemblages of green pine with such a mass of topsail that when these ships were finally captured by the British, many Royal Navy seamen refused to take them into port until the masts had been shortened. Some Down East yards kept up their jerry-built construction in the peacetime years between the Revolution and the War of 1812, and Maine vessels soon had a bad name among shipbuyers.

By 1830, however, as the cost of transporting shipbuilding materials became a matter for concern, experienced builders moved north to set up yards along the Maine coast. The state (it had become independent in 1820, no longer part of Massachusetts) found a ready market for its vessels. Between 1830 and 1860 between one quarter and one third of the ships launched from American yards came from Maine. They were not the luxury clippers and packets, which were built at Massachusetts, New York, and Philadelphia yards, but sturdy, conservatively designed cargo carriers. The usually greater value of ships constructed in the yards of more southerly regions may have brought these areas prestige, but to ship buyers it simply meant that Maine was the place to go for solid, inexpensive vessels.

The Maine coast was ideal for building wooden ships. Though large rivers—the Saco, Androscoggin, Kennebec, Penobscot, and St. Croix—are few, virtually every inlet along its convoluted and rock-bound shore is watered by a driving stream with unlimited mill sites.

Where falls were not available—as on the many islands—tide mills appeared. A mill builder would select a small inlet with a narrow entrance and dam it off. By using sluicegates and a reversing waterwheel, he could make use of the difference in water levels between the tidal pond and the ocean to power the mill for about sixteen hours each day. As times of high and low tide change each day, this power was too irregular for large-scale manufacturing, which required a large, steady workforce. Instead, the tide mills were primarily used for work that required great power but only a few attendants, such as sawing lumber, grinding grain, or cutting and polishing stone.

Coasters hugging the Maine shore saw a panorama of thriving industry:

at the mouths of countless seaward moving streams the busy mills that sawed the lumber for the yards at Rockland and Bath; mills flanked by great mounds of sawdust, which flecked the tides moving in and out, and hemmed in over veritable acres by huge piles of logs and sawn timbers.
. . . the skeletons of brigs and barques and schooners being framed upon the shingle beaches of even the smallest bays. . . . Upon the roofs of the sail lofts he saw the spread of weathering canvas to be cut and sewn and set. . . . And everywhere . . . the cheerful sounds of mallet and hammer upon wood and iron, the calls and cries of shipwrights, riveters and framers, tacklers and seamers.[11]

Bath, along tidewater downriver from the confluence of the Kennebec and Androscoggin Rivers, was destined to become Maine's greatest shipbuilding center. In the same manner that one today describes something tidy as "shipshape," sailors by the 1850s described a trim orderly vessel as "Bath-built."

Until the 1840s, when it began shipbuilding in earnest, Bath served as the market town and clearinghouse for ships bringing goods to the upriver towns or taking on timber for the West Indies trade. By 1840, the town ranked seventh in volume of trade among American ports, behind New York, Boston, Philadelphia, Baltimore, New Bedford, and Waldoboro (some thirty miles up the coast).

Although comfortable homes began to appear by this time, built by merchants and ship captains with the profits of the lumber trade, Bath was still a bit of "backwoods" Maine. Only a few houses were painted white; the rest were either a dirty yellow (as were the two Congregational churches), or unpainted, weather-blackened board. A cultivated visitor complained during a visit in a gray November of 1836:

At this season of the year, a village so dull and monotonous as Bath is anything but agreeable. There is no public amusement of any kind to beguile a weary hour; you have not even the opportunity of strolling about for exercise, unless at the peril of health and the loss of your understandings [boots] such as is the situation of the streets in wet weather. It is only here and there you can possibly get from one side of the street to the other, and it is no uncommon sight to see a person literally "stuck in the mud."[12]

In the 1840s, with its port thriving, the scarcity of good lumber elsewhere pushed the shipbuilding trade north into Maine, because hull planking could still be rafted down from upriver sawmills. Bath began to bloom. It had access to the untapped reaches of both the Kennebec and Androscoggin basins, but just as important, it had the "Long Reach."

Bath edges a deep mile-wide estuary, formed by narrows above and below the town into a magnificent basin some five miles long. The water is deep, from twenty

Clipper Ships

The epitome of the Yankee shipbuilders' art has always been considered to be the clipper ships, those Arabian stallions of ocean transports. They first appeared in the early 1840s to meet the demand for a vessel to speed tea from China to America before the salty voyage ruined the taste of the cargo. The clipper had more sails and a third less cargo space than the usual vessel its size. Its shape gave the clipper great beauty and speed, but it required a larger crew and produced less profit per voyage than other vessels. With the California Gold Rush of 1849, the clipper rocketed into public eye with its ability to get the gold-hungry easterners around the Horn to California in the quickest possible time. Soon, however, the popularity of the ships fell away to steam competition, and by the Civil War, a scant 25 years after they first appeared, they were obsolete. Though a minor footnote in the history of New England shipbuilding, they have found an honored place in the heart of Americans, for whom, then as today, speed records have a great fascination.

The clipper ship Flying Cloud, *launched from Donald McKay's East Boston shipyard in 1851. From a lithograph by Nathaniel Currier.*

to thirty feet along the shore, the banks, abrupt. The town slopes upward at an ideal angle for launching ships.

Before the Civil War, Bath's specialty was low-cost, large-cargo square-riggers. These fat, sturdy, nondescript vessels, with shallow drafts to carry them over the silt bars of the Mississippi Delta, virtually cornered the freightage of New Orleans cotton to Yankee and English mills.

When more carriers were needed to supply those who had gone west beginning with the 1849 California Gold Rush, Bath's production suddenly doubled. The 1850s saw the highwater mark of Maine shipbuilding. Bath launched about 200 vessels in that decade. By the end of the century, Bath had launched a total of some thousand vessels into the Long Reach, more than had been launched at any one location of the same size anywhere in the world.

The entire five miles of the Long Reach was a swarm of some 200 shipbuilding-related shops and yards. Bath paid the highest wages and sold the cheapest ships in America. It was an unforgettable sight from the water. As far as the eye could see there was nothing but ships upon their stocks, some only bare ribs, others nearly complete, each only a stone's throw apart from the next. Tucked in were sheds, lofts, shops, and the timber piled high along the waterfront or floating in booms moored by great ringbolts set in the bank. Everything but the hull planking arrived as unhewn logs.

Remarkably little had changed in this industry since the early eighteenth century. The basic materials, as we saw them used in Boston circa 1700, remained New England pine, oak, and maple, and Southern live oak and cedar. A crew of highly skilled laborers spent most of a year shaping into one seaworthy vessel this assorted lumber, using broad ax, whipsaw, adz, mallet, and a circular drill called a pod auger.

The only laborsaving device introduced in the prewar era was the steam box, a metal case in which planks and timbers were steamed pliable, then quickly pegged into the desired curve. After it came into use in the mid-1840s, shipyard agents no longer had to scour the forests for trees whose irregular bends matched the many eccentric shapes needed in ship framing.

Work in the Bath yards began early and ended late. Besides lunch, the men took breaks in the morning and at four in the afternoon, when the call went out for a round of rum.

There were a wide variety of workers in addition to the shipwrights who actually constructed the ships' hulls. Caulkers, painters, joiners (doors, portholes, stairs, skylights), riggers, and sometimes plankers, deckers, and cabin furnishers all moved from yard to yard in their respective gangs wherever a ship needed their services. In forging sheds, cranes lifted hot metal from the hearth onto anvils where a half-dozen blacksmiths shaped the piece in a continuous succession of

Sawyer shipyard, Bath, Maine, 1876. At left is the bark Belle of Oregon; *at right is the whale ship* John & Winthrop.

blows. Sheet-metal workers fashioned the ship's galley. Chandleries sold tar, pitch, and marine varnish. Sail lofts occupied various upper stories. Blockmakers carved out the great wooden pulleys. Ropewalks snaked their long way among the shops. Cooperages and rowboat makers, figurehead carvers: all had their small buildings. The whole Long Reach shore was one aromatic cloud from pine chips and tarred rigging.

Unlike most seafaring towns, Bath had no high warehouses lining the shore to hide the town and water from each other. The townspeople saw the sheds and open fields of the shipyards, ships in various stages of completion, vessels moored along the seabank to receive their finishing touches. In the Long Reach floated dozens of others—a most beautiful sight when, as one, they gracefully swung on their anchors with the change of tide.

Seen from the water, Bath in the 1850s presented a fine panorama of elms and Greek-columned homes. White clapboard and green shutters had replaced yellow and weathered black. The streets rose up from the water along the whole length of the reach. In summer, however, very few of the comfortable homes were visible, for the elms' leafy height rose above all but a few church steeples. The town stretched along almost the whole five-mile shore of the Long Reach, but a person could walk uphill only some half-dozen blocks before finding himself in pasture.

In the decade before the Civil War, Bath's population of 11,000-odd lived a good life not only from the sale of ships but also from their ownership. Family-owned fleets, like the Sewalls', the Houghtons', and the Pattens', carried the Bath name to every world harbor. These were merchant vessels, hired out to various shipping lines, sailing to and fro on orders from their charterers. It was a steady, burgherish business, with none of the old adventure of Napoleonic days.

The hometown family businesses of Bath and other Maine shipbuilding towns contrasted sharply with the steady migration of southern New England shore businesses to New York or Boston. A unique sort of community had developed in Maine: cosmopolitan without the problems of the larger cities. After living on the Maine coast Harriet Beecher Stowe wrote in the 1860s:

A ship-building, a ship-sailing community has an unconscious poetry underlying its existence. Exotic ideas from foreign lands relieve the trite monotony of life; the ship-owner lives in communion with the whole world, and is less likely to fall into the petty commonplace that infests the routine of inland life.[13]

Today the gracious and often intriguing old homes reflect this knowledge of the wide world. Men who traveled the seas brought back inspiration from Greek temples, English country homes, French cathedrals, and the more exotic buildings of the Far East, to vary the basic designs adapted from well-thumbed copies of Asher Benjamin's building instruction books. A nautical flavor also crept into the

Captain Edward Penniman House, built 1867, Eastham, Massachusetts. Penniman went to sea at eleven and advanced to become a successful whaling captain. When he "swallowed the anchor," he retired to a house built on plans brought from Europe. Strictly Yankee, however, is the gateway made from the jawbones of a whale.

houses of the Maine coast, as many a master shipwright built houses as well as vessels. Along the stretch of the coast between Blue Hill and Machias (not far from the Canadian border) one man, Thomas Lord, began as a joiner in 1807 and eventually took a hand in 14 meetinghouses, 84 homes, 83 vessels, 18 barns and sheds, 14 taverns, 12 schoolhouses, 12 ship's figureheads, 5 stores, and 197 coffins.[14]

Retired sea captains had a strong influence on the architectural character of many shore towns. Those who kept up the old tradition of the sea as others were abandoning it in the mid-nineteenth century often persevered their way to affluence and a "bedroom slipper" life by the age of forty-five or fifty. Those knowledgeable but still young enough to be active had the time and energy to dominate the town's social structure, keeping it from becoming provincial.

Retired sea captains' homes often incorporated unique nautical touches that enable them to be picked out with ease. With a view to the shore,

its front gate-posts were composed of the two jawbones of an enormous whale; the fence was of a most fanciful Chinese pattern; and directly in front of the house was erected that never-failing ornament of a sailor's dwelling, a tall flag staff, with cap, cross-trees, and topmast, complete.[15]

Bath's opulence did not last after the Civil War. As early as the 1840s many in Bath had made unheeded calls for the diversification of its economy. Bad weather reduces a crop, a treaty closes certain ports, new industries replace old, the nature of ships themselves changes—any one of many variables could bring sudden depression to a town that built only one style of vessel. More significantly, Bath's wooden square-riggers could not compete in a world turning in the 1860s to steel hulls and steam power.

The Maine yards ushered out the last decades of the century by perfecting the "Down Easter" design. According to one ship expert, it was "without doubt, the highest development of the sailing-ship; combining speed, handiness, cargo-capacity and low operating costs to a degree never obtained in any earlier square rigger."[16] These square-riggers took over the traffic in Maine ice, lime, and lumber, Pennsylvania coal, California wheat, and other raw cargoes. At first they relied on steam-powered tugs to tow them from dock to sea, but ultimately they fell to progress and the larger vessels spent their last days as coal barges. With this innovation, the Bath ships degenerated into the one-masted "scow-sloop" design, virtually a flat-bottomed barge, with sails and rounded ends. These oversized gundelows made their last stand in Maine's ice and cordwood trade, until they too passed away with the advent of refrigeration and gas stoves in the first decades of the twentieth century.

Bath's only salvation was its long-delayed turn to steel hulls and steam boilers. Since 1868, New York, Norfolk, Virginia, and Pennsylvania yards had been building iron ships, but it was not until Bath Iron Works put a steel-hulled coal schooner into the Long Reach around 1900 that it reestablished some semblance of its old optimism. In 1902 the Arthur Sewall Yard launched the last square-rigger built in America, the *Atlas*. It had a steel hull.

Yet Bath rallied completely, and in the early twentieth century produced battleships, grand steam yachts, and up to half of America's seagoing sail tonnage. The largest naval dreadnoughts could still steam directly up to the city wharves.

The ship Dakotah, *before its launch in 1902, at Groton, Connecticut. The largest vessel then afloat, it carried cargo between Atlantic and Pacific ports. Note the men dwarfed by its immense hull.*

Submarines

New England's major shipbuilding is today centered at the Bath Iron Works, and the yards of General Dynamics' Electric Boat Division. Bath builds various classes of naval vessels. Electric Boat, with its main yard at Groton, Connecticut, constructs the navy's nuclear submarines.

Submarine building as an industry developed in New England around 1900, but the region's history of underwater craft stretches far back even before David Bushnell's Revolutionary War *Turtle*.

In 1642, a Boston merchant named Edward Bendall contracted with the authorities to clear away a vessel that had sunk in the harbor channel. With barrel-making then a high art, he easily found craftsmen to make two great wooden diving bells, actually just oversized casks. One bell contained the diver and his half-hour air supply, and the other was used to store and raise the salvage.[a]

The twentieth-century yards were the result of expansion by companies already established in the New York Harbor area. One of these late-nineteenth-century firms had been formed by John P. Holland (1842–1914). He was an early submarine experimenter who had first sold submarines to the navy in 1900. Holland's visionary drive unfortunately led to his downfall. He dreamed of a submarine with only one man aboard—a pilot, navigator, torpedo-man, engineer, and mechanic, who would run the whole vessel while seated before an array of dials and levers. Holland's financial backers, better attuned to the realities of dealing with undersea emergencies, shifted the control of the Holland Torpedo Boat Company into the hands of some naval engineers and architects. In 1899, the old organization became the Electric Boat Company. It set up shop in the Fore River yard in Quincy, Massachusetts, and by 1905 it was launching submarines. Around 1910, Electric Boat formed a subsidiary diesel engine works, the New London Ship and Engine Company, at Groton, Connecticut. Over the next few decades the latter site grew to become Electric Boat's main yard. Here were fabricated the subs' hulls and the internal equipment manufactured elsewhere was installed.

New England's second submarine yards were those of Simon Lake (1867–1945), who brought his Lake Torpedo Boat Company to Bridgeport, Connecticut, in 1901. Lake was fascinated by vessels that could not only cruise the deep but also roll along the sea bottom on wheels. He designed his "submersibles" for both military and commercial uses. His craft were designed for such activities as wreck reclaiming, oceanographic research, and oyster harvesting. Lake's major profits however, came from his more conventionally designed navy submarines. The first sub launched at Bridgeport was the *Plunger,* in 1902, which was ultimately bought by the Russians (Electric Boat's 1905 vessels went to the Japanese). Between 1912 and 1922, Lake sold 26 subs to the United States Navy. After the military contracts petered out, Lake continued his research in such bottom-exploring vessels as the *Explorer* of 1932. The little

Simon Lake and his bottom-crawling submersible, Explorer. *The craft is now displayed at the Groton Submarine Base Museum.*

craft had both propeller and driving wheels, could move sideways, and had a mechanical arm to reach out and pick treasures off the ocean floor.

By World War II, subs were also built in other yards near Quincy, in the Boston Navy Yard, and the Portsmouth Navy Yard. Today, Groton calls itself the "Submarine Capital of the World." Here, the submarines are based at a modest complex established on the site of an old steam-warship coaling station. Downriver are the ways and giant sheds of Electric Boat, where atomic-powered submarines have been launched in a long succession since the *Nautilus* went into the water in 1954.

Everything was now imported—Pennsylvania steel and coal, Virginia oak, Carolina pine, Pacific coast pine masts—to the seven remaining Bath shipyards. Workers no longer steadily shaped wood in the old yard; the great sheds now resembled steel mills. Everything centered around the broad iron "bending floor," where long ribs of steel were taken red-hot from a furnace, to be twisted by the sledges of workmen over the curves of a mold. Giant shears and pounding knives cut the iron to fit. The whole waterfront echoed with the din of boilermakers, the cracking of steam riveters, the clang of heavy plate. Smoke and soot replaced the scent of pine and rosin. By night the foundry flames created flickering shadows.

Uphill, the town had changed little since before the Civil War. The 1900 population was about 12,000, an increase of only 1,000 since 1850. The residents were still predominantly Yankees, with the addition of a few shipbuilding families from Philadelphia, the Canadian Maritimes, Liverpool, the Clyde, and Scandinavia. There was money again in the old mansions.

Today the old shipbuilding towns of Maine's central coast are the epitome of the cultured "Down East" image, if not that of all New England. Farther south, industrialization has taken over the landscape; to the north one finds summer homes and humbler fishing villages. Here, in Bath, Wiscasset of the old wood trade, Camden, Rockport, and others (who will bristle at being left unnamed), the mansions still stand in their old settings. Elegant in design, they reflect the outward-facing vista of their builders. There is no dark suffocation of the colonial homestead here; rather, high-ceilinged rooms, large sun-embracing windows, and papered walls depicting foreign lands.

To enter these houses is not so much to be carried back into a reclusive past as to be calmed and inspired by a refined simplicity—to feel what generations have felt: that all futures are possible to those who draw their strength from such halls, and set out upon the ocean.

In the Woodcarver's Shop, *by Howard Pyle, 1895.*

With foam before and fire behind
She rends the clinging sea
That flies before the roaring wind,
Beneath her hissing lee . . .
With clashing wheel and lifting keel,
And smoking torch on high,
When winds are loud and billows reel,
She thunders foaming by.
—Oliver Wendell Holmes, from "The
Steam-Boat"

10
Voyaging by Steam, Chart, and Timetable, 1810–1920

Industrialization in New England spread inland, aided by canal lines built during the first thirty years of the nineteenth century. Canals reached into the back country from such shore cities as New Haven, Providence, Boston, and Portland, increasing rural access to these ports.

When the railroads came in the 1840s and 1850s, they at first followed the old canal lines. Soon they became a network, linking not only interior with shore but the shore communities with each other. Lines reached out along Long Island Sound, turning undeveloped villages, such as Bridgeport, into manufacturing centers where goods could be easily railed up-country. New York overtook Boston in trade both abroad and with the American interior (by way of the Hudson River and Erie Canal). By the 1850s, any community with a convenient rail link with New York City suddenly became a boom town.

This new mobility transformed the character of many towns. Wrote Thomas Bailey Aldrich of his hometown of Portsmouth, New Hampshire, in the 1840s:

The running of the first train over the eastern road from Boston to Portsmouth . . . was attended by a serious accident. . . . This initial train, freighted with so many hopes and Directors of the Road, ran over and killed—LOCAL CHARACTER. *Up to that day Portsmouth had been a very secluded little community, and had had the courage of its seclusion. From time to time it had calmly produced an individual built on plans and specifications of its own, without regard to the prejudices and conventionalities of outlying districts. . . . [With the advent of the railroad] All the conditions were to be changed, the old angles pared off, new horizons to be regarded. The individual as an eccentric individual, was to undergo great modification. . . . The last of the cocked hats had gone out, and the railway had come in.*[1]

Local speech patterns died out. Small-town people traveled to Boston and New York, expanding their interests beyond local happenings. No longer simply towns-folk, they became Americans.

Paralleling the growth of the railroads on land, steamships came into existence, churning their great paddle wheels through the coastal waters. Robert Fulton's *Clermont* marked the appearance, in 1807, in New York, of the steamship as practical transportation. In March 1815, even as the British blockading fleet was sailing back to England, the 134-foot converted sailing ship *Fulton* made its first regular run from New York City, up Long Island Sound, to New Haven.

Unlike the almost immediate enthusiasm for the railroads, public acceptance of steamships came slowly. The early rudimentary steamers were small competition for the established coastal packet lines, whose well-appointed ships provided good food, good beds, and good wine between virtually all major communities along the

Grand Trunk Railroad wharves and grain elevators, Portland, ca. 1900. Photograph by J. H. Samson. Copyright © Portland Camera Club.

coast. The first challenge by steamers came where wind, tide, and navigational conditions prevented the use of sail.

The most important of these locations lay off Manhattan Island, where the tidal forces of New York Harbor moved up the East River to meet those of Long Island Sound. During most tidal conditions the region is a mile-long stretch of eddies, whirlpools, and contrary currents. The early Dutch called it the "whirling gut," "Hoellgat," now romanticized into Hell Gate. Once steamships forced the passage, a regularly scheduled run began carrying passengers between New York and Boston. For some time the steamers stayed within the confines of Long Island Sound, letting off their passengers at Hartford (by way of the Connecticut River), New Haven, New London, or other Connecticut ports. Later they ventured on to open seas, pushing their way past stormy Point Judith to land at the Narragansett Bay ports.

These voyages, even the earlier short trips up the Sound, were overnight affairs, with primitive accommodations. A passenger describing his trip from New York to Providence on the *Chancellor Livingston* in 1830 complained that the main cabin was heated to stifling by two red-hot stoves and made unbreathable by the "discarded breath of about a hundred passengers."[2] Dinner "passed speedily as heart could desire; but the mingled odour of fish, onions, and grease, was somewhat more permanent. Whether it improved the atmosphere, or not, is a point which I could not settle."[3] Later steamers had staterooms and cabins, but at first passengers were simply divided by sex into the vessel's two large rooms. Everyone slept in the tiers of bunks rising up the wall or on cots covering the floor. Wrote our disgruntled passenger:

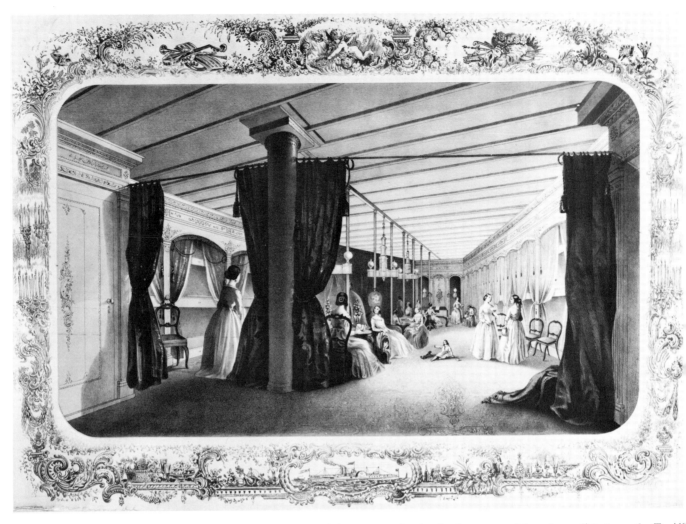

Ladies' Saloon in the Long Island Sound steamer S.S. Atlantic, *about 1846.*

Close to my right were two loud polemics, engaged in a fierce dispute on the Tariff Bill. On my left was an elderly gentleman, without shoes or slippers, whose cough and expectorations were somewhat less melodious than the music of the spheres. In the berth immediately behind, lay a passenger whose loud snorings proclaimed him as happy as a complete oblivion to all worldly cares could make him. . . . And besides me, at the table, sat a Baptist clergyman, reading, sotto voce, *a chapter of Ezekiel, and casting, at the conclusion of each verse, a glance of furtive curiosity at my paper.*[4]

The horrors of one's fellow passengers sometimes paled before the various disasters that befell early steamboating. Poor engineering design often allowed the hot smokestacks to ignite the adjoining woodwork, or the boiler to explode. If this occurred far from shore, the survivors could usually be counted on one hand. Even safely constructed ships went down as their captains pushed them beyond their limits, attempting record passages down the Sound. Those few trees along the Sound that had not been felled and sold to fire the steamboat boilers often had posters affixed to them—offering rewards for the delivery of a disaster victim's body to grieving relatives.

Still, the steamboat improved and expanded its control along the coast. By 1822, steamers bested the strong currents along the Maine shore to begin scheduled runs (virtually impossible with sailing coasters) from Portland to the landings of nearby towns. Captain Seward Porter, who soon became a dominant figure in Maine steamboating, touted his little *Kennebec* in poetic advertising:

A fig for all your clumsy craft,
Your pleasure boats and packets;
The steamboat lands you safe and sound
At Mansfield's, Trott's, or Brackets'.[5]

When the railroads began providing overland connections with the steamboat lines, passenger transport mushroomed. Various southern New England towns—Norwich and Stonington, Providence, and Fall River—all competed for the traffic. The great profits made wealthy men out of Cornelius Vanderbilt, Daniel Drew, and Jim Fisk. The boats themselves became floating palaces, each line trying to outdo the other with gilt, marble, velvet, and rooms of a size unequaled by any hotel on land.

The runs carried well into the twentieth century, with the overnight run through Fall River taking most of the business. The Fall River line ran from 1847 for another ninety years, and became quite familiar to New Englanders.

On the old Fall River Line,
I fell for Susie's line of talk,
And Susie fell for mine.
Then we fell in with a parson,
and he tied us tight as twine.
But I wish "oh Lord,"
I fell overboard,
On the old Fall River Line.[6]

The earliest Sound steamers relied on local wood for fuel, constantly putting into shore for replenishment. By 1830, they had stripped the Connecticut shore

The wreck of the Lexington, *as envisioned by Nathaniel Currier. In the worst of the early steamboat disasters, the* Lexington *caught fire and sank one wintry night some four miles from shore in Long Island Sound. This lithograph, dashed off by Currier from early reports of the sinking, brought him national attention and gave a start to the man who would later become a household word with the firm of Currier and Ives.*

The Norwich and New York Line City of Worcester *passing the ferry slip at New London, Connecticut, 1881.*

Advertising card for the Fall River Line.

of trees, and a decade later, much of the cordwood from coastal Maine had also been depleted. The vessels had to convert to coal.

New England's mills, railroads, steamers, and family stoves relied on a massive importation of Pennsylvania coal. The few local deposits in Rhode Island were of low grade. One wit, after touring a mine along the Narragansett Bay shore near Newport, pronounced it an excellent refuge for wayward sinners from the fires of the Apocalypse.[7]

The great increase in coastal traffic of all kinds—passenger steamers, ships supplying the raw material for Yankee factories, and the fleets of once-graceful clippers, East Indiamen, packets and schooners, now mastless and filled to foundering with coal—all demanded many navigational improvements. No longer was the traffic such that local skippers and hired pilots could steer vessels past their own shoreline's hazards. (Many towns, such as Woods Hole, Holmes Hole—now Vineyard Haven—of the Cape Cod and Islands region had come into existence as villages where pilots could be hired to steer passing ships.) Steamers had their schedules to keep. Storm, fog, or tide no longer dictated the movement of coastal traffic.

So in the mid-nineteenth century there was a popular outcry for improved navigational aids.

Until the federal government began publishing its own charts around 1840, the best mariners' maps of the New England coast were those made just before the Revolution under the supervision of Joseph-Frederic Vallet des Barres (1721–1824). Des Barres came to America as a British officer and in 1763 began his monumental task of supplying the Royal Navy with an accurate atlas of American waters. By 1782, the last of his charts had been published, completing his *Atlantic Neptune*—230 large, beautifully colored sheets mapping the area from the Canadian Maritimes, down to the Gulf Coast and into the Caribbean. Although sections of the less-well-known southern waters were not completely accurate, the charts of the Maritime Provinces and New England, drawn from the knowledge of their many mariners, proved highly accurate and stayed in use for half a century.

The *Atlantic Neptune* usually served as the companion piece for a constantly revised volume called *The American Coast Pilot,* published by Edmund Blunt (1770–1862). The first edition, written by a Captain Laurence Furlong, appeared

Interior of the Priscilla, *the pride of the Fall River Line. Put into service in 1894, it was the largest, fastest, and most elegant of all the Sound steamers. It ran continuously until the dissolution of the line in 1937.*

in Newburyport in 1796. At the time of Blunt's death it had reached its nineteenth edition. Unlike Des Barres's charts, the *Coast Pilot* gave written descriptions of the coast, with instructions on how to enter the harbors—all assembled from accounts by mariners familiar with each locale.

Blunt was himself a fiery individual. In one altercation he threw a frying pan at his engraver. The engraver dashed off a sketch of the incident and sent it to a British pottery firm with an order for crockery embellished with the illustration. Those pieces not purchased and destroyed by Blunt are still highly prized by old Newburyport families. Blunt moved on to New York, where his son George William Blunt (1802–1878) ultimately took over the business, reissuing *The Coast Pilot* as well as his father's other famous publication, Bowditch's *New American Practical Navigator.*

The son, George, also joined the United States Coast Survey. First authorized by Congress in 1807 to identify harbors of refuge, sheltered bays, and other inlets "where vessels may resort in stress of weather,"[8] not until the 1830s did the

Wreck of the Sparrowhawk, *exhibited on Boston Common in 1865. The little vessel, carrying passengers from England to Virginia, was driven across the shallows into Pleasant Bay, Cape Cod, by a storm in 1626. The passengers abandoned the beached vessel and it was ultimately covered by shifting sand. Rediscovered in 1863, its skeletal hull now is preserved in Pilgrim Hall, Plymouth.*

survey begin a comprehensive charting of the coast, fishing banks, shoals, and the Gulf Stream. One of its first expeditions was to chart the Nantucket Shoals, that age-old terror for New England ships sailing down the coast or making for the West Indies, and for European vessels bound for New York City. By about 1850, the Survey had moved up around Cape Cod and had published charts of the whole New England coast. Their soundings located a surprising number of submerged rocks and other unknown hazards that lay in the previously trusted shipping channels of such large ports as Boston and Gloucester. These charts formed the basis of our modern National Ocean Survey charts, which are continually updated by the National Oceanic and Atmospheric Administration.

Lighthouses and other navigational aids followed, somewhat belatedly, the appearance of the government charts. Each colony had maintained its own beacons until 1789, when the federal government took them all over. Unfortunately, the lighthouse service quickly fell to patronage, and every office, from lighthouse keeper to supervisor, was a political plum to reward party faithfuls after each election. Until the Blunts spearheaded reform around 1850, many considered the American Lighthouse Service only slightly less corrupt than the Office of Indian Affairs. Congressional investigation in 1851 brought a reformed Lighthouse Board in 1852.

At this same time one of the most infamous nineteenth-century lighthouses was being erected on Minot's Ledge, off Cohasset, south of Boston. The ledge, a constant terror for ships coming into Massachusetts Bay from the south, is only some 20 feet wide and exposed for only a few hours at calm low tide. The first design called for nine iron legs, set in holes drilled in the ledge and holding the lighthouse building itself, spiderlike, high above the waves. Work began in 1847. Wind and tide allowed 30 hours of actual work-time the first year, 157 hours the second. In 1850, the first lighthouse keeper resigned, calling the structure unsafe.

His Snakeship, the Great New England Sea Serpent

In the year 1817, an old character along the New England shore received a new name. It was a giant sea serpent, allegedly over 100 feet in length and about three feet in diameter, and it achieved great fame during a rash of sightings in 1817 and 1818 between Nahant, just north of Boston, and the Cape Ann peninsula. The press dubbed it "His Snakeship."

This creature had been known to the Indians long before the first European settlers arrived. Colonist John Josselyn was told by others, admittedly after a few drinks, of the creature's being seen on the shore of Cape Ann in 1639. In September 1641, another one was beached at Lynn following a hurricane. Wrote one Obediah Turner in his diary for September 5, 1641, "Ye witnesses being credible, and it would be of no account to them to tell an untrue tale." Turner related that the Cape Ann settlers saw one that coiled itself on a rock, much to their terror. The Indians also spoke of the creature, but, wrote Turner, they

be given to declaring wonderful things, and it pleaseth them to make ye white man stare. But making all discount, I do believe that a wonderful monster in form of a serpent doth visit these waters. And my prayer to God is it be not ye serpent spoken of in holy scripture that tempted our great mother Eve.[a]

Sporadic sightings continued over the decades, from Boston north up into Maine, but the creature's height of popularity began in August 1817, when rumors circulated around Gloucester of two women being frightened off the beach by a great serpent. Within a week, a few dozen more had seen it, and in one incident, four boats had rowed out into the harbor in pursuit. They pushed to within 30 feet of it and one man took a shot at it before it disappeared. For almost a month, the Gloucester people saw it from the shore, chased it around the harbor, set out shark hooks, and laid nets. Passing ships saw it, and it once surfaced a few feet from a small boat, sending the startled fishermen to rowing with oarlocks creaking as never before.

Broadsides depicting the great sea serpent that first made its appearance in Gloucester Harbor, to be soon pursued by the local citizenry in 1817.

Down in Boston, the city's scientific circle, the Linnaean Society, became impressed with the consistent description in all the press reports. They sent investigators up to Gloucester to examine, interview, and pass judgment. After careful work, they concluded something wonderfully new was indeed swimming off Gloucester,

to resemble a serpent in its general form and motions, to be of immense size, and to move with wonderful rapidity; to appear on the surface of the water only in calm and bright weather; and to seem to be jointed or like a number of buoys or casks following each other in line.[b]

Estimates of its length varied from 70 to 120 feet. It had a dark brown color, smooth exterior, and quickly sank, not dove, into the water when approached or provoked.

Unfortunately the Linnaean Society went on to destroy all its own careful work. Children playing on a Cape Ann beach discovered a deformed black snake, which the Boston savants quickly declared a baby *Scoliophis Atlanticus*, their new scientific name for His Snakeship. The subsequent exposé demolished both the society's credibility and any possible scientific acceptance of the sea serpent.

Despite the furor in the press, or perhaps because of it, His Snakeship was reported in 78 different sightings in the first half of the nineteenth century. Thousands of people saw it, and a few hundred wrote descriptions. The creature ultimately had quite a following around Massachusetts Bay, with its adventures featured in book-length mock-epic poems, and in cartoons like that depicting it swallowing the occupants of a sailboat, with the caption, "Through the Gut to Nahant." Sightings petered out after 1850, with a brief resurgence off Nahant around 1880. Since 1890, however, only nine reports have come in of its having been seen off the New England coast.

Was it real, mistaken identity, or hoax? The seasoned fishermen of Gloucester certainly saw something strange in their harbor. At a distance tuna or porpoise jumping in line can be mistaken for an undulating creature, but the close-up sightings are hard to discount. In the 1950s a Danish expedition in the Pacific brought up the larvae of a huge eel, but never found the adult.

The Lair of the Sea Serpent, by Elihu Vedder, 1899 (a variant of Vedder's 1864 painting). By mid-nineteenth-century, His Snakeship had entered into literature and art. Some Harvard undergraduates awarded it an honorary degree, citing it as "Magnus Serpens Maris suppositus, aut porpoises aut horse-mackerel grex." ▽

Minot's Ledge Lighthouse in 1851 — the original structure, which was washed away in 1851, taking two men with it.

A new keeper and two assistants replaced him. The whole structure flexed and bounced with each ninth wave. Everyone except the new keeper and the government knew it was doomed. Thoreau described it as

the shape of an egg-shell painted red, and placed high on iron pillars. . . . As we passed it at half-tide we saw the spray tossed up nearly to the shell. . . . Think of making your bed thus in the crest of a breaker! To have the waves, like a pack of hungry wolves, eyeing you always, night and day, and from time to time making a spring at you, almost sure to have you at last. And not one of all those voyagers can come to your relief,—but when yon light goes out, it will be a sign that the light of your life has gone out also.[9]

In 1851, a storm washed away the Minot's Ledge light and the two men within. In 1860 a new lighthouse, with fastenings deep in the ledge and its granite blocks set to interlock like a Chinese puzzle, candled its light; it has shone continuously ever since. If the first Minot's Ledge light was the greatest shame of the old patronage era, the second light was the premier engineering triumph of the reform-minded Lighthouse Board.

Despite the installation of lights, buoys, markers, and other navigational aids, the New England shore still presented a dangerous challenge to shipping. Frequent and sudden fog continued to take a great toll. The misty white played strange tricks on the eye and ear. Boston Light, despite cannon, whistles, horns, and sirens, still has its "Ghost Walk," a nearby area where no noise from the station, however loud, can be heard during fog.[10] These "silent areas" abound along the rocky bays of the Maine coast, and in the stretch of water from the eastern entrance to Long Island Sound (the "Race") past Block Island, and up to Newport.

In the 1870s and early 1880s, the Lighthouse Board made an extensive investigation into the "silent area" phenomenon. They gathered much information, but could offer no explanations, reporting:

There are six steam fog signals on the coast of Maine; these have been frequently heard at a distance of twenty miles, and as frequently cannot be heard at the distance of two miles . . . the signal often appears to be surrounded by a belt, varying in

radius from one to one and a half miles, from which the sound appears to be entirely absent. . . . This action is common to all ear signals, and has at times been observed at all the stations, at one of which the signal is situated on a bare rock twenty miles from the mainland, with no surrounding objects to affect the sound.[11]

The keepers of the light stations along the Maine coast lived particularly isolated lives on islands and rock-bound promontories. Many an author has written long and romantically of these devoted individuals. But their heroism and suffering went on far from the eyes of the general public at the time. The American press instead immortalized a more available keeper stationed on a rock in the placid waters of Newport Harbor: the "Heroine of the Lime Rock Light," Ida Lewis (1841–1911).

Ida grew up on the island as the lighthouse keeper's daughter, and in 1879 a Special Act of Congress made her keeper. Her fame rested on her lifesaving ability: a strong swimmer and expert with a small sailboat, she rescued, by various accounts, between one and two dozen people from the waters of the harbor. While her heroism has never been doubted, it should be noted that the availability of people to be rescued had much to do with the great number of "vacation sailors" at fashionable Newport, and the Lime Rock Light's position in the harbor between the barracks of Fort Adams and the Newport waterfront bars.

Ida Lewis's exemplary record at Newport did not reflect the situation of most shipwreck victims along the coast. Wrecks became so frequent, in the early days, along certain hazardous shore regions, such as Cape Cod, that many communities made a substantial livelihood from such distressed vessels. Though the colonial governments, and ultimately the Crown, had supposed title to all wrecks, the rapacity with which the local citizens rushed to loot and disassemble a derelict vessel was often truly appalling.

There runs a tale about a Maine island where everyone had a long pole with a hook on the end for pulling in salvage from the tide. To keep things equal, the town voted to standardize the poles' length. When a new minister arrived, however, in lieu of collecting for his support, the congregation decided to award him a pole two feet longer than the rest.

The trade ultimately became known as "mooncussing," since moonlit nights allowed mariners to make out the shore. Mooncussing and "bundling" are probably

Wreck of the bark W. F. Marshall *on Nantucket in 1877. Grounded in the shoal water during a fog, the vessel was later driven ashore by high winds. It was a total loss.*

the two activities most hotly debated among New England historians. In each case, a variety of opinions exists over how far matters went.

Colonial laws had threatened the death penalty for persons displaying "dangerous lanterns" along the beach at night. Such a light, tied to a rope and swung in an arc, resembled the mast-top lantern of a vessel rolling with the waves; it could lure other ships to follow its course. But the law also declared that "Where a man or dog or cat escapes alive out of a ship, neither the ship, or other vessel, or anything within them shall be judged a wreck, but the goods shall be saved and kept by the sheriff."[12] Only the pitiful survivors making their way up the beach kept the prize from the hands of the mooncussers.

By the late nineteenth century, the word "mooncusser" brought to peoples' minds the outer arm of Cape Cod, and especially the Cape's elbow village of Chatham. Here, storms, strong onshore winds, and shoal waters still defied all aids to navigation. When Ralph Waldo Emerson visited the outer Cape in 1854, he learned that the people there opposed all plans for beacons and lighthouses "as it would injure the wrecking business."[13]

A lone lighthouse had been erected in 1787 along this coast of tideswept sandbars. "Huts of refuge" were built by the pioneering Massachusetts Humane Society, beginning in 1794—as shelters for the few who made it ashore. But more common along the Outer Cape was the scavenging "wrecker," prowling the beaches for whatever washed up with the tide. Thoreau crossed paths with one as he made his way up the beach to Provincetown:

Coastal Fortifications

One of the earliest defenses from attack by sea was erected at Boston before 1634. It was simply a high wall of brush packed with mud. Over the centuries, such fortifications improved, and by the Revolution, virtually every harbor had cannon protecting the roadstead. By 1810 the new American government had erected 19 major fortresses along the New England coast, each protecting an important port. By 1850 the number had fallen to eight. Today, Fort Trumbull at New London, Fort Knox, across from Bucksport, Maine, Boston's Fort Independence, and Portland's Fort Gorges are the larger remaining nineteenth-century fortifications. The last, Fort Gorges, stands on an island off Portland. A massive wall of brick, it stands partially completed. It was abandoned during construction after authorities saw how easily its sister fort, Charleston's Fort Sumter, was demolished by Confederate shell. Many twentieth-century defenses stand along the coast in the form of great gun emplacements and lookout towers, which can be found in large number at the entrance to Narragansett Bay and near Boston.

Fort Trumbull, New London, Connecticut, *by Seth Eastman, ca. 1870–1875.*

Lifeboat manned by Cohasset crew, April 2, 1918.

Old Harbor Lifesaving Station, now at Race Point Beach, Cape Cod. Built around 1875, it contained nine rooms and housed two beach carts, two surf boats, and a life car. It was abandoned in 1944 and purchased by the National Parks Service for a museum in 1975. ▽

He looked as if he sometimes saw a doughnut, but never descended to comfort; too grave to laugh, too tough to cry; as indifferent as a clam—like a sea-clam with hat on and legs, that was out walking the strand. He may have been one of the Pilgrims . . . who had kept to the back side of the Cape and let the centuries go by.[14]

In 1872, the newly organized Life Saving Service placed nine fully manned stations along the outer Cape, each three to five miles from the next. Eventually thirteen stations were built. The men of the service walked the beaches, on the lookout for distressed ships. If a vessel in danger was sighted, the men took to the sea in rescue boats, or if the vessel were caught in rough surf, they fired a line out to bring in the survivors on a breeches buoy. The "surfmen's" pay was $65 a month with no medical, convalescence, or disability benefits.

The wreckers also began organizing themselves. By the turn of the century well-crewed ships worked out of Block Island and Provincetown, ready to take, for a sizable fee, stranded vessels into safer waters. If the captain declined the costly service, the wrecking boat would stand by, ready to claim the endangered ship if it were later abandoned.

The Cape Cod wreckers lost their prizes with the completion of the Cape Cod Canal in 1914. This passage, contemplated since earliest colonial days, had long been rejected because sailing ships would not be able to fight the tidal currents that would be set up between Buzzards and Cape Cod bays. It took the advent of swift steamboats and the drive of financier Augustus Belmont finally to make "doubling the Cape" an unnecessary horror.

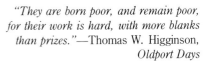

11

Mending the Nets: Living off the Sea, 1860–1920

As the many New England nautical trades died away, fishing became the last holdout. The Revolution and later difficulties with England kept fishing on the Grand Banks erratic (the final questions of American rights were not resolved until 1910), and after the War of 1812, many towns turned from working the Banks to chasing the elusive schools of mackerel that frequent coastal waters from Cape Hatteras to the Maritimes. By the mid-nineteenth century, the fishing boats, hailing from many little seaports, made up a fleet of over a thousand, which followed in like manner the mackerel swarming beneath them. The schools bit unpredictably, which often left the crews with little to do: "Some sleep, some read, some talk over old times, and a few old fishermen sit upon the quarter [deck], hour after hour, spyglass in hand, watching the fleet and wishing for fish."[1]

Nearly every fisherman went to sea well stocked with dime novels (then called "penny dreadfuls") and the more lurid newspapers.

When bad weather blew in, the fleet made for protected harbors, huddling at anchor to await the end of a ragged nor'easter. Wrote a historian of Gloucester in 1860:

In the course of the year, many hundred vessels, mostly of the coasting and fishing classes, find here a refuge from the dangerous easterly gales and storms by which the coast is often visited; and in autumn, when a favorable wind in clear weather follows an easterly blow, it is not an uncommon sight to see a fleet of two or three hundred sail working out of the harbor at the same time, and presenting a scene of surpassing interest and beauty.[2]

It was one of the most impressive events of any age along the New England coast, when this forest of vessels, their green hulls embellished with gilt scrollwork, tacked about with white duck unfurling against a sky clearing to blue, and rounded Eastern Point to meet the gray ocean swells.

By the 1860s, some two hundred of the "mackerel catchers" called Gloucester their home port. This once-sleepy town, whose vessels had unloaded at Boston docks until the railroad arrived in 1846, grew from some 6,000 in 1840 to 12,000 in the 1860s as it became America's most important fishing port during the last half of the nineteenth century.

Gloucester and its harbor sit on the south side of Cape Ann, a rocky peninsula north of Boston. Ocean breezes perpetually sweep the Cape, dispersing many of the fogs that settle into the mainland harbors. Before its growth, the old seaport climbed irregularly up a rocky hillside to the ancient highway to Salem. Narrow crooked lanes connected both large homesteads and fishermen's cottages. Outside the village, farmers worked the rocky soil, and flake fields gave off their fishy scent.

Coastal New England

What the town lacked, the harbor made up for. A perfect harbor for shallow-draft vessels, it has a small inner haven and an outer area of bolder water some two by three miles, where the wind and ocean rollers are broken by the granite bedrock of Eastern Point. Behind the town, hills rise to create a lee for the harbor during the dangerous northeasters.

Gloucester's rise coincided with the shift from hunting the migrating mackerel up and down half the coast of North America, to working the swirling shoal waters of Georges Bank, 100 miles east of Cape Cod. Other Gloucester vessels made for the cod of the Grand Banks off Newfoundland. The town of Gloucester, with its railhead and large fogless harbor, attracted an ever-growing fleet. The ships set out in late February for the Banks to anchor in ranks among strong tidal rips.

Gloucester Harbor, *by Childe Hassam, 1909.*

If a vessel dragged her anchor in a winter storm, it was a certainty that any other vessel she ran down would join in the common doom. If a ship bore down on you, your only chance was to cut your own anchor, ride with the storm, and pray. Not until the turn of the century were Gloucester vessels designed to weather storms, not just to hold as much fish as possible.

Fog banks and line squalls on the Grand Banks often scattered the dories used in working the cod lines, too. Wrote a Gloucester man, not himself a fisherman:

One would think that common sense, if not law, would make each dory carry a [bottle] of water and pilot-bread; but none do, and either experience does not teach or the fishermen like chances, for year after year comes the same old story of a lost dory and two men starved or dead of thirst. When fog lifts they are miles from their schooner, and are carried by the swift tides they know not whither. Then comes days of hunger and thirst; hands are frozen to the oars; madness haunts them; and then—

death. . . . I have sat under the trees on a morning when returning spring softens and lights up everything. . . . Slowly a schooner rounds the Point, with her flag at half-mast. It is impossible to be careless in thought for that day; no matter what joy may be in your heart, you feel with the skipper and his crew, and the dread that must be theirs of telling who it is that is missing.[3]

In the 1860s investors began looking at the fishing trade to turn it into an industry. They underwrote the cost of vessels, established large packing factories, advertised nationwide, and forced the fishermen themselves to take greater care with their catch. Gloucester-caught and -packed fish was soon the best in the country. The fishermen worked on the whalers' familiar lay system; their profit was a certain percentage of the vessel's take. "It's curious, the way we manage," said one captain,

I take this vessel which belongs to a firm here, and go off with it and handle ten or twelve thousand dollars that the fish we catch during a year sell for, and never give any security. It's the same with the rest of the skippers. There's no class of shore people who could get trusted that way.[4]

The improvement of business by consolidation brought fishing into two ports: Gloucester became the center of the packaged fish industry (canned, salted, smoked, cured), and Boston took in the fresh fish. Soon the aroma of packing

Gloucester Harbor and Dory, *by Winslow Homer, 1880. Watercolor.*

The Boston Fish Pier, ca. 1940.

plants and glue factories had transformed Gloucester by the sea to "Gloucester by the Smell."

When Banks fishing came to dominate the industry, the lone fishermen of the other New England fishing villages found themselves in financial straits. They could move to Gloucester, fall back to subsistence fishing—supplying only a local market—or give up the sea. The sons of the old Marblehead and Beverly fishermen now joined their counterparts farther down the coast at Lynn, to live an inshore life, working leather into shoes. By the 1890s, most shore towns were similarly affected.

The old fisherman finds the vessels which at different times he sailed scattered. Some lie at wharves, falling apart from disuse; others have been pressed into service as coasting craft, carrying freights of lime, brick, or lumber, their hulls appearing in old age like worn out bodies, already almost ready to lay down the overheavy burden.

Others are broken up on some barren shore, or thrown high above the tide line on a bleak waste of sand to bleach in sun and rain. More modern vessels have taken their place in the fishing business; but they hail from central ports, and are manned by strangely assorted crews.[5]

In the twenty years between 1875 and 1895, the New England Yankee virtually relinquished the fisherman's calling to foreign-born fishermen. In 1876, there were fifteen Yankees to one immigrant fisherman; by 1896 the ratio was reversed.[6] What sprouts of the old family stock remained in the business had risen to managerial positions ashore. These departures, and the regular mortality of Banks fishermen, forced Gloucester first to rely on green hands from inland farms, who were soon replaced by seafaring foreigners: island Portuguese, Nova Scotians, and Swedes.

Of these groups, the island Portuguese formed the largest ethnic influx. The first had come to America in the forecastles of whalers, and by the 1850s their immigration was brisk. Most came to work in the New England mills or the California gold fields, but a few kept to their hereditary fishing. In the late nineteenth century, Portugal changed to a blanket military draft rather than conscripting one out of every three youths, and soon the cream of the Cape Verde, Madeira, and Azore islands' youth took passage to America in preference to eight years in the mainland army.

The Gloucester Yankees found them an exotic people, and this 1868 description probably says as much about the Yankee observers as the Portuguese newcomers:

Former home of Cotton Mather as it appeared in 1896. The house of Boston's great Puritan divine had by then become a boardinghouse for Azorean immigrants.

They come from the Western Islands, and are, for the most part, frugal, industrious citizens, fond of garlic, intense in their religious belief, which is Roman Catholic, and very superstitious concerning Friday, which they consider an unlucky day; and they will never sail on that day if they can possibly avoid it. They are passionately fond of pictures representing Catholic saints, and the walls of their dwelling-houses are profusely decorated with such, very elaborately framed. . . . They are very saving of their money, and, as soon as they get enough ahead, generally purchase a piece of land, build themselves a house, get married, and open a boarding establishment.[7]

Portuguese fishing colonies soon began working out of Boston, New Bedford, Fall River, Gloucester, Provincetown, and other, smaller communities. Here they erected their churches, such as Gloucester's Church of Our Lady of the Good Voyage, and while the men fished, the bronze-faced, serious-eyed women took their children to say the rosary, praying that the sea would not claim their men.

The Nova Scotians followed the Portuguese in numbers. They often came just for the fishing season, returning to their homes for the colder months. Others became naturalized in order to become masters of American vessels. They were a rollicking sea-chanty crowd, of the same stock as the Yankees they replaced, but far livelier. They often helped lift the lid on the waterfront bars when the fleet came in from the Banks.

Gloucester required a constant yearly influx of these newcomers. Poor ship design, dangerous fishing practices, and ocean steamers pushing through the foggy Banks trying to keep on schedule, claimed many lives.

There is one permanency in Gloucester. The sea still takes men and ships. Women are widowed, children are made fatherless. The records vary but little. Now and then a storm takes so many that the world pauses and comments. One wonders how life can move on with this constant shadow descending or just passing away from the community.[8]

Packing room of a sardine cannery, Eastport, Maine.

In *Captains Courageous,* Kipling described Gloucester's annual gathering after the return of the fleet, to mourn its dead and read off the names added in the last year:

> *The fishermen began to mingle with the crowd about the town-hall doors—blue-jowled Portuguese, their women bare-headed or shawled for the most part; clear-eyed Nova Scotians, and men of the Maritime Provinces; French, Italians, Swedes, and Danes, with outside crews of coasting schooners; and everywhere women in black, who saluted one another with a gloomy pride, for this was their day of great days.*[9]

Seldom did the annual list toll out under one hundred names.

The fatalities began to decrease with improved vessel design and the use of auxiliary gasoline motors, finally freeing the fishermen of the wind's caprices. The first vessels with auxiliary motors accompanied the Gloucester fleet in 1900. One fisherman reported: "There was the fish, millions of them, and not a breath to move a boat. Chug-a-chug, away she went, and scooped 'em in. We looked on."[10] Soon everyone had gasoline engines, though they still relied on sail for their main power.

Despite its seagoing renown, by the turn of the century, pressure from both fish-processing factory owners and the industrious immigrants had made Gloucester very much a modern town. Half a dozen large packinghouses dominated the town. New streets, broad and well-paved, spread out from the old center. On the heights, fine Victorian homes opened their airy piazzas to the sea view and the sea breeze. Electric trolleys, lights, telephones, modern schools, churches of all denominations—all put the lie to any image of Gloucester as a little saltwater town. The fishermen lived with their families in boardinghouses three or four stories high. Wives could no longer peer out to glimpse the sea; they had to thread their way through packinghouses, storehouses, and fish-drying lofts to find shore space on which to stand and watch the horizon.

One had to go down to the harborside to find the old Gloucester. Each morning the rowboat fishermen, often elderly Bankers who could not entirely give up the sea, set out with their nets. Mackerel schooners entered the harbor, anchored, and their crews set to cleaning the catch. Often they worked into the night, with lights and flares hung from the rigging to reflect across the water. Other vessels arrived to throw their hawsers out to young boys lining the docks, awaiting the day when they too would go for the Banks. "Lumpers" (hired for a lump sum) came and went, unloading fish and transporting it to flakes and packinghouses, "after which they [the fish] are ready to serve up to good Christians either for fish-balls on Sunday or for hash on Friday."[11]

Today Gloucester is still much the same, a modern city with an ancient trade. The vessels are now diesel fueled, but the men still work the nets in the cold Atlantic waters. The Portuguese flavor has permeated the town, as it has in New Bedford, Stonington, Connecticut, and other still-active fishing ports. No longer do ships named *Lucky Sally* or *Fighting Quaker* set out for the Banks. Now they are named after Portuguese patron saints. The fishermen do not turn the town on its ear with their arrival home, for (though every port has its notable exceptions)

Interior of a fishermen's shack, Monhegan Island, Maine.

most are now somber family types. Once a year the priest leads the faithful to wharfside for the blessing of the fleet. Unchanged are the elderly women in the crowd, some in traditional mourning black. They stand and pray for the safety of their grandchildren, as they once did for their husbands and sons.

In 1896 the magazine article quoted above, "The Passing of the New England Fisherman," chronicled the decay of many formerly prosperous fishing towns, their wharves dilapidated, the homes—fish merchants'—all unpainted, empty mansions and fishermen's shacks alike, warehouses and the village fleets long departed.

In reality, fishing did not disappear entirely from the small towns; it merely became less profitable. Those fishermen who did not move to Gloucester, or land their catches at Boston, where the lack of old sailing vessels allowed the fishing boats to take over the docks, retreated to the level of subsistence fishermen. They fished and farmed in season, chopping firewood in winter. Many men still fished local waters, supplying fresh catch to milltown markets. Along the Maine coast, canneries appeared in sheltered harbors. Tinned lobster prepared at Eastport, Maine, in 1843 was America's first canned food. Soon the sardine industry took hold, the fish being caught in weirs along the shore. Smoked herring also came from the more rural shores, and the dark smokehouses could be seen from Connecticut to Maine.

The fishermen still had their various vessel types and techniques for catching the fish; trawling for halibut, cod, haddock, and hake; hand-lining for cod; purse-seining, hooking, and gill-netting the mackerel; spearing swordfish; seining menhaden; and gill-netting and weiring herring. The list is as extensive and sophisticated as the parts of a ship's rigging.

Whatever the type of fishing, life on shore had much the same character in every little town that edged the water. Often even a good anchorage was wanting. There the men put their boats in through the surf, sometimes having to break through man-high walls of shore ice pushed up in winter when fresh runoff met the frigid seawater. Life in these towns was invariably slow-paced. Along the Maine coast:

Still another characteristic of the inhabitants was their serene lack of haste. "Forced-to-go never gits far," was a sentiment that seemed to have found universal acceptance in the rustic fishing villages. . . . Yet the people were not incompetent or thriftless. In their plodding way they nearly all made a decent living, and some accumulated modest wealth.[12]

On Cape Cod:

The people don't care to exert themselves. There's no hurry and no worry. They live simply and the necessaries can be had with astonishingly little effort. A man who goes out raking up clams can earn from three to six dollars a day. But he can't go out when it's rainy, and he can't go out when it blows hard, and other days he won't go because those are nice days to loaf.[13]

And the Connecticut shore:

The people are content if they have sufficient capital invested to return them a comfortable living and save them the necessity for undue exertion.[14]

As the fishing gave out, often the population dropped, and houses stood vacant. The young moved from outlying farms into the village or went off to the cities.

The fisherman who fought wind and water far from land typically had little enthusiasm for the shore. His farm was minimal: a small vegetable plot to supply

The Indians in the Nineteenth Century

By the beginning of the nineteenth century, not many New England Indian tribes remained. Pockets existed here and there, and many had intermarried with white and black New Englanders. Only the Menemshas at the western end of Martha's Vineyard and the Passamaquoddies and Penobscots of Maine still worked the coastal waters. Others had adapted to the Yankee's industries, and some, like the Wampanoags and what was left of the Pequots after the colonial wars, took passage aboard the whaling ships.

New England Indians never lost their identity, however. In 1859, the Rhode Island government took a census of its Narragansett tribe, and found only 244 persons of at least partial Indian descent. In 1882, they held hearings as to whether the tribe should be allowed to divide up its land, and if so, how it should be apportioned. A surprised commission reported:

While the many persons who appeared before the commission differed from one another in almost everything else, they agreed in believing it to be a distinguished honor to have descended from Narragansett Indians; and the rivalry, which at times became intensely exciting, in establishing their claims to what they regarded as the honor of tribal membership, was beyond the pecuniary interest they had in the proceeds of the tribal lands. . . . Some of them bearing no indication they were not of pure African descent, while others it was difficult to distinguish from persons of equally pure Caucasian origin.[a]

Despite their tribal allegiance, many nineteenth-century descriptions seem to suggest that the Indians had lost their old spark after centuries of oppression and dislocation. Nathaniel Hawthorne describes how the Penobscots descended to the mouths of rivers in summertime to set up wigwams beside roaring millsites, where their ancestors had hunted deer and caught salmon; how they paddled out to the coasting schooners in their canoes to drive a little trade in basket work.

The Penobscots still went offshore to fish, spearing porpoise from their canoes. Others ranged the coast, combining fishing with curio selling. A vacationer at Nahant around 1850 watched such a group beach their canoes in a cove not far from the hotel:

In a short time, men, women and children had disembarked the scanty baggage and cooking utensils. . . . Three or four stakes stuck upright into the earth, close to the sheltering rocks, with a couple of old sails hung above and at the side from which the wind blew, and some skins spread upon the ground, formed the "parental roof," . . . under and around which groups of dark haired Indian boys and girls quickly began to disport, some amusing themselves with bows and arrows, while the women and older children, wrapped in loose cotton gowns . . . squatted down before the tents and began with a mechanical air, and in melancholy or moody silence, to make wicker baskets from material ready at hand. The men, who were dressed in the ordinary garb of fisherman, were busy at preparing their cargoes for the market, or in spreading their nets to dry. . . . They are little other in character and habits than the gypsies of Europe, but without their vagabond vivacity. These Indians, with their dark brown skins, and lunging [lounging] and listless air, are far different from the people among whom they exist in precarious sufferance; and it requires no stretch of fancy to see in them a tone of hereditary regret for the soil which was theirs by natural right.[b]

Indian porpoise hunters, Passamaquoddy Bay: canoe, rifle, and lance for capture. From Goode's Fisheries, 1887. *For much of the nineteenth century, the Passamaquoddies caught and "tried" the porpoise, selling its oil to towns along the Maine coast.*

the table, summer pasture and salt meadows to fodder the horse and cow, a small woodlot, and room for pigs and fowl. If he had too much land, he would be tied to it year round. Instead, as in Massachusetts, Rhode Island, and Connecticut, the male population took its annual "vacation" at sea after the late summer crop of salt hay had been cut and left stacked in the marshes. Up in Maine, the boys plowed the spring fields and dropped the potatoes with sure knowledge that, once done, it was off to the Banks till harvest. Here, "All the weather-beaten houses face the sea apprehensively, like the women who live in them."[15]

The income of the fishermen–shore farmers along the Rhode Island coast, circa 1875, broke down into these totals: shellfish, $800,000; fish for food, $300,000; fish for oil and fertilizer, $100,000; wood from seadrift, $60,000; fish for manure, $40,000; and salt hay, $16,000.[16]

These people often had an amphibious existence simply because their land was

too barren to support life without help from the sea's bounty. In some places they developed new livelihoods for greater security. As ice and saltmaking had benefited Maine and Cape Cod, later generations turned to Maine peat and blueberries and Cape Cod cranberries.

In Maine, the shoreline bogs were drained, cut into large loaves of peat, and sent off down the coast. Blueberries grow just inland, on the barrens where forest once stood along the far eastern part of the Maine coast. In some places, after the pines had been logged, the moist loam beneath dried up and blew away, leaving a gravelly underbase. No trees could root in such a niggardly soil, and blueberries and alpine vegetation now cover the land. The blueberry region yields 90 percent of the nation's crop. First sent out in cans in 1866, almost the whole crop is now shipped out frozen.

On Cape Cod, the cultivation of the cranberry began in the early nineteenth

century but did not become extensive until the 1880s. Before that, the people largely ignored the berry in its wild state:

Us old-time Nantucketers would let them berries rot on the vines, but we've got a colony of Cape de Verde negroes here, and they go in whole families after the berries and bring 'em to the town to sell. The children pick the same as the grown-ups. Why, heavens and earth! those kids are 'bout ten years old when they are born, and all ready to go right to work. The negroes are poor and live in little shacks of homes often, but they dress better'n the whites do.[17]

By the turn of the century, cranberries had replaced the failing saltworks as the region's chief landside industry.

The cranberry is a bog plant that grows wherever peat underlies the vegetation. Cape farmers, and those on the sandy scrub of adjoining Plymouth County, would mortgage their land and use the money to clear their swamps and marshes of large trees and roots. Once the land had been leveled, dikes were constructed to control the water levels. A layer of sand, which promoted cranberry growth, was then laid down. When the crop was ready to be harvested, the whole town turned out.

Dwellings are closed from morning till night. Cooking is done in the evening or on rainy days, and in fair weather every one is on the marshes all the hours of daylight. The pickers wear their oldest clothes, and the women draw stocking-legs over their arms as a defence against the briars.[18]

It was a colorful sight—the pickers, clad in sunbonnets and a patchwork of old clothes, moving slowly down the bog, combing out the autumn berries with wooden scoops. It was an exhausting, back-breaking activity.

We begin picking here early in September, and the last of the berries ain't gathered until toward the end of October. Often the bogs are three or four miles from a village, and then the pickers have to make an early start. They all go together in a truck cart. It's quite a ride, I tell yer, bumping along, and they say they feel as if they hadn't had any breakfast by the time they get there. We pay thirty cents an hour for grown people and twenty cents for children; and they're expected to hustle and keep steady at it. We ain't got no use for loafers.[19]

While the harvest was perhaps an inspiring sight for the vacationing artist, the local people gladly turned to catering to summer visitors once the owners found that simply flooding the bogs would cause ripe berries to rise to the surface for easier gathering with floating push-brooms.

The shore villagers also found traditional sustenance from the tideline. Where land was poor, seaweed, gathered from beaches long ago divided into individual holdings, was spread as fertilizer or to prevent winterkill. As always, clams provided food when all else failed.

Generation after generation of New Englanders have made their way to the mucky brown ooze between sea and land to hoe the flats into a profusion of muddy hills, which are leveled by the first wet touch of the flowing tide. In the 1930s the Depression witnessed many families out on the clamflats, too proud to ask for government relief.

In the years before the Revolution the popularity of this humble bivalve had waned in favor of a deeper-water shellfish, the oyster. When politics made drinking tea anathema, and coffee was yet to become popular, many communities sported oyster houses, where men came to relax and talk (as in Boston's Union Oyster House, where they made plans to form an independent American nation). By the early nineteenth century, oystering had become a lucrative trade.

Oysters are found in many shore waters, and the industry centered in New York Harbor, off the Connecticut shore of Long Island Sound, and in the shallows of Wellfleet Harbor on the outer arm of Cape Cod. Reported a traveler going through New Haven in 1800:

In Quinnipiac River, near its mouth, is a very large and most prolific bed of oysters. These shellfish are annually caught between the months of September and May in vast quantities. Many of them are put into casks and sent, during the cold season, over large tracts of Connecticut, New York, Massachusetts, Vermont, and New Hampshire. As women and children are extensively employed in opening them, the expense of this fishery, which is quite profitable to the inhabitants, is inconsiderable.[20]

While the women and children shucked, the men and the boys went out in boats to rake the oysters off the bottom with "oyster tongs," which resemble two long-handled garden rakes fastened together like the parts of a scissors. The perfection of insulated ice packing allowed the industry to be pursued year-round.

About 1870, oystermen learned how to raise oysters in deeper water. Connecticut parceled out its coastal waters, and by the 1880s, some 5,000 acres of Long Island Sound was being worked by small oysterboats, modeled after dugouts used by the ancient Quinnipiac Indians, and by more modern steam dredges. By the time the industry peaked about 1900, Connecticut, though second to New York in actual production, had the largest oyster fleet. However, twentieth-century development of the shoreline doomed oystering in the Sound. Pollution made many of the oyster beds toxic. Industrialization of the shore cities raised waterfront land values and brought an end to the picturesque huts, with thatched roofs and cluttered gear, where the oystermen lived in winter with telescope and warm fire, keeping lookout for poachers on their beds.

A Long Island oysterman, Henry Treat of Black Rock (Bridgeport), Connecticut, aboard the oyster sloop Nena A. Rowland. *The shotgun was for dealing with poachers on his oyster beds.*

Oyster huts on Milford Point, Connecticut. A sketch ca. 1830 by John Warner Barber.

The heir of the quaint oysterman is the lobster fisherman, who with his traps, buoys, and slicker forms probably the most traditional image of the seacoast Yankee. Today, the number of lobster pots made to be sold for export atop carracks is estimated to outnumber those now in use beneath cold Gulf of Maine waters.

The lobster is a cannibal and scavenger, eating whatever it can find on the sea bottom, including, if they do not put up too much of a struggle, its fellow lobsters. It prefers cold waters, anything except muddy bottoms, and frequents waters from Delaware north. Lobsters proliferate in the Gulf of Maine. Lobstermen catch them close to shore for the ease of hauling up the lobster pots on shorter lines.

Indians and the early colonists found lobsters incredibly abundant, and heavy storms often left foot-high walls of them along the beach to mark the reach of the storm tide. They could be picked out of knee-deep water if it were cold enough. The simplest way to catch a few was to leave some fish trash in a tide pool before the water rose, then collect the congregation trapped after the tide fell. The first records of Europeans' eating New England lobsters is a 1605 report by John Weymouth extolling the virtues of the region's fisheries. This date, however, is no "famous first," as a smaller type of lobster was common to northern European waters.

The first New England lobsters for nonlocal consumption came out of the traps in the 1840s. (A trap, at that time, consisted of a circular grid, lowered flat onto

Writers

The abundance of unusual characters along the New England shore first attracted chroniclers in the 1830s and 1840s: now-forgotten writers such as Nathaniel Ames, Delia Bacon, Sylvanus Cobb, Joseph Holt Ingraham, John Neal, Seba Smith, and Alonzo Tripp. Only a few, like Nathaniel Hawthorne and Harriet Beecher Stowe, have stood the test of time. But by the late nineteenth century, many well-known writers were adding to the celebration of the New England shore.

Thomas Bailey Aldrich wrote about his boyhood home, Portsmouth, New Hampshire. In Maine, perhaps the best characterization of coastal life came from Sarah Orne Jewett. Thomas Wentworth Higginson wrote about Newport. A few spent their lifetimes novelizing certain regions, like Elijah Kellogg in Maine and Joseph C. Lincoln on Cape Cod. With a few notable exceptions, the curious quaintness of local folks seemed to be the books' selling points. One novelist, Sarah Pratt McLean Greene, was a little too accurate in her descriptions of local color in *Cape Cod Folks.* When it was published in 1881, the people she romanticized were chagrined to find their real names used in the text. Needless to say, a few lawsuits ensued

and the publisher opted for fictitious names in later editions.

Yet despite the variety of life on the Maine coast and on Cape Cod, perhaps the coastline most fascinating to writers lay along the North Shore, that stretch between Boston and Cape Ann. Many of Boston's literati had summer homes there—the Lowell, Holmes, Peabody, and other families. Here these leading writers of the day heard, firsthand, traditions and tales that harked back to colonial days—stories of witches and the supernatural straight out of the Salem witch-craze of the late 1600s or Cotton Mather's *Wonders of the Invisible World.* The region always had a heritage of superstition. Salem colonists, upon a death in the family, would smash in the backs of dressers and highboys, lest the departing spirit lodge in them. Marblehead children, in post-Revolutionary times, turned their jackets inside out after bringing home the cows, this to get rid of pixies from the fields.[c]

This region so rich in folklore inspired a great variety of literature, from Nathaniel Hawthorne's *House of the Seven Gables,* set in mid-nineteenth-century Salem, to "The Wreck of the Hesperus," Whittier's tale of death on the Gloucester reef Norman's Woe—once every schoolboy's favorite ditty.

Even Hawthorne, it may be argued, was not so much a chronicler of the Puritan past as he was a brooding Dante, reflecting on the departed glory of Salem. Though the murky waters of his tales wash Puritan shores, nowhere in his work does one find other aspects of Puritan life: the lyrical piety of poet Anne Bradstreet, the tongue-in-cheek accounts of tritons, mermaids, and sea monsters of John Josselyn's drinking companions, or Roger Williams's descriptions of the Indians' comradeship and dignity.

In general, wit and humor seem to dominate most tales of the nineteenth-century coast. Even the philosophical Thoreau delighted in the panorama he encountered in his travels there. Probably his most beloved character sketch is "The Old Wellfleet Oysterman," whom he encountered on his walk up the outer arm of Cape Cod in 1849. When Thoreau met him, this grizzled old gentleman, a retired merchant who had profited from harvesting the oysters in the nearby shallows, was living, along with his retarded son, under "petticoat government." "These women," he told Thoreau and his walking companion, "are both of them poor good-for-nothing critturs. This one is my wife. I

the bottom with bait attached.) In 1843 tinned lobster began to be shipped from an Eastport cannery to points throughout America. Everything with claws (and a few creatures without) went into the can. Not until the 1890s did legislators put size and licensing restrictions on the lobster trade.

The cost of a modern lobster today almost makes one believe that the stories of the colonists' and Indians' indifference to the lobster must be fables concocted to dupe the city folk. Yet colonial accounts rank them low, on a par with the lamprey as food. Unless times were hard, or the winter long, they considered lobsters better bait than feast.

Today the demand for the sweet flesh of claws and tail provides an occupation for some 5,000 lobstermen in Maine alone. The far northern coastal section of Maine has many little lobstering towns, best visited when fogs descend, obscuring the colorful lobster buoys and keeping the men ashore. Lobster fishermen in their Day-Glo slickers haunt the new cooperative building down on the wharf. Others, especially the older ones, sit on their front steps awaiting a break in the weather.

Today lobstering is still dangerous work. The men often go out alone. The best craft are specially designed, some thirty feet long, with winches for bringing up the traps. But many lobstermen use whatever craft is available and lean out to haul in each trap by hand. One slip will leave a man floating among his buoys, and the boat to be found hours later, its still-idling motor giving evidence of a recent tragedy.

---

married her sixty-four years ago. She is eighty-four years old, and as deaf as an adder, and the other [his daughter] not much better."[d] Spending the night, Thoreau received an evening's lecture on subjects ranging from local shipwrecks to the changing sound of surf before a storm, from the oyster business to the cannon roar from Bunker Hill rolling across the bay when the old man was a child. "We

were a rare haul for him," Thoreau wrote. "He could commonly get none but ministers to talk to him, though sometimes ten of them at once . . . the evening was not long enough for him."[e] The evening's entrancement was shattered the next morning as Thoreau and friend watched the old man casually spitting tobacco juice into the fireplace, oblivious to the breakfast heating there.

I ate of the apple-sauce and the dough-nuts, which I thought had sustained the least detriment from the old man's shots, but my companion refused the apple-sauce, and ate of the hot cakes and green beans, which had appeared to him to occupy the safest part of the hearth. But on comparing notes afterward, I told him that the butter-milk cake was particularly exposed, and I saw how it suffered repeatedly, and there-fore, I avoided it; but he declared that, however that might be, he witnessed that the apple-sauce was seriously injured, and had therefore declined that.[f]

Such tales created a ready group of travelers eager to visit this fabled land, be it the Maine coast, North Shore, old sea-port city, or Cape Cod. All the public needed was ease of transportation.

Northeastern view of Provincetown, Massachusetts, ca. 1839, as Thoreau would have seen it. The town was then simply one street two miles long, hugging the shore. In the background are the Province Land dunes. The windmills are for raising sea-water to the town's many saltworks.

12

Along the Bathing Sands: Vacationing, 1870–Present

In the age of sail and the early years of steam, New England's tourists first explored the cities and surrounding countryside. In the decades preceding the Civil War, those with time and money to spare visited New Haven, Newport, Portland, and, most of all, Boston. Crowds strolled the Common, viewed the Athenaeum's works of art, walked the crooked streets down to the waterfront and Faneuil Hall, and even visited a forerunner of our modern aquarium—complete with trained seals.

Boston, unlike breezy Newport, has a damp, hot summer. Once a steamboat began running in 1817, moneyed Bostonians started taking their summers on Nahant, a nearby rocky island connected to the mainland by a sandspit beach. This was the region then reportedly inhabited by "His Snakeship," the great New England sea serpent. The creature could have not picked a more socially acceptable location to disport himself. What better credibility for the monster than to be reported by a Beacon Hill Cabot? What better pastime for a vacationer, than lolling about the hotel veranda, scanning the horizon for a sea serpent?

We had rather by half have you come to our doors,
And eat all the boarders who take the first floors,
Than to have you keep off at such wonderful distance,
As to make people doubt your Honour's existence,
At all events, now, if you cannot stay long here,
We shall have, while you do, a terrible throng here.[1]

The Nahant Hotel, one of New England's first attempts at a summer resort, had little to offer beyond a possible view of His Snakeship. A gigantic ugly structure,

Constructed for the purpose of stowing away as many lodgers as possible, it was nothing better than a huge pigeon-house, with a number of sleeping cribs wretchedly furnished, a couple of drawing-rooms . . . and a dining-hall capable of accommodating about two hundred persons.[2]

The building was ringed by verandas on the first and second floors,

On the upper of these the ladies congregated in groups for walking, or in gossiping parties on the settees; while the lower one was destined to the exclusive use of the gentlemen to smoke, chew, and drink drams, early morning to late at night.[3]

The men left each morning by stage or steamboat for their Boston offices, "When

James Ambrose Cutting with "Ned" and "Fanny," trained seals at the Boston Aquarial Gardens, 1859. Cutting, a photographer and the inventor of the Ambrotype, gave up the photography business and opened the city's first aquarium. Here brother "Ned" stands guard duty, while "Fanny" sleeps.

Interior of Cutting & Butler's Grand Aquaria, Boston. The 41 specimens in the collection varied from snails to a stuffed kangaroo. A small band played music from the balcony.

*The Nahant Hotel, Boston's first summer
resort, in Nahant, Massachusetts.*

*Marble House, Newport. Built in 1892 for
William Vanderbilt. The name describes the
facing used in the formal rooms within. It
is the most sumptuous of Newport's
"cottages."* ▷

they return in the evening they are tired and not much inclined for anything but
indulgence in the bar room or the lower balcony."[4]

Nahant never fully blossomed as a resort, and by the Civil War its peak had
passed. Despite its location close to Boston, its sea air, mists, and mirages, it
never caught the public's fancy. Its rocky shore did little to invite those enjoying
the new vogue in sea bathing, and its staid Boston attitudes discouraged the fun
seekers.

More successful at attracting the summer crowd was Newport. Since colonial
times a retreat from the damp heat of the South for plantation owners, Newport
began actively to lure vacationers after its maritime economy collapsed during the
eras of the Revolution and the War of 1812. As a first step, the town fathers did
what they could to make the town more attractive, which included relocating many
destitute townspeople. In 1822 the Newport Asylum was opened to house these
poor. The asylum sat on Coasters Island, some 150 feet out in the harbor. (The
building is now part of the Naval War College Museum.) Deep water prevented
the inmates from coming ashore to wander the town without permission, thus
relieving Newport "from the disgrace of having the streets infested with beggars,
as formerly, to the great scandal of the citizens and annoyance to strangers."[5]

By the century's middle, Newport had become the preeminent seaside resort.
Activity centered around one great hotel, the Ocean House, dubbed by one wit a
huge, yellow pagoda-factory. Visitors however, came for the beach. It was a great
wide strand with a gently sloping sea bottom that provided 100 yards of shallow
water. From a carriage along the beach one could watch others take their first
mouthfuls of seawater. A lady wrote in 1854:

*We drove by Newport to the bathing sands, where gentlemen take charge of ladies
in the surf; it was to me a very singular and amusing scene—numerous carriages,*

Along the Bathing Sands: Vacationing 1870—Present

Great Summer Attraction.

The Landlord of the Crystal Lake and Little Falls Hotel determined that his guests shall not be disappointed in the matter of a snake this year, has therefore engaged a stout swimmer, and has him fixed up for the part.

From Yankee Notions, *August 1856.*

drawn up before a semicircle of small bathing houses, containing gaily dressed occupants, who had taken their marine walk, or were waiting for the ladies, young and old, still frolicking among the waves, children dancing in and out, gentlemen handing about their pretty partners as if they were dancing water quadrilles, and heads, young and old, with streaming hair dripping in and out; it was very droll, very lively, and I dare say very amusing to all engaged.[6]

Newport slowly grew into the most fashionable summering place for America's very rich. At first, the moneyed families had little sophistication, and an 1852 observer wrote how Mr. Croesus (as the species became called), moves in and "builds a house in the most fashionable street rather larger than his neighbor's, but a reproduction of it in very upholstered detail."[7] But as their sophistication grew, Newport changed, and by the early twentieth century, Mr. Croesus, Jr.,

commands the services of the ablest architects, who have transformed Newport from a city of commonplace cottages to one of rare architectural distinction. . . . He will overdo things occasionally—or at least Mrs. Croesus will; as when once she built a temporary ballroom next to her stately summer house, at a cost—so the newspaper said—of some forty thousand dollars, and tore it down after a single evening's entertainment.[8]

Newport, like less-publicized Bar Harbor, Maine, had become the watering place for America's pre–income-tax rich. Bar Harbor had great wooded estates and large hotels, while Newport was a patchwork of large mansions, often built on quite small lots.

At the turn of the century, some 5,000 came to "summer" at Newport. Millionaires who owned entire railroads, banks, and industries—Vanderbilts, Astors, Belmonts, Grosvenors, Morgans, and other, now-forgotten names— lived in a collection of 100-odd mansions which had, said one reporter, "a measure of luxury men have not witnessed since the fall of Rome."[9]

The most legendary of these edifices line the high bluff over the ocean along the Cliff Walk. This shore path, "the vested right of the humblest citizen of Newport in the Atlantic Ocean,"[10] skirted the expanses of lawns and gardens behind the big houses. On one side of the walk, gulls wheeled and screamed about the crag face, and far below the surf boomed, folding and refolding its breakers against the barrier before it; on the other side, regally fortified from nature's fury, flourished the "Gilded Age," among reflecting pools, terraces, croquet lawns, and roses.

They called these summer homes "cottages": oversized reproductions of Louis XIV chateaus, or round-towered castles out of medieval England. Wrote one witty admirer of the latter style:

. . . in a half-light, when the whitish smears on the brick, and the cold curtainless windows are not too much in evidence, and while you are still laboring under the delusion that it is a state asylum for the criminally insane, and not a house, you admire the mighty mass of it upon its foundation of undulating rock against the noble background of sea and sky.[11]

Less pretentious homes surrounded themselves with formal gardens and masses of purple hydrangea, which grow lush in the salt air.

From their palaces, the "cottagers" vied among themselves in extravagance, the wives plotting and intriguing for social predominance. Butlers clad in satin knee breeches and powdered wigs rode miniature railway cars to carry the silver tea service from the main house to the Oriental teahouse overlooking the sea. Society

"Breakwater," the Newport home of Governor Charles Lippincott of Rhode Island.

dinners often had so many courses that a truly hungry guest had to stab for morsels as liveried servants served from the left, while others simultaneously cleared from the right.

Sea bathing was out of fashion for society by the 1870s. "Strangers and servants may do so, but the cottagers have withdrawn their support from the ocean. Salt water may be carried to the house and used without loss of caste, but bathing in the surf is vulgar,"[12] wrote William Dean Howells. Many observers of the period attributed this to the style of women's bathing dresses, which made even the comeliest belle a caricature.

The fashionable carriage drive along the beach was by now a ritual. People dressed in their formal best. The servants, in livery, sat stiffly atop and behind. No one spoke to those in other carriages; one never even made eye contact outside one's own vehicle. One simply sat and rode.

Newport itself was a strange mixture of classes. The townspeople ignored the rich.

The fixed population, absorbed with the past, have a serene contempt for the fripperies of the present. Odder creatures than many of the fishermen and seafarers can scarcely be met. Weird and dreamy in appearance, they never rub their eyes lest they should awake to the unpleasant fact of the latter half of the nineteenth century.[13]

Coming into the town by steamer at the turn of the century, one saw a typical New England shore town—a hillside of gray-cedar-shingled or white painted homes, elms, and white church steeples—which upon closer look revealed odd

From Yankee Notions, *December 1857.*

Something Else.

Anxious Mother (to her son, at fashionable party).—CHARLIE, MY BOY, WHY DO YOU STAND THERE? GO IN AND EN-JOY YOURSELF; YOU LOOK LIKE A STATUE! THERE'S MISS JONES, SHE'S A SPLENDID CREATURE, PLUMP AS A PARTRIDGE SHALL I INTRODUCE YOU?

Son.—NO, I THANK YOU; I SAW THE LADY IN BATHING AT NAHANT LAST SUMMER! EXCUSE ME!

anomalies. Among the weatherbeaten shipping vessels were racing yachts of international renown, and on the dilapidated docks alongside old horse-drawn hacks were the most expensive automobiles in the world.

Many of the cottagers, especially the Boston crowd, in contrast to the New York magnates, frequented the Reading Room, a nondescript verandahed club, and surrounded it with their modest rented 6-mph electric buggies.

Newport's high society gathered in two other places: the Casino, the premier lawn-tennis club, set behind a line of storefronts built in imitation Tudor design, and Bailey's Beach, early twentieth-century society's concession to the enjoyment of swimming once more aesthetic bathing costumes appeared. Since the public had taken over the large beaches, society gathered behind a barrier of bathhouses in a little cove for which even the most sympathetic Newport enthusiast found few positive words.

Bailey's Beach, where society swims, dives, palavers, and rides the surf in canoes, is crescent-shaped and white, too white for the eye's comfort, and too crescent-shaped for the seaweed that drifts into it to drift out. For fifty or sixty feet the water is a kind of thick gruel: seaweed, floating sand, and seawater, but beyond it is clear, lively, and swimmable. [14]

Newport changed in the early twentieth century. Newspapers had long feasted on Newport's rich, while socialist agitators labeled them American Romanovs, but, in truth, the arrival of trust-busting and the income tax did away with much of the ludicrous extravagance. No matter, the Model T still brought a good part of Fall River and New Bedford over on Sunday afternoons to picnic and gawk. Newport retired behind closed doors. Today the town is still a summer colony for the very rich. Those who could not beat the changing times joined them, opening their palaces as museums to the once-abhorred public.

Yachting

Pleasure boating in New England has had a long history. In 1797, Timothy Dwight joined his hosts in Portland, Maine, for an excursion to one of the harbor islands. "Our business," he said, "professedly was fishing, in which we were completely successful. It is true, we neither caught, nor attempted to catch, any fish; but we made an excellent dinner of very fine ones."[a] Throughout the eighteenth and nineteenth century, New Englanders kept up the tradition of a fishing voyage across the waters to some deserted beach, where later a bonfire warmed the evening.

As New England's maritime economy began to wane, by the mid-nineteenth century, many families deserted fishing, shipping, and whaling for mercantile livelihoods, but kept up their seagoing tradition through yachting. During the last half of the century yachts lay at anchor off the club piers at Marblehead, Boston, Newport, and elsewhere. Like Nantucket Harbor today, Newport in the late nineteenth century symbolized the epitome of pleasure boating. It was the destination of wealthy yachtsmen and the finish line for the New York Yacht Club's annual regatta. The town today still retains one vestige of that era, the America's Cup Race, named for the ship that in 1851 defeated 15 British yachts in a race around the Isle of Wight. It today takes place a few miles off Newport. Newport's race week today is an experience even for those who never leave the docks. The harbor is filled with vessels of every description, a flotilla skippered by boatmen of all levels of competence. The salty yachtsmen congregate together, casting disdainful comments at those who would foul the waters with their gas-burning stinkpots. Millionaires relax upon the afterdecks of their floating palaces. Experienced crews stand by to weigh anchor or hoist the Rolls-Royce onto the dock should the owner decide to take a spin onshore. Surrounding these vessels is a great anthill of weekend party boaters, careening through the harbor, oblivious to even the most basic rules of the nautical road. Minor collisions are common. (One vessel often punctures another when a skipper fails to put the gears in neutral before starting the motor. The typical casualty is the larger yacht, which offers a more extensive target.) Personal injuries are infrequent, however, as help is almost always anchored only a few yards away. Yet it can be suggested that, given a fast boat and waterproof binoculars, Ida Lewis could surpass her whole career of lifesaving during one Newport Race Week.

Fishing Party in Boston Harbor, 1855.

1881 · TIME TABLE · 1881

BOSTON & HINGHAM
STEAMBOAT CO.
AND
NANTASKET BEACH
RAILROAD CO.

Covers for the 1881 timetable of the Boston
& Hingham Steamboat Company and the
Nantasket Beach Railroad Company.

The coal-fired cities along the shore had attracted a large work force, which was soon eager for temporary escape from its industrial environment. By the 1870s, short-line railroads and steamers carried urban daytrippers to the nearest sands and sea breeze. Sometimes the voyage was an end in itself.

> *There's a place down the bay, a few miles away,*
> *Down at the end of the Cape;*
> *Where sea breezes blow that make your face glow,*
> *Where from heat and all care you es-cape;*
> *There's a fine steam-boat too, that's strong, staunch, and true,*
> *That's wait-ing to car-ry you there,*
> *She's called the Cape Cod, af-ter his-tor-ic sod*
> *That's known the world ev-'ry where.*
> *Then take your best girl, from the city's mad whirl,*
> *O-ver the wa-ter so blue;*
> *Bring a big box lunch and a bot-tle of punch,*
> *You'll enjoy your-self sure if you do;*
> *On the deck you can spoon the whole after-noon*
> *'Till the sun in the West has gone down.*
> *As homeward you go, no regrets will you know*
> *From go-ing to Prov-ince-town.* [15]

Easy access by steam soon brought the summering crowds to more remote locations, where they rented homes or built cottages for "the season."

A Gloucester resident complained in 1875:

> *At present the cape [Cape Ann] is overrun annually for three or four months by an army from the cities. The era of boarding-houses, shanties, and shooting-boxes has fairly set in. The trim yacht is seen lying in the coves alongside of some rusty old pink or granite drogher; the weather-worn and quaint gambrel-roofed farm-houses are turned for the nonce into villas. They are garnished with new porches, lace curtains, and croquet grounds; and cottages presenting a cross between an Italian villa and Chinese-joss-house are perched on the hill-tops and planted among the buildings of the early settlers, not always with perfect success as regards effect.* [16]

In Rhode Island, the town of Narragansett Pier combined little summer cottages, interspersed with a few mansions—the overflow from Newport society. It soon became a famous resort for Victorian summer vacationers.

Connecticut had a boom in the beach town of Westbrook, beginning in 1878. Unfortunately the major part of that state's shore contained only a few pocket beaches, the rest being insect-infested marshes. Even the railroads and steamship lines that promoted the joy of vacationing in New England had little good to say about the Connecticut shore. The New York, New Haven and Hartford Railroad, in a tour book published annually between 1890 and 1910, went so far as to assure prospective visitors to Ridgefield, some 17 miles inland, that "Of malaria, that pest of the New England lowlands near the seashore, it knows nothing."[17] Other guides recommended the Connecticut shore as a pleasant autumn side trip, once a hard frost had killed off the mosquitoes.

The Connecticut shore finally came of age after two New York land developers bought, sight unseen, the small peninsula of Groton Long Point, near New London. After they had inspected this marshy tract, their glee at getting the land away from the local Yankees at a cheap price quickly evaporated. Undaunted, however, they began a program of ditching and draining the marshes, a practice that slowly spread to other sites along the coast. As the mosquito infestations receded, the

Connecticut shore took on at least a partial semblance of a resort area.

Massachusetts fared better. The sandy islands in warm Nantucket Sound attracted visitors as soon as the railroads and steamers began service. The trains first made connection to New Bedford, transferring vacationers to steamers for the run across Buzzards Bay and Vineyard Sound to the Martha's Vineyard landing of Holmes Hole, later given the more appealing name of Vineyard Haven. Other steamers pushed on across Nantucket Sound to that faraway isle of the whalemen. Once this happened, never again would these sandy wastes ever face the depression that followed the demise of whaling.

Vacationers now paid ready money to stay in fishermen's shacks and examine the whalebones, scrimshaw, and other relics exhibited for the veneration of the faithful and the entertainment of the tourists.

The gradual infiltration of city people into the remote shore regions brought an end to the isolation of many of the remaining coastal communities. At first, vacationer and old Yankee circled warily, inspecting each other from a polite distance. A visitor to Biddeford Pool, Maine, wrote in the 1880s of how the fishermen set out nets to catch small bait fish and of their constant problem of disentangling frenzied sharks from the nets, confiding to the reader, "and I am informed that the fishermen do not always use mild language on these occasions."[18] To the shoreline locals, the summer visitors were known as "rusticators." In 1877, a Block Island historian, chronicling the island's past for the summer visitor, observed that the Block Islanders built their homes with a view toward the ocean, enabling them to note the movement of ships with the powerful telescopes owned by nearly every household. He added, "It might be well for some visitors to remember these far seeing instruments, especially at the bathing beach."

Friction inevitably developed. Complained a Nantucket landlord,

You take these vacation visitors lookin' for a lodging-place . . . they don't want this and they don't want that. We have to deal with a good many blame cheap people, and it's something fierce the way they talk to you. . . . They come into our house and tell us how much they admire old-fashioned homes and furnishings . . . lastly they say "Now let's see what kind of beds you've got;" and they'll punch their fists into 'em to see whether they've got the latest springs. If you was to show them a corded bed they'd drop dead. . . . Our Massachusetts people put up the worst kick of any on God's earth. They are kickers from way back. They want everything old, and they also want all the modern improvements.[19]

By the time "good" beds predominated, new controversy had arisen over vacationers' demands that modern plumbing replace the old outhouse.

One of the last regions to submit to a vacation economy was Cape Cod, which did not fall into its dubious embrace until the 1920s. A railroad pushed up the Cape, connecting to Provincetown in 1873, but only after its promoter had toured the Cape, convincing the happily isolated inhabitants that if the British ever again invaded, they would use Cape Cod as the first foothold if there were no rail connection to the mainland. In the late nineteenth century, the Cape had little to offer that could not be found closer to home. Only Provincetown and Hyannis attracted any sort of summer colony. Some fine summer mansions were built in the southeast, along Buzzards Bay and across from Martha's Vineyard, but they were isolated enclaves for rich Bostonians.

By the 1920s the Cape was locked into hard times. The fishing had peaked in 1860, cranberrying had shifted to Plymouth County on the mainland, and mass-produced items were being trucked in more cheaply than the local shops and farms could produce them. The Cape's population around 1920 of 26,000 was 10,000 fewer than in 1860.

All the Cape now had to offer was the evidence of centuries of marginal living: one-and-a-half-story Cape Cod houses, windmills, old fishing wharves, lighthouses, quaint hamlets, and their even quainter inhabitants.

What ultimately saved the Cape and made tourism flourish was the automobile. In 1901 the first motor car, a Stanley Steamer, made it through the sandy ruts to Provincetown, but it was not until about 1938 that macadam covered the whole route.

Unlike the more centralized vacation spots, with their hotels and "cottage cities," the Cape provided individual tourist homes, roadside cabins, and other accommodations easily accessible by auto. The Cape Codders saw nothing demeaning about such work. Hooking in the tourists could be compared to the old custom of driving in the willing blackfish that congregated along the shore. Soon the old farmer-fishermen were pumping gas, building cottages, or selling homemade fishnet curios at gift shops such as the "Merchant of Dennis." Cape Cod life fell into its present schizophrenic cycle: nine months of peace, followed by the hectic twelve-week "season," when the elderly no longer crossed streets, and children were told to play in the backyard, away from the road.

Tower of the Ocean House, Westerly, Rhode Island, one of the last of the Victorian hotels that once populated every New England beach resort. Begun in the 1850s, it today has over 200 rooms. ◁

Vacationers in front of the "gazebo" on the beach at Westbrook, Connecticut, just after the town became the state's first beach resort, in 1872.

Prosperity and population increased during the twenties and thirties. There were a few scares; once it was rumored that land speculators were moving in to start a northern counterpart to the Florida land craze (when everyone was driving south to move into the Everglade swampland they had bought, sight unseen). Development at this time centered around Hyannis, along the middle part of the Cape's southern shore. Here, abutting Nantucket Sound, family vacationers found the perfect combination of warm waters, southern exposure, excellent shallows for wading children, and a mild sea breeze out of the southwest. Most of the prewar tourism congregated here, leaving the northern Cape Cod Bay side to the natives. Only up in Provincetown was there any other influx of "mainlanders." Here bohemians, artists, and other exotics mixed with the old Portuguese and Yankee stock.

Gas rationing during World War II brought the Cape commercial expansion to a halt, beginning some ten years of inactivity in which the sandy peninsula contemplated its future. Many towns made plans to keep public their stretch of the Cape's 300 miles of beach; others revised (or initiated) their zoning and building codes. The most monumental accomplishment of the postwar years was the formation of the Cape Cod National Seashore, officially created in 1956, which today holds almost half of the Cape's outer arm as a public trust.

In postwar years, the permanent population was joined by retirees, who tolerated the "season," or opened small businesses to profit from it. They settled more evenly through the Cape than the beach-hugging tourists had.

In the late 1950s the boom resumed. The neon-lit lion lay down with the cedar-shingled lamb. Along the old main roads, "Leaning Towers of Pizza" abutted the slightly frayed homes of old Cape Codders. The mixture was in itself characteristically seashore-tourist-funky, and not at all repellent to the vacationer. As the

natives had been bemoaning their homeland's "hell-in-a-handbasket" course since well before the Revolutionary War, few paid them any attention.

The cracks in the high-density, automobile-dependent economy began to widen in the 1970s. At the height of the season, the south coastal artery approaches gridlock. The hamlets, to preserve their quaint character (as the brochures advertise) and simultaneously accommodate population needs, have become small oases of rustication between vast stretches of shopping centers catering to the needs of man, car, and cottage. The vacationer is usually provided with great leisure to study the pretourist architecture as he sits in endless traffic, bottlenecked by a pair of unsynchronized lights at the village center.

For all its problems, the Cape still draws enthusiasts. Summer cottages now extend from Nantucket Sound to Cape Cod Bay, and the population of year-round dwellers is still growing. The permanent residents and returning vacationers can see the changes, but newcomers look beyond the modernization toward what has kept the oldtimers from moving out and the cottagers coming back: Cape Cod's climate and scenery.

Nature still dominates the Cape's character whether the land is covered with stores or has been restrictively zoned to allow only classic Cape architecture: cedar-shingled, white-wood-trimmed, green-shuttered "Capes" of age-old proportions. Warm sea breezes invite the bather. From the bluffs of the outer shore one

A cottage at the Methodists' Camp Meeting Grounds, Oak Bluffs, Martha's Vineyard, ca. 1880.

*Fishermen's shacks, Provincetown, now
vacation cottages.*

*The Provincetown waterfront. The wharves
are dilapidated, but the summer homes are
bright and tidy.*

can look down on ocean rollers built up by storms a thousand miles away. The flats at low tide along the bay side invite the idle hour but wet the careless shoe as the water returns swiftly over the miles of sand. Everywhere twisting wisps of scrub pine show lichen and green moss from the constant mists. At Chatham, the Cape's "elbow," retired naval men glory in the dense fog created from the meeting of the cold Atlantic and the warm Nantucket Sound. Bird life, encouraged in sanctuaries, carries on a semblance of its wild state (aided by vacationers' handouts) among the tidal rivers and ponds, only yards from summer cottages.

All these attract people to the Cape: Bostonians to Osterville and Cotuit; tourists to the old villages of Barnstable and Brewster along the north shore; vacationers to Hyannis, Dennis Port, and Harwich Port; surgeons, psychiatrists, and other professionals to Wellfleet; and to Provincetown come the outsiders (and people-watchers to marvel at the outsiders), keeping up the tradition begun by the colonial pirates and smugglers who made the location their refuge. Until removed by the highway department a few years ago, the most photographed subject on the Cape was a highway sign near Provincetown, informing the motorist that both the divided highway, Route 6, and the old shore road, now 6A, led into the village. The sign stated simply, "Provincetown. Either Way."

The Artists

While the rich found congenial spirits at Newport, the North Shore above Boston, or Bar Harbor; the religious at Eastham and Oak Bluffs; so, too, did the artistic folk set off certain coastal sites as their own.

An artist on a summer cruise sketching a maid on a Nantucket wharf. From Harper's Monthly, *1882.*

In early instances, such "art colonies" became popular through the fame of a single artist who lived there; Prout's Neck, Maine (just south of Portland) is a well-known example. Here, in the 1880s, Winslow Homer, already famous, took up residence in an unheated stable adjoining a plot of land his family had bought in the hope of developing it into a resort. A recluse whenever the opportunity arose, Homer divided his time between lending his prestige to the family business, and painting in a style that, though impressionistic in its lack of detail, was scientifically accurate in its representation of atmospheric effects. Of one painting, Homer pointed out:

The picture is painted fifteen minutes after sunset—not one minute before—as up to that minute the clouds over the sun would have their edges lightened with a brilliant glow of color—but now the sun has gone beyond their immediate range & they are in shadow. . . .[b]

When the season for tourism and amateur artists ended in early fall, Homer had Prout's Neck to himself, his art, and his alcohol. In response to a letter accusing him of a lack of sociability, he wrote:

I deny I am a recluse as is generally understood by that term. Neither am I an unsociable hog. I wrote you its true that it was not convenient to receive a visitor. . . . I have never yet had a bed in my house. I do my own work. No other man or woman within half a mile & four miles from railroad or P.O. This is the only life in which I am permitted to mind my own business. I suppose I am the only man in New England who can do it. I am perfectly happy and content. Happy New Year.[c]

As Homer kept to himself on the rocky peninsula of Prout's Neck, farther down the coast the more gregarious of his brother artists congregated at such locations as Provincetown and Gloucester, Massachusetts, and Old Lyme and Cos Cob, Connecticut.

Old Lyme, at the mouth of the Connecticut River, had, at the turn of the century, been "discovered" by painters of the American Impressionist style: Childe Hassam, Maurice Prendergast, John Twachtman, and Willard Metcalf, to name a few. Old Lyme was then a quiet backwater of past glories. Like many a once-prominent shore town, it was a quaint combination of frugal yet lethargic common folk, interspersed with the old families living off the wealth amassed by an earlier generation. The painters who summered there saw in its rocky fields, tidal rivers, wide marshes, and shoreline, an answer to the Fontainebleau of the French Barbizon School.

These artists shared an old mansion-turned-boardinghouse, dispersing each morning to paint classics of American Impressionism, images of high color and suggested detail, which rank foremost of all the attempts to record the wonderful sense of open shadow and brilliant sunlight beloved by those who know the New England shore.

Many of the same artists who summered at Old Lyme also frequented the town of Cos Cob on a year-round basis; it was not far by train from New York. As Lincoln Steffens the "muckraker" (today read "investigative reporter"), a frequent visitor to the town, observed: "Cos Cob, Conn., is a little old fishing village strung along one side of one long street facing Cos Cob Harbor. . . . Quiet, almost dead, it was a paintable spot frequented by artists who worked, painters who actually painted."[d]

As at Old Lyme, the group had taken over a former mansion, and boarded there in extended social contact. In Cos Cob, it was the Holley House:

a great, rambling, beautiful old accident—so old that it had its slave quarters up under the roof; and it looked out from under elms as high as oaks upon the inner harbor and an abandoned boat-building house with sail lofts. There was a long veranda where breezes blew down from the river, up from the sound. . . .[e]

Here the group argued art and other matters, often falling into debating traps laid by Steffens and Twachtman, who would create sides to an issue, gather supporters, then spend the evening getting their respective sides to swing around unknowingly until they argued against their original propositions. In one incident, the controversy was not so subtle. Steffens wrote: "One spring we found the railroad building a new bridge over the neck of the harbor. Everybody was disgusted. It was a busy scene of noisy, steaming, smoking activity."[f] Steffens defended the intrusion on the grounds that action, as well as scenic repose, was a proper subject of the artist; he predicted that his colleagues would ultimately agree with him. Soon he left on business and returned a few weeks later. Walking up from the station, he "passed all the Cos Cob school with their easels set and painting the noisy, dirty bridge improvement. None of them greeted [him]; they wouldn't look up at [him]. . . . Twachtman alone spoke . . . and all he said was, 'Ah, go to hell.'"[g]

While Old Lyme's artistic fame brought it rebirth as home for the cultured wealthy, Cos Cob soon became immersed in the flood tide of commuters' homes as it gradually developed into a bedroom community of New York City.

Another art colony with close ties to New York City was bohemian Provincetown, which, during World War I, became an extension of Greenwich Village. Beginning around the turn of the century, a number of accomplished artists had discovered Provincetown and by the war about a half-dozen schools took on aspiring painters for the summer-long course.

This "portrait painting on the docks each morning with a 10 o'clock break for tea" atmosphere was soon shattered by an influx of Left Bank expatriates forced from their Parisian garrets by the German invasion. Such revolutionary painters as Charles Demuth organized art associations to discuss bolshevism, the role of the artist in the upcoming socialist world, and how to champion the new ideals of modern art—cubism, futurism, and other "modernisms"—brought to the public eye in the widely publicized Armory Show of 1913 in New York City.

Among the artists there was a small circle of aspiring playwrights. This group founded the Provincetown Players, giving performances in an old wharf building, beneath which the tides could be seen ebbing and flowing through the gaps in the floorboards. It was they who in 1916 invited a young author living in a shack down the beach in Truro to show them some of his efforts. The man was Eugene O'Neill, and his plays soon brought fame to the Provincetown Players when they staged his dramas in Greenwich Village. The solitary O'Neill, a lover of the sea, found himself considered a suspicious character when the town constable began fearing that O'Neill's beach wanderings might be attempts to signal enemy submarines. Despite a subsequent arrest, and a continued shadowing by the police, O'Neill fell in love with the Cape and in 1919 acquired an abandoned and isolated lifesaving station among the dunes of the Atlantic side of the Cape. Here he stared at sea and sky, and wrote his tragedies. He said:

I feel a true kinship and harmony with life out here. Sand and sun and sea and wind—you merge into them, and become as meaningless and as full of meaning as they are. There is always the monotone of the surf on the bar—a background for silence—and you know *that you are alone— so alone you wouldn't be ashamed to do any good action. You can walk or swim along the beach for miles and meet only the dunes—Sphinxes muffled in their yellow robes with paws deep in the sea.*[h]

The sea claimed O'Neill's Peaked Hill Bar house in 1931.

As the population of Cape Cod and the southern New England shore grew during the twentieth century, the artist searching for a refuge from civilization gravitated toward the Maine coast. The Wyeth family, George Bellows, and Rockwell Kent, among many others, produced works that portray people struggling out their existence in a rugged yet beautiful environment. Other artists found Maine an ideal place for coming to personal terms with the revolutionary concepts of modern art being spread throughout the Paris and New York studios: artists such as John Marin, Edward Hopper, Maurice Prendergast, and William and Marguerite Zorach, drew great vitality from the Down East landscape. Wrote John Marin, whose work is concerned with the depiction of feeling, rather than realistic detail, "This day is a peach, clear and snappy, the tide is in, the water a crystal green, the sky coming down to the waters, indescribable brilliancy. The boats dance. Everything is dancing. To Hell with Gloom. Even my boat feels the day. It has a jump to it."[i] Abstractionist or Realist, different eyes see different things, each mind produces a different interpretation, yet the inspirational beauty of the land and sea pervades them all.

13

The Shore Today

There are few Americans today who are such strangers to the fabled history of the New England shore that they can approach the region with an unaffected eye. This stretch of land, where Yankees abode with the sea, somehow perpetually evokes its past. One's view of it today has become an inseparable mix of present physical character and the enduring ghosts (both real and imaginary) of history. Trim Nantucket, for example, with its yachts, vacation homes, and mid-nineteenth-century mansions, is conjured by our minds into colonial Quaker Nantucket, the sandy, unadorned "gray lady of the sea."

With this in mind, it is perhaps best to tie off this tapestry of the New England shore's history with a look at the region as it stands today.

As one moves eastward from the Connecticut–New York border, the first leg of the trip along the shore takes one through the "Gold Coast," prestigious Fairfield County, where residential shoreline real estate is the world's most expensive. In little Byram, hard by the New York line, one can peer across well-guarded estates to glimpse among the trees impressive homes, some Victorian, some of the dignified colonial revival style, and a few so hilariously palatial that the visitor might expect one of Louis XIV's mistresses to come walking out the front door.

Before World War II, Fairfield County, the western third of Connecticut's shoreline, was a scattering of industrialized cities among sleepy little villages, which were the haunts of artists, bohemians, and summer people. Just before the war, business executives discovered the region, and they were followed after the war by the Madison Avenue advertising crowd. By the mid-1950s, the scene was set—enter the gray-flanneled commuter with his newspaper to await the train at the Darien or Westport station.

Today, giant corporations are moving their headquarters into Stamford and other shoreline cities, greatly urbanizing the bedroom-town image. The Old Post Road, as Route 1 is commonly called, now guides motorists past the colonial town greens before swinging them out into the mayhem of Post Road shopping centers, car dealerships, and fast-food restaurants.

Moving farther east, one finds the middle class being allowed to approach the shore as the commuting distance to New York becomes too long. Small vacation houses fill the somewhat oily beachfront. Land values remain high, and a cottage is considered to have a respectable yard if a car can be parked between adjoining houses.

East of New Haven, the terminus of the commuter trains, life relaxes back to communities typical of Connecticut "steady habits." Colonial houses line the shore road at dignified intervals, then begin to clump together to mark a village centered around a white-steepled church. Outside town, the road is often the solitary intruder through a salt marsh spanning a tidal river by a small bridge before again

Three Sons, one of the fishing fleet of Point Judith, Rhode Island. ▷

making high ground. The marshlands are Connecticut's last true wilderness, although over half have been bulldozed into building lots since the century began. Like the windmill raising water to make America's prairies into lush farmland, so too did the modest sump pump transform life along the marshy Connecticut shore. The summer homes, set on pilings, now were given dug foundations and became year-round homes. Here, as elsewhere along the coast, the interstate highway system of the 1950s and 1960s awoke many sleepy little towns. After this sudden entry into the twentieth century, they either became part of the region's growing suburban area or were saved from "progress" by the liberal application of time and money by the old families and concerned newcomers who attempted to preserve the towns' old character.

While cottages crowd the little roads leading down to water, there is still much untouched land. It can best be seen from the windows of the shore train from New York to Boston. The roadbed runs past villages, to cut through rocky woods and over the many salt marshes. In season, one looks out on ducks and swans in surprising numbers, trailing their young behind them as they paddle up a tidal creek. Ospreys nest on poles set up for them in the marsh, glaring and fluffing out their feathers at the noisy intruder that rushes by. At dawn, raccoons wash at the river bank, and twists of morning fog lie in the still-shadowed coves.

Rhode Island comes next on the northeast journey. The marshlands here are now fronted by barrier beaches, for the shore has passed out of the placid Long Island Sound and now faces the open sea. Those Connecticut bathers who come here suddenly realize how dilute their home waters are as they feel the sea salt drying on their bodies. The ocean has its hazards, however, since hurricanes have decimated many beach colonies and shifting beachfronts have tumbled many cottages into the surf. The population here allows room for the old industries, and little inlets at Point Judith house active fishing fleets.

The rough southern shores turn north in Narragansett Bay, a separate world of islands, passages, and small bays, lying in placid protection from the open ocean. It combines a portion of the rugged grandeur of the Maine coast with its own balmy climate. It is no wonder that the Indians of the southern New England region chose to center their activities here. From atop the high Newport Bridge can be viewed the grandest sweep across this region, a sight that rivals the vista of dawn from the summit of Cadillac Mountain on Mount Desert Island. The bridge at Newport replaced an old ferry, which itself provided an inspiring view from its upper foredeck as the ferry threaded through the vessels in Newport Harbor to dock at the old waterfront.

The next region the traveler sees is the shores of misty Buzzards Bay, dividing Cape Cod from the mainland. For most, the bay is simply a way station to the Cape. The residents of its shore villages live content that few recognize the beauty of some of the old communities, leaving them relatively unbothered. Fall River and New Bedford are the population centers of the region. New Bedford remains an active fishing port. Deep-sea vessels line the docks, a few foreign cargo ships tie up alongside the fish packing plants, and the cats that prowl the waterfront are sleek and well fed.

Cape Cod soon looms into the landscape. The traveler must now actively avoid the new to locate the more timeless. Venture down the small side roads that wind down to the shore in the less commercial towns. Here are the old homes built around windmills. Cedar-sided Cape houses are set off by yards ornamented with purple hydrangea and bordered by wild roses. Farther inland, the scrub pines, knurled and covered with lichen, twist up out of the sand in stunted, toylike forests, reminiscent of the improbable pines in ancient Chinese paintings. As the traveler moves up to Boston along what is known locally as the South Shore, the

landscape combines comfortable suburbs and more rural sections like those along the Connecticut shore into a pleasant homogeneous blend.

When Boston approaches, the scene changes. One sees the classic image of the New England seaport city that has turned its back on the sea. The smell of petroleum distillates from offloading oil tankers has long ago replaced the smell of dockside hemp and tar. Tankers and a few container ships are the majority of the vessels here, for over 85 percent of all New England–manufactured goods marked for overseas go through New York. The cargo vessels that do enter Boston Harbor now tie up across the harbor in East Boston, far from the eye of the citizenry. The city inhabitants see a dockside of crumbling warehouses, textile mills, and shoe factories, all left over from earlier eras. Restoration has come only in the last few years. Boston's waterfront has been refurbished into an impressive condominium section and a tourist attraction. The old buildings have been stripped, scrubbed, and urethaned back to their original appearance—but not their original use. The old Quincy Market has been partitioned off into boutiques. It is a developer's paradise.

Farther north the industrial wasteland tapers off into the "North Shore," where seaside estates are owned by families whose names would have been as familiar to Massachusetts citizens a century before the Revolution as they are now.

Old Town Mill, New London, built for John Winthrop in 1650, rebuilt 1712; now lying beneath the eastbound and westbound lanes of Interstate 95 as it approaches the Thames River bridge. "On the grounds is an old weather-stained mill, its gambrel roof green with the moss of time; the stream that turns the wheel falls through a rocky ravine from a considerable height. The water dashes and foams over its bed of large boulders, singing merrily as it rushes through the lonely glen. It is overshadowed by great forest trees, which cause a dark impenetrable gloom; a picturesque spot, seemingly as wild to-day as when the Indians—that mighty Pequot tribe—owned the land." From "At the Old Winthrop Mill," in The Old Harbor Town, *by Augusta Watson Campbell, 1907.*

The Hurricane of 1938

At about 3:00 in the afternoon of September 21, 1938, the worst hurricane of the century to strike New England hit the Connecticut shore. The afternoon had begun with a sunny sky and a slight breeze out of the northeast, then, with little warning from weather forecasters, it came in on a high tide. The wind soon swung around, coming out of the south with enough strength to topple small buildings and tear off roofs. It roared like a siren. From Long Island Sound to Buzzards Bay, the winds, with gusts measured at up to 186 mph, brought storm-driven "tidal waves," which pushed houses a half-mile inland, sank the fishing fleets at anchor, took almost 700 lives, and destroyed many thousands of homes.

It was an hour and a half of hell, which lasted much longer for those caught in the rubble. The unimaginable horror it brought was not without its freakish aspects. The shoreline New-York-to-Boston train had to push a cabin cruiser and house off the tracks at Stonington, and even then it became stalled in the high water. The 275 passengers spent the night huddled in the cars, before being rescued in the morning. A woman in Somerset, near Fall River, looked out her window to find an oil tanker wedged between her house and garage. Most stories were less freakish, but more harrowing—tales of how a wave, estimated to be about thirty feet high, came in out of the howl-

The 1938 hurricane at Stonington, Connecticut. A storm wave (the wind-driven equivalent of a tidal wave) can be seen approaching in the distance. The vessel is the fishing boat Laura. *The series of storm waves flooded the town, flattened buildings, and pushed vessels far inland.*

ing rain to smash away all the buildings and summer homes that lined the water's edge. Many houses, like the 44 homes along the sand spit of Napatree Point at Westerly, Rhode Island, had been placed with little regard for the elements. This line of homes, dubbed "Suicide Shores" by the weatherwise fishermen, disappeared entirely; even their foundations were swept away. The story was the same up and down the coast. Even those who had built on "guaranteed hurricane-proof pilings" came to realize that this meant only that the pilings would still be standing after the house was washed away.

Out of the horror came a new realization of the ocean's dangers. Cities like New Bedford, which had been drowned by the waters, constructed sea barriers, dikes that could be closed to protect the inner harbors and the waterfronts. Small towns began to pay more attention to the little beach houses being built at the edge of the tideline. When the hurricane of 1955 struck, the caution paid off in reduced loss of life and property damage.

Once around Cape Ann and its touristy "artists' colonies," the flat beaches stretch north into Maine. Resort towns still retain a vestige of their Edwardian origins, though they are perhaps a little tawdry now. The boardwalks have their video game arcades, but on the beach, children play on the wide sandy flats and hillocks that are exposed as the tide falls. They search for sand dollars or splash along the ankle-deep rivulets that meander along the flats at low tide.

North of Portland, with its own more utilitarian waterfront restoration, comes a region of headlands and estuaries. Here is the genteel shore at its best. Towns that grew to wealth from the lumber or shipbuilding trade now strike a dignified balance between old and new with a foreground of lobstering and fishing against a backdrop of nineteenth-century homes, now preserved as museums, and summer homes.

Penobscot Bay is next, a great indentation in the shore that is masked on maps by its islands and the many smaller inlets surrounding it. Its name also presents a problem to the uninitiated. If in New England the Indians have left any legacy by which they exact their vengeance upon the white settlers, it is the innumerable similar-sounding place names. For those who have not actually visited the places, and thus fixed their location in their minds, it becomes a maddening task to differentiate between such places as Penobscot, Pemaquid, Presumpscott, Passamaquoddy, Piscataqua, Pawtucket, Pawcatuck, and the like.

Edging the east side of Penobscot Bay is the lovely Blue Hill peninsula, with Deer Isle at its tip. Next on the route east comes Mount Desert Island. Here, tucked in around the mountains of Acadia National Park, are summer hideaways of many rich and famous. Lobster boats and sleek yachts intermingle in the little pine-sheltered harbors. Occasionally a gaily painted rendition of a Chinese junk, or some equally gaudy craft, will be anchored among them, standing out like the proverbial hooker at a church picnic.

America's hurried life-style makes its last stand on the road to Mount Desert Island—with an asphalt strip lined with fast-food restaurants and discount department stores. The effect of all this is not so pronounced when one is traveling east, since one is usually well down the road before realizing that the last of the parking lots is far behind. If one is coming from the northeast, however, the abrupt return from a landscape of quiet villages into what could easily be a giant shopping center in a suburb of a large city leaves the traveler—who until then had been reveling in the beauty of a pastoral countryside—emotionally shattered.

After this, the last of Hancock County leads into Washington County, and, finally, the border. Route 1 here becomes an inland road, crossing a landscape of engaging bleakness, with rolling blueberry barrens suggesting the wilds of the Scottish Highlands. Side roads wind down the slopes to the fishing hamlets—often centered around a cannery set on a wharf along the inlet. These towns have much starker character than those farther south, where such communities would be overshadowed by the beautiful old shipbuilding and lumber towns. This is a deceptive region. At first glance it looks not only unspoiled, but untouched—forgotten, utterly bypassed by the changes that have overtaken America since midcentury. In actuality, many of the homes are owned by retirees and summer people. Yet those "outsiders" who come this far north do so with the express intent of becoming a part of this no-frills life, with its personal pride and quiet dignity. There are few ostentatious summer homes and no tourist industry here, only the pursuit of age-old occupations—eking out a living from the sea because the land holds no promise. The old traditions continue, seemingly unchanged. For those seeking the character of life along the New England shore during centuries past—here is the place.

Site List
by Town from South to North

The sites are listed under the appropriate town or location as shown on the road maps published by each state. These are the most detailed maps that are readily available to the general public. They can be obtained free of charge at each state's many tourist information centers or by mail from their departments of tourism.

The directions are typically given from the nearest adjacent highway exit or from the center of the town under which the site is listed. If the community is small and the site is in the village's center, no directions are given.

For up-to-date locations of ferry lines to the many islands, consult the most modern state map.

This list is, of course, a selective collection of sites. There are many other locations that may provide great enjoyment to the visitor. The places identified below, however, have been chosen on the basis of being perhaps the most entertaining and enlightening for the out-of-state visitor, and intriguing for local residents who may be unaware of the fascinating places in their own backyard.

Connecticut

BYRAM. "Lorelei" Tower, on Northern Calf Island. *Can be seen in winter from Byram Harbor docks.*

GREENWICH. Indian Harbor Yacht Club (1889).

RIVERSIDE. Riverside Yacht Club (1888).

NOROTON. Mill and Customhouse (1737). "Gold Coast" estates. *From I-95 take exit 10, south on Noroton Avenue; go left (east) onto Route 1 (Boston Post Road), right (south) onto Ring's End Road to buildings by water.* For homes: *continue across bridge, then left (south) onto Long Neck Point Road.*

SOUTH NORWALK. Oyster fleet, shell piles and dragger boats. *Take Route 136 to Water Street, then left (east) to waterfront.*

NORWALK. Lockwood-Mathews Mansion Museum (1864); French chateau. *Northeast of junction of Routes 7 and I-95, on West Street.*

WESTPORT. Cedar Point Yacht Club (1888).

SOUTHPORT. Village along the water with opulent mid-nineteenth-century homes.

FAIRFIELD. Penfield Reef. Imposing sight during storms. *From I-95 take exit 21, and go south, at Route 1 (Boston Post Road), turn left (east), then second right (south) onto Reef Road.*

Powder House (1812). *From I-95 take exit 21, go north onto Mill Road, right (east) onto Unquowa Road. The Powder House is on left (to east) just north of I-95.*

BRIDGEPORT. Fishing fleet. *From I-95 take exit 29, go south to waterfront.*

MILFORD. Tombolo to Charles Island, exposed at low tide. *Off Silver Sands State Park.*

NEW HAVEN. Peabody Museum, salt marsh diorama. *170 Whitney Avenue.*

Lighthouse. *From I-95, take Townsend Avenue exit (50 from west, 51 from east), go south on Townsend Avenue to Lighthouse Point Park.*

SALT MARSHES. *From New Haven eastward, marshy estuaries push inland from Long Island Sound. The best overall view of them can be had aboard the Amtrak train as it passes from New Haven to Westerly.*

STONY CREEK. "Down East fishing village." A little hamlet seemingly transplanted from Maine and saved from progress by a low narrow underpass on the one road into the community. *From I-95 take exit 56, go south on Leetes Island Road, continue through the stop sign to the village.*

Thimble Islands. A complex of rocky islands just offshore, many just big enough to fit the mansion sitting atop them. *Tour boats leave from the Stony Creek dock.*

GUILFORD. Marshes and marsh island views. Rock outcrops. Tidal rivers. *They occur along Route 146 between Stony Creek and Guilford village.*

Henry Whitfield House ("1639"): stone manor house, reconstructed in the 1930s. *From the village green, go south ½ mile on Whitfield Street. Bear left (east) at "Y" in the road. The house is immediately on the left.*

CONNECTICUT RIVER.

ESSEX. Mid-nineteenth-century port village. Scenic.

Connecticut River Maritime Museum. In it there is a reconstruction of the *Turtle*, Bushnell's submarine. *At the foot of Main Street.*

WETHERSFIELD. Old Cove Warehouse (1692). *From I-91, take exit 26 west to Marsh Street. Turn right (north), then right (north) again onto Main Street. Continue to the warehouse, at Cove landing.*

HAMBURG. Nineteenth-century shipbuilding and lumber town. Picturesque houses along northeast end of cove.

OLD LYME. Florence Griswold House Museum. Turn-of-century headquarters of American Impressionist painters. *Route 1, north of I-95 exit 70, on left (west).*

Houses along Main Street are sea captains' retirement homes.

WATERFORD. Harkness Memorial State Park. A mansion (1902) and landscaped ground overlooking Long Island Sound. *Take Route 213 to the park.*

NEW LONDON. Coast Guard Academy. Square-rigger *Eagle.* There are tours. *It is north of I-95 on the east side of Route 32.*

Old shipyard with a marine railway. They are presently being restored by the city. *Turn off I-95 onto Route 32 north, pass the Coast Guard Academy, turn right (east) onto Monhegan Avenue, then left onto Naumkeag Avenue, descend to shipyard.*

Hempstead House (1640, 1678, and later additions). Museum. *From west: take I-95 exit 83 onto Route 1A west (Huntington Street), follow Route 1A right onto Jay Street. The house is on the right at the intersection with Hempstead Street. From east, take I-95 exit 84 onto Williams Street (south), turn left (east) onto Broad Street, right (south) onto Hempstead Street, to the house on the left.*

Old Town Mill (1650, rebuilt 1712). *From Route 32 south of I-95, left (east) onto Crystal Road, then right onto State Pier Road. The mill sits beneath I-95.*

Lighthouse (1760, rebuilt 1801). *Take Route 213 south from the center of the city to the shore. The lighthouse is on point at left (east).*

UNCASVILLE. Tantasquidgeon Indian Museum. Dwelling reconstructions. *From I-95, go north on Route 32. The museum is at 1819 New London Turnpike.*

NORWICHTOWN. Agricultural village at head of tidewater, beside falls. Eighteenth- and nineteenth-century homes surround a green, at the northern edge of Norwich. The city grew up at the docks to the south during the nineteenth century.

GROTON. Electric Boat Company. Submarine yards.

U.S. Navy submarine base. *Both base and yards may best be seen from tour boats or bus tours.* A public submarine museum is now being planned to accompany the *Nautilus.*

Fort Griswold State Park. Revolutionary War fort, scenic view of New London.

Bluff Point State Park. Seaside wilderness hiking. Beach cliffs. High surf during storms. Tombolo. Marshland. *From I-95 take exit 88 south to Poquonock Bridge. Park south of the railroad tracks.*

NOANK. A nineteenth-century fishing village.

MYSTIC. A nineteenth-century shore town. It contains the Mystic Seaport Museum.

STONINGTON. A nineteenth-century seaport. The fishing fleet and dockside steam-powered factory are still active.

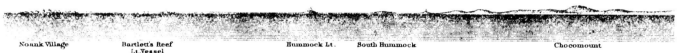

Noank Village   Bartlett's Reef   Hummock Lt.   South Hummock   Chocomount
Lt.Vessel

View of Approaches to Fisher's Id. Sound from the Westward, Race Rock bearing E. by S.⅓ S, distant 5⅞ Miles.

Rhode Island

WATCH HILL. Victorian resort town.

Ocean House Hotel (begun ca. 1860, added to ca. 1890). *It is at the top of the town's hill, best seen from beach to east.*

CHARLESTOWN. Fort Ninigret. Although tradition calls this an Indian fort, it is most likely that these earthworks were thrown up by Dutch traders before 1660. *Take Route 1 to the exit for routes 2 and 112 south. At the stop sign, turn right (west) onto Route 1A. Fort Ninigret Park will be approximately 1 mile on left (south).*

GALILEE. Tuna fishing port.

POINT JUDITH. Lighthouse (1816). Scenic views. Coastal defense gun emplacements from both World Wars. *In camping area off Sand Hill Cove Road (the beach road between Point Judith and Galilee).*

BLOCK ISLAND. Bare rolling landscapes. Sea cliffs. Old Harbor: Victorian hotels.

NARRAGANSETT PIER. The Towers (1882): remains of a casino designed by Stanford White. *At the shore just south of village center, straddling Ocean Road.*

JAMESTOWN. Windmill (1787). *On North Road, south off Route 138 along west side of the island.*

Wright Museum of Indian Artifacts in Philomenian Library, *North Road.*

Beavertail Lighthouse (1856). Ocean panorama. *At the southern tip of Beavertail Road.*

Naval communications towers. *Beavertail Road.*

Ruins of nineteenth-century fortification. *West off Beavertail Road, just west of Mackerel Cove Beach.*

SAUNDERSTOWN. Silas Casey Farm Museum (1750). South County plantation. *On Route 1A, west side, north of the village.*

WICKFORD. Nineteenth-century port. Scenic village.

Smith's Castle Museum (1678): a seventeenth-century shore farm. *On Route 1 north of the town, on the east side of the road.*

PROVIDENCE. John Brown House (1786): a merchant's mansion. *On Benefit Street, near Brown University.* Lovely streets in immediate vicinity.

View of Approaches to Fisher's Id. Sound from the Eastward

Spindle Lt.Ho.Watch Hill Hotel

PAWTUCKET. Old Slater Mill (1793): a restored factory and museum. *From I-95, take exit 28 onto Prospect Street (Route 114). Go north, cross the Sekonk River, then turn right onto Roosevelt Avenue.*

BRISTOL. Scenic town.

Coggeshall Farm: a restored eighteenth-century farm. *Take Route 114 north from village, turn left (west) at Asylum Road to grounds of Colt State Park.*

Herreshoff Marine Museum, honoring the builders of *America*'s Cup yachts. *On Burnside Avenue.*

Blithewood Gardens: a Victorian estate with 33 acres of gardens and landscaped grounds. *South of the village on Route 114 (Ferry Road).*

Indian petroglyphs: a broad flat rock with Indian markings. *On grounds of Roger Williams College, southern tip of island, between Mount Hope and the narrows.*

MIDDLETOWN. Prescott Farms: a restored nineteenth-century plantation. *On Route 114, east side, at Portsmouth-Middletown line.*

Whitehall (1729): restoration of Bishop Berkeley's home. *From Route 128, Middletown center, go south on either Route 214 (Valley Road) or Route 138A (Aquidneck Avenue), then left (east) onto Greene End Avenue, then left (north) onto Berkeley Avenue, where the house is.*

Purgatory Chasm: deep cleft in a beach cliff. *Go east from Newport on Memorial Boulevard along Easton's Beach. Continue straight onto Beach Road to the chasm, near the intersection of Tuckerman Avenue.*

Paradise Rocks (Hanging Rocks, Berkeley's Seat): picturesque (and often-painted) overhanging rocks. *In Norman Wildlife Sanctuary, north of Sachuset Beach.*

Tombolo. *At tip of Sachuset Neck.*

NEWPORT. Victorian mansions. Colonial buildings. Fort Adams. Harborside restoration. Naval War College Museum (originally the poorhouse). Old Stone Mill. Cliff Walk. Ocean Drive. Steam factories. *Consult abundant local promotional material.*

TIVERTON. Sin and Flesh Brook, a scenic tidewater brook. *Take Route 77 south, turn left (east) at north end of tidal inlet (Nannaquaket Pond) to the view from the little bridge over the brook.*

Massachusetts

ATTLEBORO. Bronson Museum: Indian and colonial artifacts. *At 8 North Main Street (Route 52).*

BERKLEY. Dighton Rock: thought to be either an Indian petroglyph or a runestone or a message inscribed by Miguel Corterreal, shipwrecked in 1502. *In Dighton Rock State Park, east bank of Taunton River.*

FALL RIVER. Battleship Cove Museum: U.S. Navy battleship, destroyer, submarine, and PT-boat, all open for exploration. *They are beneath Route I-195 at waterfront. Follow "Battleship Cove" signs.*

Fall River Marine Museum: its emphasis is on steamboats and the Fall River Line. *On Water Street, just south of the I-195 bridge. Follow signs from Battleship Cove.*

Saint Anne's Church and Shrine: Old World cathedral. *On South Main Street.*

Textile mills. *Straddling a stream downhill, near Route I-195.*

SOUTH DARTMOUTH. Picturesque village and harbor.

NEW BEDFORD. Whaling Museum of the Old Dartmouth Historical Society. *From I-195, take exit 15 to the downtown connector, take the "Downtown" exit, then follow signs.*

Seamen's Bethel (1832). It contains a chapel with marble cenotaphs to those lost at sea from the 1830s to 1980s. *Across from the Whaling Museum.*

Renovated waterfront: nineteenth-century houses and other buildings. *It is in streets surrounding the Whaling Museum.*

Coast Guard Lightship *New Bedford.* It is a museum. *At the waterfront, the foot of Union Street, downhill from the Whaling Museum.*

Whaling merchants' mansions. *From the Whaling Museum, go uphill (west) on Union Street. The houses are on the left (south) along Sixth, Seventh, and County streets.*

Fort Taber (1860). This restored seacoast fortification is a museum. *At Fort Rodman Park, Clarks Point. Take the downtown connector/JFK Highway south to the end, continue straight onto First Street, then left onto Brock Avenue to the fort.*

Hurricane barrier, harbor section (1966). Giant stone breakwater with sea gate. Land door at East Rodney French Boulevard. *Take JFK connector south, continue onto First Street, then turn left (east) onto Scott Avenue to the barrier at the water. The land door is to the south at Frederick Street.*

Hurricane barrier, Clarks Cove Section (1966). *Take JFK connector south onto First Street, then turn right (west) onto Brock Avenue/Clarks Cove Road to the barrier. The land doors are at the ends of the barrier.*

Modern fishing fleet. Packing plants. Fishing vessels. Ocean cargo vessels. *Along Water Street, south of I-195.*

Textile mills. Large brick complexes along the Achushnet River. *Along the waterfront, north of I-195.*

Martha's Vineyard

An island with a barren rolling landscape of peat, sand, and clay.

WESLEYAN GROVE. At Oak Bluffs, Victorian gingerbread cottages, often tent-shaped, of the nineteenth-century Methodist camp.

EDGARTOWN. A pristine nineteenth-century seaport town.

MENEMSHA. A fishing village.

GAY HEAD CLIFFS AND LIGHT. Clay cliffs dropping into the ocean. Impressive colors at sunset. Indian community.

OAK BLUFFS STATE LOBSTER HATCHERY.

Nantucket

NANTUCKET TOWN: a former nineteenth-century seaport, now an upper-class summer resort. Mansions. Brick stores. William Rotch warehouse (1772). Old windmill (1746). Coffin House (1686). Whaling Museum. Restored waterfront. Yachts in harbor. Lightship *Nantucket*. Lifesaving museum. *Use local maps.*

SIASCONSET. Old fishing village, which since about 1880 has been a place for a rich person (the first to come were Quaker merchants) to rent a fisherman's cottage for the summer.

BUZZARDS BAY. At the western end of the Cape Cod Canal.

Cape Cod

BOURNE. Aptucxet Trading Post (1627) reconstruction and saltworks. Saltworks are a re-creation of the Cape's standard nineteenth-century design. *Follow signs from Bourne village, go west on Monument Beach Road, then turn right (north) onto Aptucxet Road.*

WOODS HOLE. Woods Hole Oceanographic Institute (private). *Drive through the Institute to see oceanographic vessels at docks.*
Woods Hole Aquarium.
Nobska Lighthouse. *Go north from Woods Hole on Woods Hole Road, then take first right (east) onto Beach Road, to lighthouse.*

COTUIT. Oystermen's shacks. *From Route 28, turn south onto Putnam Avenue, left (west) onto Old Post Road, right (south) onto Little River Road to shanties at the harbor.*

OSTERVILLE. In summer, a village of well-to-do people.
Crosby boatyard. *At the harbor. Go south on Main Street, turn right (east) to the docks by Bridge Street.*

SOUTH YARMOUTH. Baxter Mill (1789 and 1840): a restored water-powered gristmill. *On the north side of Route 28, east of the village.*

BASS RIVER. Old windmill (1791). On ground sloping down into scenic Bass River. *From Route 28 at South Yarmouth, turn south onto Main Street, then left onto River Street, then left onto Willow Street, where the mill stands.*

WEST DENNIS. Scenic view: tidal river with barrier dunes at the shore upon which sits a windmill now converted to a summer home. *From the junction of routes 2 and 134, turn*

south and continue to the end of the road, then turn left (east) onto Lower County Road. The view is on the right at the first bridge, over Swan Pond River.

HARWICH. Wychmere Harbor: a picturesque harbor. *Take Route 28. The harbor is just east of Harwich Port village.*
Old Powder House (1770). Harwich Center. *Go east on Main Street. The powder house is on the right (south), one house beyond Brooks Library.*

WEST CHATHAM. Fishing shanties. *At Route 28 opposite Chatham Airport, turn south onto Barn Hill Road. The shanties are at the base of a bluff along tidal river.*

CHATHAM. Stage Harbor: a scenic location. *At the intersection of Route 28 and Main Street, west of the village, turn south onto Stage Harbor Road.*
Chatham Light. On a bluff, overlooking Chatham Harbor, a barrier beach, and the ocean. *Take Route 28 to Main Street, continue east to Shore Street, then right (south) to the lighthouse.*
Old windmill (1797). *From Main Street, turn south onto Cross Street, then onto Shattuck Place to Chase Park and the mill.*
Fish Pier. *North of Chatham Light on Shore Road.*

ORLEANS. Rock Harbor: a small inlet that is almost dry at low tide, at which time the exposed beach flat reaches miles out into Cape Cod Bay. Excellent location for watching sunsets.
Jeremiah's Gutter. Tidal rivers that in colonial times connected across the Cape, allowing small boats to row across the Cape's "forearm." *From the traffic circle at the junction of routes 6, 6A, and 28, go south on routes 28/6A a short distance, then onto Canal Road, where there is a historic marker.*

EASTHAM. Old windmill (1793): an operating gristmill and museum. *On the west side of Route 6, at the center of the town.*
Captain Edward Penniman House. The ornate home of a whaling captain. *Turn east off Route 6 onto Fort Hill Road.*
Cape Cod National Seashore Visitors' Center. Museum, interpretive displays, a marsh walk with a view of Henry Beston's "Outermost House." *At the junction of Route 6 and Nauset Road.*
Nauset Light and Nauset Light Beach (not to be confused with Nauset Beach, in Orleans and Chatham). A scenic lighthouse on a high bluff with a beach at the base of a cliff. Impressive surf during storms. *Follow signs east from Route 6 at the National Seashore Visitors' Center.*
S.S. *James Longstreet*, a target ship. A World War II Liberty Ship grounded on flats on the Cape Cod Bay side, used for aircraft target practice. *Can be seen from any of the town's beaches on that side.*

WELLFLEET. Picturesque village and harbor. *In the center of the town*: Victorian architecture, a fish pier, a footbridge over the Duck River.
Sunset Hill: scenic view. *From the Town Wharf, go west on Kendrick Avenue, continue west onto Chesquesset Neck Road to the end.*
Nature walks. *Starting from the Marconi Station site, Cape Cod National Seashore. South of the village on the east side, off Route 6.*
Ocean View Drive. A scenic route along the Atlantic side of the

Cape past bluffs, hollows, ponds, and the vegetation of the outer Cape. *From Route 6 south of the village at the town information building, go east onto Lecount Hollow Road, then left (north) on Ocean View Drive. Return to Route 6 by turning left (west) at Grass Hill Road.*

TRURO. Cape Cod Lighthouse: a scenic vista. This lighthouse is on the Cape's highest bluff. *From Route 6 at North Truro, go east on Highland Road.*

Old shipwreck: the remains of the sugar carrier *Francis*. *From Route 6 just north of Highland Road, turn east onto Head of the Meadow Road. The wreck can be seen at low tide at the north end of the beach.*

Hill of Churches. Up to thirty years ago this was a famous landmark, a group of churches atop a barren sandy hill. Replanting has left only the towers visible above the forest. *On the top of the hill, just north of the village.*

Highland House Museum: a small Victorian hotel converted to a historical museum. *On Highland Road near the lighthouse.*

Pilgrim Lake and dunes. Beginning of the Province Lands. *Along Route 6 approaching Provincetown.*

PROVINCETOWN. A picturesque town of Victorian cottages and Cape houses. It is quaint despite massive commercialism.

Pilgrim Monument. Tower with scenic panorama. Museum.

MacMillan Wharf. Fishing fleet.

The harbor is virtually dry at low tide, leaving vessels scattered about the flats.

Provincetown Art Association, Chrysler Art Museum: exhibitions by Provincetown artists.

Playhouse-on-the-Wharf, 83 Commercial Street. The converted sail loft of the Provincetown Players.

Province Lands. An awesome region of dunes, hills, and hollows, all covered by a tenuous growth of scrub pine and bushes. *West and north of Provincetown, and on the right side of Route 6 approaching the town. To get to the National Park Service's Province Lands Visitors' Center, turn north off Route 6 on Race Point Road. There are hiking, biking, and auto routes through the dunes.*

Lifesaving Station. One of the Cape's original stations, built in the 1870s, was moved here from Cahoon Hollow and is being converted into a museum. *Take Race Point Road to beach, then right (southeast) along beach to station.*

BREWSTER. Cape Cod Museum of Natural History: nature exhibits, marsh walk. *Route 6 at West Brewster.*

Stony Brook Mill: a scenic location. Water-powered mill. The last remnants of a nineteenth-century Cape Cod factory village. *Go south off Route 6 onto Stony Brook Road, or onto Setucket Road, to West Brewster village and the mill.*

BARNSTABLE. A scenic village center.

SANDWICH. Dexter Mill (1654), a water-powered gristmill. *On Route 130 at the west end of the town green.*

Hoxie House (ca. 1637): the earliest surviving Cape house. *From Route 6A, turn south onto Route 130 or School Street to the museum, which is on the west side of Route 130 by the junction of School Street.*

Scorton Creek. A scenic location, high dunes, a salt creek, marshes, a beach. *Route 6A east, just before Barnstable town line turn left (north) onto Sandy Neck Road, continue to end.*

End of Cape Cod Section

CARVER. A center of the cranberry industry. There are bogs throughout the town.

PLYMOUTH. Plimoth Plantation, the restoration of a 1627 village. *It is 3 miles south of the town on Route 3A.*

Mayflower II. At the pier just north of Plymouth Rock.

Pilgrim Hall, a museum of Pilgrim relics. Ribs of the *Sparrowhawk.* On Court Street.

Old houses, mills, etc., throughout the town.

Plymouth Rock.

Gurnet Point. A haphazard community of Victorian cottages set on a sand spit extending across Plymouth Harbor. *It is accessible by four-wheel-drive vehicles only. From Green Harbor take Beach Road south.*

BRANT ROCK. A World War II lookout tower. *It is beside the beach at the center of the village.* (One of many such towers along the coast. For a complete list consult William B. Matthews, Jr., *Marine Atlas Series.*)

COHASSET. Minot's Ledge Lighthouse. It is most impressive in rough weather. *Best seen from Atlantic Avenue.*

Moore's Rock Reservation: a scenic location overlooking the ocean. *From the village, go west on North Main Street, then right (north) on Jerusalem Road to the Reservation.*

SHARON. Kendall Whaling Museum. *It is on Everett Street.*

NANTASKET and HULL. Glacial drumlins. Tombolo. At Hull, glacial drumlin-formed harbor islands shaped over the centuries by waves and currents into beaches, tombolos, spits, etc.

MEDFIELD. Peak House (1651, rebuilt 1680). While *not* in a coastal location, this steep-roofed little house best exemplifies the typical home of seventeenth-century New England. *Go east from the center on Route 109. The house is on the north side ½ mile away.*

WEYMOUTH. Indian dugout canoe that was found in a local pond. *At Tufts Library, 46 Broad Street. Weymouth is on Route 53, northwest of Route 3.*

Minot Ledge Lt.Ho.   Cohasset

Coast between Cohasset Entrance and Scituate Harbor; Minot Ledge Lt.Ho. bearing S.by E.distant 2¾ Miles.

QUINCY. Modern shipyard of General Dynamics Corporation. *Take Route 53 back to Route 3A, turn south. The yards are near the Quincy–North Weymouth bridge.*

SQUANTUM. Squaw Rock: a cliff undercut by the sea to form a "face." *From Route 3A in North Quincy, turn north onto Squantum Street, then continue onto Dorchester Street to Chapel Rocks Park. Rock at land's tip.*

MILTON. Governor Hutchinson's Field. A view from heights down across marshes with Boston Harbor in the distance. *From Milton Lower Mills, go south on Adams Street for ½ mile to the field, on left (east).*

Museum of the China Trade. Restored home of the Federalist era. *Adams Street opposite Hutchinson's field.*

BOSTON. Beacon Hill, Back Bay: nineteenth-century row houses.

Boston Tea Party Ship and Museum. *At Museum Wharf.*

Fort Independence. *Castle Island, South Boston.*

Waterfront restoration: brick warehouses, stone wharves, Faneuil Hall (1742), Quincy Market.

John Hancock Observatory: an observation floor near the top of the John Hancock Insurance Company Building. *Copley Square.*

Boston Fish Pier. *South Boston. Northern Avenue, by Commonwealth Pier.*

Museums, homes, libraries. The Massachusetts State House can supply local brochures.

WARNING! *One-way signs, winding streets make Boston a driver's nightmare.*

WESTON. Norumbega Tower. Fanciful recreation of a "Viking site" discovered by a Harvard Professor in the late nineteenth century. *Beside the Charles River. From Route 128, take exit 49 (Route 20) west, take second left (south) onto Summer Street, then turn left (east) over the highway onto South Street, then right (southeast) onto Norumbega Road before reaching the river. The tower is at the far side of a clearing.*

CAMBRIDGE. Tory Row. Mansions of pre-Revolutionary Loyalist merchants. *From Harvard Square go northeast along Garden Street, then left onto Mason Street, then right onto Brattle Street.*

Fort Washington. Revolutionary redoubt that stood where the Charles River once entered into the Back Bay. Over the centuries, the Back Bay was filled in and built upon. The waterfront fortress now lies many blocks from the water, surrounded by parked trailer trucks. *On Massachusetts Avenue at the Massachusetts Institute of Technology buildings, continue west across railroad tracks, then left onto Albany Street; continue onto Waverly Street. The fort is on the left, between Reardon and Talbot streets.*

CHARLESTOWN. Bunker Hill Monument. Panorama from the tower.

U.S.S. *Constitution* (a U.S. frigate, built 1794–1797, used in War of 1812).

Charlestown Navy Yard.

EAST BOSTON. Modern cargo vessel port.

WINTHROP. Winthrop Great Head: a high drumlin eroded into a cliff. *From Route 1A, take Route 145 southeast to Winthrop Shore Drive; go south to Great Head. Also visit Grover's Cliff at the North end of Winthrop Shore Drive.*

NAHANT. Scenic location. Nineteenth-century "cottages." Tombolo beach. *Virtually no public parking.*

SAUGUS. Saugus Iron Works (ca. 1650). A restoration. The museum and iron furnace are at the head of the tide, Saugus River. *Take Route 1 to the Main Street exit, go east on Main Street, then left (north) onto Central Street to the Iron Works.*

LYNN. High Rock Park. Scenic views of the city and shore. *From interchange Routes 1, 128, and I-95 at South Lynnfield, take exit 30 onto Route 129 east (Lynnfield Street). Go east 2 miles, through Wyoma Square, and continue onto Broadway. Turn right (south) onto Boston Street (if you reach Western Avenue/Route 107, you have gone too far on Broadway). Go south ¾ mile on Boston Street to third left (east) onto Washington Street. Continue to third left onto Beacon, then right onto Lawton, then left onto High Rock, and finally right onto Circuit Avenue to the park.*

Pirate's Dungeon Rock. A cave, closed by a 1658 earthquake, which supposedly entombed a pirate and his loot. In the nineteenth century, a father and his son tunneled hundreds of feet through the rock in search of the fabled treasure. *In Lynn Woods Reservation. From Route 1, take North Saugus–Walnut Street exit. Route 129, (not to be confused with next exit north, Route 129–South Lynnfield exit), turn east onto Walnut Street and proceed to Lynn. Park ½ mile beyond Saugus-Lynn town line at Penny Brook Road on left (north), the southern entrance to the reservation. Walk north on Penny Brook Road. Turn onto the first trail on the right leaving the unpaved portion of Penny Brook Road. Follow trail north for ½ mile to wood road. Cross wood road and follow path a short distance to Dungeon Rock.*

MARBLEHEAD. Scenic town with narrow winding streets. *Use local maps, available at museums and many stores in town. Park your car and walk.*

Lee Mansion (1768). Merchant's house.

"King" Hooper Mansion (1728, 1745). Merchant's house.

Old Town House (1727).

Wharves along the harbor.

Fort Sewall (1742 and later additions). *Front Street.*

Old Powder House (1755). *37 Green Street.*

Alley steps to Washington Street from High Street at the corner of Elm Street.

Old Burial Hill (1638): panorama.

Corinthian and Eastern yacht clubs. *Marblehead Neck, facing the harbor, off Harbor Avenue.*

The Churn, Castle Rock: a bluff with an ocean view, and spouting hole when the wind is out of the northeast to east. *Take Ocean Avenue on Marblehead Neck. Park car and go east across a field at Castle Rock Lane, next to French chateau mansion.*

Fountain Park, Orne Street. Panorama.

SALEM. A scenic city. Colonial homes, Federalist mansions. *Consult local maps available free in museums and many stores throughout the town.*

State Ho.in   Boston Lt.Ho.   Great Brewster I.   Bunker Hill
Boston   Monument

Entrance to Boston Harbor by the Main Channel, Boston Lt.Ho. bearing W. N. W. distant 5 Miles.

Chestnut Street Historic District. Post-Revolutionary mansions on Chestnut, Essex, and Federal streets.

House of Seven Gables (1668). *On Turner Street.*

Peabody Museum, New England's greatest museum of the maritime trade. *Essex Street Mall.*

    Pioneer Village. A re-creation of Salem ca. 1630. *From the junction of routes 1A and 114, go north, then right (east) on Clifton Avenue to the end.*

    Custom House (1819), where Nathaniel Hawthorne worked, and Derby Wharf. *Derby Street.*

BEVERLY. Nineteenth-century summer mansions of Boston Brahmins. *Along Route 127, at Beverly Farms.*

DANVERS. Glen-Magna Farm. Summer home (beginning in 1814) of Salem Peabodys. Gardens. Has a two-story temple-like teahouse built for Elias Derby by Samuel McIntire in 1793.

MANCHESTER. Fashionable North Shore town.

Singing Beach. The sands squeak or "sing" when stepped upon. *Park at the center of town and walk to the beach (there is no public parking in summer).*

Powder House (ca. 1812). *It is in woods above the village, below a park.*

GLOUCESTER. Modern fishing port.

Stage Fort. *In a shore park, on Route 127, just south of the junction with Route 133.*

Fitz Hugh Lane House. Perhaps the last remnant of nineteenth-century Gloucester's waterfront. *128 Main Street.*

Fisherman's Museum. Small exhibit devoted to Grand Banks fishing. *On the corner of Rogers and Porter streets.*

Cape Ann Historical Society: over 30 paintings by Fitz Hugh Lane. *On the corner of Federal and Pleasant Association streets.*

Waterfront. Vessels. Gorton Fish Plants.

Church of Our Lady of the Good Voyage: church (built 1915) of Gloucester's Azorean congregation. *Prospect Street.*

Wingaersheek Beach: a long beach backed by dunes and marshes. *From Route 128, take exit 13, turn north on Atlantic Avenue.*

Bass Rocks and Good Harbor Beach. Scenic rock islands. *From Main Street, go east on Bass Avenue to beach.*

Beauport: museum. 40 rooms of different periods transplanted from various homes into one great house. Little gardens overlook the harbor. *Take East Main Street to Eastern Point Boulevard.* (The house is closed on weekends.)

Mount Ann Park: a scenic panorama, at an elevation of 270 feet above sea level. *It is along Route 128 near exit 4 in West Gloucester.*

ROCKPORT. Harbor. Bearskin Neck. Quaint but utterly touristy.

James Babson Cooperage Shop (1658): a last link with the era when barrels were as important as ships. *On Route 127, between Gloucester and Rockport.*

Loblolly Cove and view of twin lighthouses on Thacher Island. It is a scenic cove, where a "baby sea serpent" was discovered. *From Route 127A, go south from the village, turn left (east) onto Loblolly Cove Road.*

Gott House (1702) and Halibut Point. This is a fisherman's house on a scenic outlook. *From Route 127A, go north on Granite Street, then turn right (northeast) onto Gott Avenue; continue to the house and the park.*

Stone Harbor: a small harbor formed by a granite-block mole, an abandoned quarry, *on Route 127 at the north end of the village.*

ANNISQUAM. Scenic Cape Ann village and harbor. *Off Route 127.*

LANESVILLE. Another Cape Ann hamlet. *Off Route 127.*

ESSEX. Story Shipyard: an active shipyard (founded 1813) along tidal marshes. *Along Route 133 (Main Street) at village.*

IPSWICH. Crane's Beach and Reservation: Castle Hill, a nearby landscaped estate by the sea. The beach is backed by extensive dunes, marshes, and marsh islands, which extend far inland. *From the town green on the south side of the river, go east off Route 1A onto Argilla Road to the beach.*

John Whipple House (1640). *On Route 1A (South Main Street).*

ANDOVER. Peabody Foundation for Archaeology: museum of Indian artifacts. *On Route 28, opposite Andover Academy.*

NEWBURY. Extensive marshes.

Old Town Hill: a scenic outlook. Depressions at the base of the hill are reported to have been dugouts of early settlers, ca. 1635. *From the end of the town green off Route 1A, go west on Newman Street to the reservation.* Climb the hill for a panoramic view from Cape Ann to Maine.

NEWBURYPORT. Federalist era, ca. 1760–1840, town overlooking the tidewater part of the Merrimac River.

Market Square: brick shops constructed after a fire in 1811.

Old lighthouse. *Along Water Street, east of Route 1.*

Federalist mansions and churches. *High Street/Routes 1A and 113.*

Plum Island: extensive beach dunes and marsh. *Go east on Water Street to the Parker River Wildlife Refuge and Plum Island State Park.*

AMESBURY. A nineteenth-century milltown along the tidewater part of the Merrimac River.

Coastal New England

New Hampshire

HAMPTON FALLS. "Runic stone." *Go west from Hampton Falls 5 miles on Route 84 to Falls River. The stone is on land belonging to a house on the right along the river embankment.*

RYE (including RYE BEACH, WALLIS SANDS, and RYE NORTH BEACH). Great Boar's Head. Eroded sea cliff.

Fosses Beach: sand dunes.

Parson's Point: excellent surf.

JENNESS BEACH: drowned forest. Tree stumps visible at low tide.

NEWCASTLE. Picturesque village streets.

Wentworth-Coolidge Mansion (1695 and later additions): colonial governor's mansion, 42 rooms. *From Portsmouth, go south on Route 1A, then left (east) onto Wentworth Road to the mansion.*

Fort Constitution (1808): ruins overlying earlier forts. *From Route 1A in the village, go east onto Walbach Street to Fort Point.*

Wentworth-by-the-Sea: massive Victorian seaside hotel. *On Route 18.*

PORTSMOUTH. Colonial and Federalist mansions. *Middle Street/ Route 1. Also at Haymarket Square, on Market Street, State Street, Court Street, and scattered locations throughout the city.*

Strawberry Banke restoration: a 10-acre section of colonial homes along an inlet.

Shaef's Warehouse (1705): dockside warehouse.

Christian Shore: colonial homes — Richard Jackson House (1664) — and Federalist mansions.

Moffat-Ladd House (1763) and extensive landscaped grounds (1862).

PISCATAQUA RIVER, LITTLE BAY, and GREAT BAY. Drowned river valley. Colonial homes. Scenic locale.

DOVER. Dam Garrison House (1675). *At Woodman Institute on Route 16, just south of junction with Route 9.*

ISLES OF SHOALS. Picturesque islands.

Maine

SOUTH BERWICK. Tidewater factory town. Colonial homes.

Hamilton House (ca. 1785) Museum: the giant mansion of a Portsmouth merchant on a scenic site overlooking the Piscataqua River. *From town, go south on Route 236, then right (west) onto Vaughan's Lane at the junction of routes 236 and 91.*

KITTERY. Picturesque town.

Portsmouth Navy Yard. No visitors. *It can be seen clearly from Route 103.*

Fort McClary (1715, 1812): a colonal fort topped by a blockhouse dating from the War of 1812. *On Route 103 at Kittery Point.*

Colonial mansions at Kittery Point, William Pepperrell House (1682, 1720). Lady Pepperrell House (1760).

Fort Foster (ca. 1870–1945). *Take Route 103 at Kittery Point, then go south onto Chancey's Creek Road, left (east) onto Pocohontas Road to the fort.*

YORK. Sewall's Bridge: restoration of a 1761 pile bridge. *From the junction of routes 1 and 1A, go south on Route 1A, then left (west) onto Organuy Road; continue to the river and bridge.*

John Hancock Warehouse and Wharf: a colonial building, now a museum. *From Route 1A in York Village, west onto Lindsay Street to building along east side of river.*

Old Gaol (1653) Museum. *York Village, on the west side of Route 1A.*

Shoals House: a house floated on a raft from the Isles of Shoals during the evacuation in 1752. *Along Route 1A, York Harbor.*

Nubble Light. Cape Neddick. Scenic lighthouse on a rocky promontory. *From Route 1A, Cape Neddick village, go south on Broadway onto Nubble Road.*

Bald Head Cliff. Scenic location: gorge. *From Route 1 at York Beach, go south onto Route 1A, then left (east) onto Shore Road to Bald Head.*

McIntire Garrison House (1640s). Private. Heavily timbered refuge from Indian attacks. *On Route 91, 2½ miles north of the junction of routes 1 and 91.*

Mt. Agamenticus. The mountain (elevation 682 feet) gives a panorama of the shore. *Take Route 1 north from York Beach; turn left at signs.*

OGUNQUIT. Marginal Way: a mile-long walking trail along sea cliffs *from Onzio Hill to Perkins Cove.*

Museum of Art: scenic view in addition to exhibits. The town has long been an artists' colony. *On the Shore Road, at Narrow Harbor.*

Foot drawbridge. *Across the river at the cove.*

WELLS. Storer's garrison house. *Go north on Route 1 from the junction with Route 9. It is on your right side.*

KENNEBUNK. Victorian mansions.

Wedding Cake House: a brick house with an overlay of wooden scrollsaw "gingerbread." *Go south on Route 9A/35. The house is 1 mile from the junction of Route 1.*

KENNEBUNKPORT. Pristine seaport town. Fishing fleet.

Spouting Rock and Blowing Cave: surf spray during heavy waves at half-tide. *Go south from the Route 9 bridge along the river on Ocean Drive, then go straight onto Shore Drive. The rock is at Cape Arundel. The cave is at Walkers Point.*

Perkins tidewater gristmill (1749 and later additions). Now a restaurant. *Go north on Main Street to Mill Lane on Grist Mill Pond.*

BIDDEFORD POOL. Scenic harbor. Homes of wealthy people.

Fletcher's Neck Lifesaving Station (1874): one of the first stations constructed by the U.S. government. *On Ocean Avenue, in the village.*

SACO and BIDDEFORD. Tidewater mill towns.

West Point Pepperell Company: *factories along river and on Factory Island.*

OLD ORCHARD BEACH. An active resort around a Victorian beach town. Maine's longest beach. Impressive sand flats at low tide.

SCARBOROUGH. Maine's largest salt marsh. The Audubon Society gives guided canoe tours. *Nature Center on Route 9, east of the junction of routes 1 and 9.*

PROUT'S NECK. Winslow Homer's studio. Museum.

CAPE ELIZABETH. Two Lights State Park. Rocky shoreline. Impressive surf. *Take Route 77 south from Cape Elizabeth village.*

Portland Head Light (1791) and Fort Williams. The lighthouse tower is open to visitors. *Go east off Route 77 onto Cottage Road, between Cape Elizabeth and South Portland.*

SOUTH PORTLAND. Portland Breakwater Light (1855): A cast-iron lighthouse in the ornate Greek Revival design. *At the northeast corner of the South Portland waterfront, at the end of the breakwater.*

PORTLAND. Old seaport city, now actively restoring its picturesque nineteenth-century downtown and waterfront areas. Mansions. *Consult local maps.*

Portland Observatory (1807). View of harbor and the White Mountains from the lookout tower. *138 Congress Street.*

Fort Allen Park (1814). View of nearby islands in Casco Bay. *Fore Street and Eastern Promenade.*

Longfellow Square: early nineteenth-century mansions.

Fort Gorges (ca. 1860). *It can be seen on Hog Island in Casco Bay.* Built according to the most advanced design just before the Civil War, it was quickly abandoned when its twin, Fort Sumter, was demolished by Confederate cannon.

Maine Historical Society. Extensive maritime collection. Includes pirates' loot.

FREEPORT. Desert of Maine: glacial sand breaking through and spreading over topsoil. *Near Route 1 south of town; follow signs.*

Casco Castle Tower: remains of a hotel in medieval style. *At South Freeport village.*

Brunswick-Rockland Region

Drowned coastline of peninsulas and estuaries. State roads lead southwest from Route 1 to picturesque towns, harbors, inlets, islands, and rocky points.

TOPSHAM. Tidewater mill town. Early nineteenth-century homes.

BRUNSWICK.

Bowdoin Pines. Maine's last grove of "mast pines." *In the town, east of Bowdoin College between Bath Street (Route 24) and Pine Street.*

Androscoggin Falls, Pejepscot Paper Mill (1869). Delightful early Victorian architecture. *On Route 201 at the Androscoggin River.*

Mere Point: a peninsula with views of the bay.

ORR'S AND BAILEY ISLANDS. Actually a scenic peninsula. *Take Route 24 south off Route 1 at the Cook's Corner section of Brunswick.*

The Gurnet. Tidal gut with water roaring through at changing tides. *Route 24, between Orr's and Great islands.*

Bailey Island bridge (1928). Honeycomb cobwork construction. *Route 24 between Orr's and Bailey islands.*

RICHMOND. A small town with an unusually large number of Greek Revival mansions.

BATH. Mid-nineteenth-century shipbuilding town. Mansions throughout the town.

Bath Marine Museum. Devoted to maritime Maine. *On Washington Street, north off Route 1.*

Percy and Small Shipyard (1894–1920). Builds wooden ships. Museum. *At 263 Washington Street, south of Route 1.*

Bath Iron Works. Still active shipyard. *On the waterfront, south of Route 1.*

There is an excellent view of the town from the tall Carleton Bridge (Route 1).

Winnigance tidal mill. Private. An operating tide-powered sawmill. *From Route 1 at Bath, go south onto Route 209 for 3 miles, to tidal inlet, then first left to the mill. Can be seen from Route 209 just north of hamlet of Winnigance.*

WEST POINT. Scenic fishing village.

POPHAM BEACH. Fort Popham State Memorial. *At the end of Route 209.* Off a side road is the site of the 1607 settlement. Exhibits. Scenic locations. There are remains of later forts (1865, 1912), by the point.

PARKER HEAD. Reversing falls over an old tidal milldam. *Between Parker Head and village, and Parker Head promontory.*

West Lt.   East Lt.
Mt.Washington

Cape Elizabeth from the Southward, East Lt.bearing N.NW,distant 6½ Miles.

GEORGETOWN. Reid State Park: ecxceptionally beautiful combination of headlands, dunes, beach, and marsh. Unusual vegetation.

WISCASSET. The perfect image of a Maine coast nineteenth-century town. Mansions. Several old public buildings have become museums.

Two derelict schooners, *Hesper* (1918) and *Luther Little* (1917), abandoned during the Depression, may be seen along the waterfront south of Route 1.

Nikels-Sortwell House (1812) Museum. *On Route 1.*

Powder House (1813).

NORTH EDGECOMB. Fort Edgecomb (1808–1809). A restored octagonal wooden blockhouse. *Take Route 1 east from Wiscasset across bridge, then turn right (south); 1½ miles to fort.*

BOOTHBAY HARBOR. Resort and yachting village.

Modern yachtbuilding yards.

Grand Banks Schooner Museum. The Grand Banks fishing schooner *Sherman Zwicker* at the harbor is open to the public.

DAMARISCOTTA. Indian shell heaps: a 30-foot-deep layer of oyster shells discarded by Indians. *Off Route 1, east of the village.*

SOUTH BRISTOL. Thompson ice house (1825). *On Route 129.*

PEMAQUID. Colonial Pemaquid museum. Excavations. Fort William Henry (1692) reconstruction. Fort house (1731). *Take Route 130 south from Pemaquid Village, turn right (west) onto Huddle Road, proceed to the harbor.*

Pemaquid Point, the southern tip of the peninsula, has rocks and a lighthouse. Magnificent breaking surf after storms.

NEW HARBOR. Often photographed fishing village.

THOMASTON. "Montpelier." Replica of General Knox Mansion (1795). *East end of town at the junction of routes 1 and 131.*

PORT CLYDE. Another scenic fishing village. Artists' colony.

OWL'S HEAD. Scenic locale. Owl's Head, a headland, is 100 feet above the water. *At Owl's Head Light State Park, at the eastern end of peninsula which forms park.*

ROCKLAND. Old and still active port.

Farnsworth Art Museum: exhibitions of landscapes and seascapes of the Maine coast. *19 Elm Street.*

Breakwater across harbor. Scenic view. *Go north from the town on Route 1, then turn right (east) after passing the waterfront, onto Waldo Avenue, then turn right (south) to Jameson Point.*

The harbor usually contains an assortment of Grand Bankers, sardiners, yachts, and naval vessels.

ROCKPORT. Summer town for the affluent. Yachts in harbor. Yachtbuilding yards.

Lime kilns. Nineteenth-century kilns for burning lime before barreling it hot (and thus dry and powdery) and sending it south on coastal schooners. *At the bridge over the river, on either side of the shore, where the Goose River opens to become Rockport Harbor.*

CAMDEN. Another summer resort.

Marine park, landscaped gardens. *On Atlantic Avenue at the harbor.*

Camden Hills State Park. Mountaintop view of Penobscot Bay. *Take Route 1 going north, then turn left (west) on the road that goes to the summit of Mt. Battie (elevation 800 feet). Other nearby mountains can be climbed on foot.*

BELFAST. Many nineteenth-century homes.

Excellent view of the town from the bridge on Route 1 over the river/inlet.

SEARSPORT. Commercial port: tankers and potato carriers. *The Anchorage is east of the center.*

Penobscot Marine Museum. *On Main Street (Route 1).*

Tombolo to Sears Island. *Take Route 1 east, pass Long Cove, then turn right (south) to Penobscot Park.*

PROSPECT. Fort Knox (begun 1846, never finished). State Park. Massive bastion overlooking the Penobscot River. *Route 1A, west side of river.*

BUCKSPORT. Tidewater industrial town. Paper mills.

CASTINE. Historic area, settled in 1626. Scenic village and summer colony.

Fort George (1779): British fort defended against American colonists. *Top of hill, above village.*

Maine Maritime Academy. Ocean-going training vessel *State of Maine* often at docks.

Canal cut across marshes by British during Revolution. *From the junction of routes 166 and 166A, go south to the marsh and coves.* Historical sign marks canal.

CAPE ROSIER. Goose Falls: scenic location. Waterfalls dropping into cove.

STONINGTON. Working seaport town. Lobstering. Sardines.

Cannery.

Victorian hotel.

BLUE HILL. Quiet seaport village turned to artists' and artisans' colony.

Blue Hill Falls. Reversing falls, stationary waves created by tidal currents. *Route 175 south of Blue Hill, at mouth of salt pond.*

ELLSWORTH. Black Mansion (ca. 1820). *From Route 1 at center (bridge over Union River) go west, then bear left (south) onto Route 172. Mansion is a short distance on right.*

MOUNT DESERT ISLAND. Island of mountains sloping into the sea.

Acadia National Park. *Get information at Visitors' Center at Hulls Cove entrance.*

Cadillac Mountain (elevation 1,530 feet). Grand vista at sunrise. Tallest peak on Atlantic coast.

Somes Sound. Glacial fjord.

Thunder Hole. Booming noises and high spray with heavy waves at rising half-tide, especially in bad weather.

Ocean Drive. Scenic road.

Otter Cliffs.

Sieur de Monts Spring and Robert Abbe Indian Museum.

BAR HARBOR. Late eighteenth- and early nineteenth-century resort town.

NORTHEAST HARBOR. Many summer homes of wealthy and well known.

Approaches to Camden and Rockport

Rockport

Camden
Mt. Megunucook

Hancock–Eastport region

Currently the true "Down East." The summer vacationing economy fades into the background and the towns appear to live almost exclusively off the land and sea. The communities are primarily small "no frills" villages where low tide leaves pile wharves towering above stony flats.

HANCOCK. View of Mt. Desert Island. *Follow Route 1 northward (east), look toward the ocean.*

WINTER HARBOR. Affluent summer colony. Views of Mt. Desert Island. *From Route 1, turn right (south) onto Route 186. Follow the west side of Schoodic Peninsula.*

Panoramic view from summit of Schoodic Head (400 feet), part of Acadia National Park.

PROSPECT HARBOR. Sardine cannery town along inlet. Scenic. *On Route 186.*

COREA. Much-photographed lobstering port. Best seen at sunset. Military radar domes west of the village.

MILLBRIDGE. Blueberry barrens. *Along Route 1.*

Sand Cove. Small cove created by an enclosing curved sand spit. *From Route 1, go west from Millbridge, take your second left (south) to Petit Manan Point, continue south onto the Point, pass Pigeon Hill and Carrying Place Cove on right (west). Cross peninsula to the west side, then take your first right to Over Cove. View south from Over Point.*

ADDISON. Scenic outlook. View across hillside of blueberry barrens down onto village and meandering tidal river. *From Columbia Falls, go east on Route 1, then turn right (south) onto Route 187. The view occurs where Route 187 turns left (east) at the first junction. The road straight ahead leads to Addison.*

JONESPORT. Fishing village.

Lobster Co-op. *Just east of bridge to Beals Island.*

Peat diggings. *On Route 187 east of Jonesport.*

BEALS. The Flying Place. Spectacular surf during high waves. *Go south from Beals to the bridge over the gut between Beals Island and Great Wass Island.*

COLUMBIA FALLS. Ruggles House (ca. 1818) Museum. *On Route 1, in the village.*

JONESBORO. Little church at head of small tidal river. Scenic.

ROQUE BLUFFS. Scenic location.

MACHIAS. Old milltown at falls and head of tide.

EAST MACHIAS. Interesting village set on steep slopes along a tidal river. Post-Revolutionary-era buildings.

CUTLER. Lobstering wharf.

Forest of communication towers (approximately 1,000 feet high) at the naval signal station on Cutler Peninsula. *Private, but can be seen from Route 191, North Cutler.*

WEST QUODDY HEAD. Lighthouse. Much photographed candy-striped.

Scenic panorama.

"Arctic" Tundra peat bog. *North of lighthouse at Flying Place in Quoddy Head State Park.*

LUBEC. Sardine factories. Herring sheds.

DENNYSVILLE. Scenic view, looking across a tidal river to a church on a bluff. *From the west side of Route 1 at Dennys River.*

WEST PEMBROKE. Reversing "falls": standing waves created as the tide enters or empties through a passage between the mainland and an island. *From Route 1, turn southeast to the village, then follow signs south to the park on Leighton's Neck. The "falls" are off Mahar's Point.*

EASTPORT. Rustic town.

Fort Sullivan (1808) barracks and ruins. Museum. *At 74 Washington Street.*

Old Sow. A whirlpool during changing tides. *From the stores at the center of Eastport, go north along the waterfront to end of road. The whirlpool, one of the world's largest, forms to the north by Dog Island just offshore.*

QUODDY VILLAGE. Pleasant Point Indian Reservation.

RED BEACH. View of Dochet's Island in St. Croix River. Site of Champlain's 1604 settlement. Small park with explanatory plaques *just off Route 1 at north end of cove.*

Silhouettes of the coastline from Volumes 1 and 2 of the Atlantic Coast Pilot *(1878–1879).*

Notes

1 The Shape of the Shore

a. Sidney Perley, *Historic Storms of New England* (Salem, 1891), 190.

b. Ibid.

c. Rev. Samuel Peters, *General History of Connecticut* (London, 1781; reprint, New York, 1877), 164.

d. John Winthrop, *The History of New England, 1630–1649,* 2 vols. ed. James Savage, (Boston, 1853), 1: 184–85.

e. S. T. Livermore, *History of Block Island* (1877; reprint, Forge Village, Mass., 1961), 124–25.

2 Red Men on the Ocean

1. Bartholomew Gosnold, in George P. Winship, *Sailors' Narratives of Voyages Along the New England Coast, 1524–1624* (Boston, 1905), 45.

2. Howard S. Russell, *Indian New England Before the Mayflower* (Hanover, N.H., 1980), 200, 202.

3. Rev. William Hubbard, *A General History of New England* In *Mass. Hist. Colls.,* 2nd ser., vol. 5–6: (Cambridge, 1815) 31.

4. Dwight B. Heath, ed., *A Journal of the Pilgrims at Plymouth . . . Mourt's Relation . . . 1622* (Reprint, New York, 1963), 78–79.

5. Christopher Leverett, in Winship, *Sailors' Narratives,* 286.

6. W. L. Grant, ed., *Original Narratives of Early American History: Voyages of Samuel de Champlain* (New York, 1907), 63.

7. Giovanni da Verrazano, *Voyages.* Old South Pamphlets (Boston, 1920), 11.

8. Champlain, in *Original Narratives,* 66.

9. Roger Williams, *A Key into the Language of America* (London, 1634), 104.

10. George Waymouth, in Winship, *Sailors' Narratives,* 148–49.

11. Claude M. Simpson, ed., *Nathaniel Hawthorne: The American Notebooks* (Ohio State University Press, 1972), 169.

3 Explorers and Entrepreneurs

1. "Second Letter of Raimondo de Soncino to the Duke of Milan. London, December 8, 1497," quoted in *Original Narratives of Early American History: The Northmen, Columbus, and Cabot* (New York, 1906), 426–27.

2. Verrazano, *Voyages.* Old South Pamphlets (Boston, 1920), 6.

3. Ibid., 7.

4. Ibid., 9–10.

5. Ibid., 9.

6. Ibid.

7. See Samuel Eliot Morison, *European Discovery of America: The Northern Voyages* (New York, 1971).

8. Richard Hakluyt, "A Discourse Concerning Western Planting (1584)," in James Phinney Baxter, ed., *Documentary History of the State of Maine,* 20 vols. (Cambridge, Mass., 1877), 2:37.

9. Ibid., 38–39.

10. Ibid., 13.

11. Ibid., 96.

12. Ibid., 161.

13. Gabriel Archer, in *Mass. Hist. Colls.,* 3rd ser., vol. 18 (18-13): 73.

14. Ibid., 86.

15. W. L. Grant, ed., *Original Narratives of Early American History: Voyages of Samuel de Champlain* (New York, 1907), 46, 52.

16. Samuel Purchas, *Purchas His Pilgrims,* 4 vols. (Glasgow, 1905–1907), 19:271.

17. Maverick, quoted in Charles K. Bolton, *The Real Founders of New England: Stories of their Life Along the Coast, 1602–1628* (Boston, 1929), 24.

18. John Smith, *A Description of New England,* in *Mass. Hist. Colls.,* 3rd ser., vol. 6 (1837):103.

19. Ibid., 103–04.

20. Ibid., 109.

21. Ibid., 110–11.

22. Ibid., 109.

23. Ibid., 117–18.

24. Thomas Morton, *The New English Canaan* (London, 1632), 23.

25. Ibid.

26. William T. Davis, ed., *Original Narratives of Early American History: Bradford's History of Plymouth Plantation, 1606–1646* (Reprint, New York, 1908), 118.

27. James I, *Great Patent of New England,* granted November 3, 1620. Reprinted in William Brigham, ed., *The Compact with the Charter and Laws of the Colony of New Plymouth* (Boston, 1836), 3.

a. David Ingram, quoted in B. F. De Costa, *Ancient Norumbega* (Albany, N.Y., 1890), 5–7.

b. Ibid.

c. Ibid.

d. Ibid.

e. John Clarke, in Richard Hakluyt, *Principal Navigations,* 12 vols. (Reprint, Glasgow, 1903–1905), 3:182.

f. Edward Hayes, in Hakluyt, *Principal Navigations* 8:47.

4 The Foothold Colony: Plymouth

1. Quoted in Samuel Eliot Morison, *Builders of the Bay Colony* (Cambridge, Mass., 1930), 344.

2. Dwight B. Heath, ed., *Mourt's Relation* (Reprint, New York, 1963), 16.

3. Ibid., 47.

4. Farmer and Moore, *Collections* (Concord, N.H., 1824), 281. Also *Mass. Hist. Colls.,* 3rd ser., vol. 8.

5. James Truslow Adams, *The Founding of New England* (Boston, 1921), 120.

6. Rev. John White, *The Planters Plea* (London, 1630), 74.

7. Samuel Purchas, *Purchas His Pilgrims,* 4 vols. (Glasgow, 1905–1907), 19:311.

5 Deepening Roots: Life in Four Colonial Settlements

1. William Wood, *New England's Prospects* (London, 1634), (in part 1, chapter 10).
2. Wood, *Prospects,* (in part 1, chapter 4).
3. Letter of William Hilton, 1622, in Samuel Purchas, *Purchas His Pilgrims* (Glasgow, 1905–1907), 19:306.
4. Wood, *Prospects,* (in part 1, chapter 2).
5. As quoted in Michael Zuckerman, "Pilgrims in the Wilderness, Community, Modernity and the Maypole at Merry Mount," *The New England Quarterly* 50 (June 1977):277.
6. *The General Laws and Liberties of Connecticut Colonie* (Cambridge, Mass., 1673), 23.
7. E. T. Fisher, trans., *Report of a French Protestant Refugee in Boston, 1687* (Brooklyn, N.Y., 1868), 16.
8. John Josselyn, *An Account of Two Voyages to New England* (London, 1674), in *Mass. Hist. Colls.,* 3rd ser., vol. 3 (1833):266.
9. William T. Davis, ed., *Original Narratives of Early American History: Bradford's History of Plymouth Plantation, 1606–1646* (Reprint, New York, 1908), 256.
10. John Wingate Thornton, *Ancient Pemaquid* (Portland, 1857), 65.
11. Josselyn, *Two Voyages,* 91.
12. Quoted in James Phinney Baxter, *Documentary History of the State of Maine,* Vol. 3 (Cambridge, Mass., 1877), 137.
13. Quoted in Federal Writers' Project, *New Hampshire* (Boston, 1938), 32.
14. E. B. O'Callaghan and Berthold Fernow, *Documents Relative to the Colonial History of New York,* 15 vols. (Albany, N.Y., 1856–1887), 3:101.
15. John Winter, quoted in James Phinney Baxter, *Trelawney Papers* (Portland, 1884), 171.
16. Quoted in John Johnston, *History of the Towns of Bristol and Bremen in the State of Maine* (Albany, N.Y., 1873), 152.
17. Josselyn, *Two Voyages,* 351.
18. Cotton Mather, *The Fishermans Calling* (Boston, 1712).
19. Ibid.
20. Quoted by Nathaniel Hawthorne in his *American Notebooks* (Columbus, Ohio, 1972), 547–48.
21. *Records and Files of the Quarterly Courts of Essex County, Massachusetts 1656–1681,* 8 vols. (Salem, 1912–1921), 1:170.
22. Capt. Robert Goelet, quoted in *New England Historical and Genealogical Register* (1870):57.
23. J. Reynolds, M.D., *Peter Gott, the Cape Ann Fisherman* (Boston, 1856), 30–31.
24. Quoted in Samuel A. Drake, *Nooks and Corners of the New England Coast* (New York, 1875), 247.

a. "The Company's First General Letter of Instructions to Endecott and His Council," in *Transactions of the American Antiquarian Society* 3 (1857):83.
b. "Captain Struttingham," "To Old Master Janus," in *The New England Courant,* no. 122 (Nov. 25–Dec. 2, 1723).
c. Charles Nordhoff, *Whaling and Fishing* (Cincinnati, 1856), 351.

6 Voyages of Trade and Adventure: The Eighteenth-Century City

1. William Wood, *New England's Prospects* (London, 1634), 38.
2. John Josselyn, *An Account of Two Voyages* (London, 1674), 180.
3. Samuel Breck, *Recollections of Samuel Breck* (London, 1877), 86.
4. Cotton Mather, "Diary," ed. W. C. Ford, in *Mass. Hist. Colls.,* ser. 7, vol. 7–8 (1911–1912), 2:484.
5. "Travel Diary of Dr. Benjamin Bullivant (1697)," in *New York Historical Society Quarterly* 40 (1956), 59.
6. Carl Bridenbaugh, ed., *Gentleman's Progress: The Itinerarium of Dr. Alexander Hamilton* (Chapel Hill, N.C., 1948), 157.
7. Quoted in Edward Peterson, *History of Rhode Island* (New York, 1853), 129.
8. Bridenbaugh, ed., *Gentleman's Progress,* 151–52.
9. Ibid.
10. Ibid., 157.
11. R. N. Toppan and A. T. S. Goodrick, *Edward Randolph: Including His Letters and Official Papers . . . 1676–1703,* 7 vols. (Boston, 1898–1909), 7:275.
12. Quoted in William B. Weeden, *Early Rhode Island* (New York, 1910), 183.
13. Timothy Dwight, *Travels in New England and New York,* 4 vols. (Reprint, Cambridge, Mass., 1969), 3:33.
14. John C. Gray, "Remarks on New England Agriculture," in *Essays Agricultural and Literary* (Boston, 1856), 35.
15. Clifton Johnson, *Highways and Byways of New England* (New York, 1915), 38.
16. Edward Johnson, *Wonder Working Providence 1628–1651* (Reprint, New York, 1910), 208–09.
17. Charles Molloy, *De jure maritimo* (London, 1676), 247.
18. Samuel Adams Drake, *Nooks and Corners* (New York, 1875), 343–44.
19. Quoted in Everett U. Crosby, *Nantucket in Print* (Nantucket, 1946), 142.
20. Ibid., 127.
21. Ibid., 74.
22. William E. Gardner, *The Coffin Saga* (Cambridge, Mass., 1949), 48.
23. Robert A. Douglas-Lithgow, *Nantucket: A History* (New York, 1914), 235.
24. Quoted in Crosby, *Nantucket in Print,* 94.

a. G. B. Hutchins, *The American Maritime Industries and Public Policy, 1789–1914: An Economic History* (Cambridge, Mass., 1941), 152.
b. Howard I. Chappelle, *The History of American Sailing Ships* (New York, n.d.), 10.
c. William T. Davis, ed., *Bradford's History of Plymouth Plantation* (Reprint, New York, 1908), 118.
d. W. T. Salter, *John Salter, Mariner* (Philadelphia, 1900), 10.
e. From a broadside, "An Account of the Behaviour and Last Dying Speeches of the Six Pirates . . . Executed on Charles River . . . June 30th 1704 . . ." (Boston, 1704).
f. Bridenbaugh, ed., *Gentleman's Progress,* 163, 98, 98, 136.

7 The Revolution to the War of 1812

1. Quoted in Henry C. Kittredge, *Cape Cod* (Boston and New York, 1930), 123.

2. Sir Joshua Child, *A New Discourse on Trade* (London, 1694), 198.
3. John Mitchell, *The Present State of Great Britain and North America . . .* (London, 1767), 163–164.
4. Letter of Gilbert Deblois to Samuel Curwin, Boston, August 6, 1759. Reprinted in Henry Wells Lawrence, *The Not Quite Puritans* (Boston, 1928), 208.
5. Mitchell, *Present State,* 158–59.
6. Anne Hulton, *Letters of a Loyalist Lady* (Cambridge, Mass., 1927), 71.
7. As quoted in Alden T. Vaughan, ed., *Chronicles of the American Revolution* (New York, 1965), 200.
8. Jacob Bailey, "Letter of Mr. Bailey," in *Collections of the Maine Historical Society,* vol. 5 (Portland, 1857), 444.
9. Ibid., 447.
10. Ibid., 449–50.
11. Ebenezor Fox, *The Adventures of Ebenezor Fox in the Revolutionary War* (Boston, 1838), 33–35.
12. Letter from Brigadier General John Sullivan to George Washington, Portsmouth, October 29, 1775. In Jared Sparks, ed., *Correspondence of the American Revolution* (Boston, 1853), 1:71.
13. Elijah Cobb, *Elijah Cobb. 1768–1848: A Cape Cod Skipper* (New Haven, 1925), 21.
14. Timothy Dwight, *Travels in New England* (1821–1822; reprint, Cambridge, Mass., 1969), 1:367.
15. Ibid., 330.
16. Esther Forbes, *The Running of the Tide* (Boston, 1948), 76.
17. Letter of Timothy Pickering to George Cabot, Jan. 29, 1804, in *The Life and Letters of George Cabot,* ed. Henry Cabot Lodge (Boston, 1878), 337–340.
18. Robin D. S. Hingham, "The Port of Boston," *The American Neptune* 16, no. 3 (July 1956):220.
19. Jonathan Weston, quoted in W. H. Kilby, *Eastport and Passamaquoddy* (Eastport, Maine, 1888), 66–67.
20. *The Columbian Centinel* [Boston], June 11, 1808.
21. Quoted in William H. Rowe, *The Maritime History of Maine* (New York, 1948), 95.

a. Lord Timothy Dexter, *A Pickle for the Knowing Ones: or, Plain Truths in a Homespun Dress* (Newburyport, Mass., 1802).
b. "The Late Timothy Dexter," *The Western Reserve and Miscellaneous Magazine* 3 (1820):278–285. Reprinted in *The Filson Club* [Louisville] *Historical Quarterly* 34, no. 4 (Oct. 1961):357–66.
c. *Niles' Weekly Register* [Baltimore], vol. 4, no. 20 (July 17, 1813):326–327.

8 Seafaring's Indian Summer

1. Mrs. Elizabeth D. B. Stoddard, *The Morgessons* (New York, 1862), 181.
2. Nathaniel Hawthorne, *American Notebooks* (Columbus, Ohio, 1972), 155.
3. Nathaniel Hawthorne, "The Custom House.—Introductory," *The Scarlet Letter* (Boston, 1850).
4. Ibid.
5. Thomas Wentworth Higginson, quoted in William S. Rossiter, ed., *Days and Ways in Old Boston* (Boston, 1915), 29.
6. Charles Nordhoff, *Whaling and Fishing* (Cincinnati, 1856), 22–23.
7. Herman Melville, "The Carpet Bag," *Moby Dick* (New York, 1852).
8. J. S. Buckingham, *The Eastern and Western States of America,* 3 vols. (London, 1842), 3:521.
9. Melville, "The Street," *Moby Dick.*
10. Nordhoff, *Whaling and Fishing,* 24.
11. George C. Homans and Samuel Eliot Morison, *Massachusetts on the Sea* (Boston, 1930), 9.
12. For a thorough study of labor practices in whaling, see Elmo P. Hohman, *American Whaleman* (New York, 1928).
13. Rowland G. Hazard, ed., *The Jonny Cake Papers of "Shepherd Tom" . . . by Thomas Robinson Hazard* (Boston, 1915), 272.
14. Melville, "The Carpet Bag," *Moby Dick.*
15. N. W. Taylor, *Life of a Whaler* (New London, Conn., 1929), 22.
16. Melville, "The Street," *Moby Dick.*
17. Nordhoff, *Whaling and Fishing,* 26–27.
18. D. H. Strother, "A Summer in New England," *Harper's Monthly Magazine* 21:8.
19. Ibid., 745.
20. Melville, "The Spouter-Inn," *Moby Dick.*

a. Henry David Thoreau, "The Pond in Winter." *Walden* (Boston, 1854).
b. Samuel Eliot Morison, *The Maritime History of Massachusetts* (Boston, 1941), 284–85.
c. William Dean Howells, *A Woman's Reason* Boston, 1883), 47.
d. "Hawser Martingale" [John S. Sleeper], *Tales of the Ocean* (Boston, 1841), 9.
e. *Selections from the Court Reports originally published in the Boston Morning Post, from 1834 to 1837. Arranged and Revised by the Reporter of the Post* (Boston, 1837), 205.
f. "Martingale," *Tales of the Ocean,* 51.
g. William Bradford, *History of Plymouth Plantation* (Reprint, New York, 1908), 177.
h. Timothy Dwight, *Travels in New England* (1821–1822; reprint, Cambridge, Mass., 1969), 3:53.

9 Spindles and Ship Hulls: Manufacturing Towns

1. Timothy Dwight, *Travels in New England* (1821–1822; reprint, Cambridge, Mass., 1969), 1:320.
2. George A. Rich, "The Cotton Industry in New England," *The New England Magazine,* n.s., vol. 3 (1890), 173.
3. Thomas Hamilton, *Men and Manners in America* (Philadelphia, 1833), 88.
4. Quoted in Dane Yorke, *The Men and Times of Pepperell* (1945), 10.
5. Rev. Jonathan Cogswell, "A Topographical and Historical Sketch of Saco, County of York, District of Maine," *Mass. Hist. Colls.,* 2nd ser., vol. 4 (1816):187.
6. Ibid., 186.
7. Roy P. Fairfield, *Sands, Spindles, and Steeples* (Portland, Maine, 1956), 34.
8. Jonathan Thayer Lincoln, *The City of the Dinner-Pail* (Boston and New York, 1909), 18.
9. T. M. Young, *The American Cotton Industry* (New York, 1903), 20.
10. William Dean Howells, *A Woman's Reason* (Boston, 1883), 48–49.
11. Mary Ellen Chase, *Silas Crockett* (New York, 1935), 7–8.

12. *The Boston Traveler*, November 12, 1836.
13. Harriet Beecher Stowe, *The Pearl of Orr's Island* (Boston, 1862), 257–58.
14. Talbot F. Hamlin, *Greek Revival Architecture in America* (New York, 1944), 162.
15. Nathaniel Ames, *An Old Sailor's Yarns* (New York, 1834), 16.
16. Howard I. Chappelle, *The History of American Sailing Ships* (New York, n.d.), 287.

a. John Winthrop, *The History of New England, 1620–1649*, 2 vols., ed. James Savage (Boston, 1853), 1:73.

10 Voyaging by Steam, Chart and Timetable

1. Thomas Bailey Aldrich, *An Old Town by the Sea* (Boston, 1893), 105–109.
2. Thomas Hamilton, *Men and Manners in America* (Philadelphia, 1833), 78.
3. Ibid.
4. Ibid.
5. Quoted in Seymour Dunbar, *A History of Travel in America* (Indianapolis, 1915), 410.
6. William Jerome, Andrew B. Sterling and Harry Von Tilzer, "On the Old Fall River Line" (New York, 1913).
7. Edward Peterson, *History of Rhode Island* (New York, 1853), 288.
8. F. A. P. Barnard, *Report of the History and Progress of the American Coast Survey up to the Year 1858 . . . American Association for the Advancement of Science* (N.p., n.d.), 10.
9. Henry David Thoreau, "Provincetown," *Cape Cod*.
10. H. C. Adamson, *Keepers of the Light* (New York, 1955), 97.
11. Report of Gen. J. C. Duane, 1871, quoted in John H. Morrison, *History of American Steam Navigation* (1903; reprint, New York, 1958), 580–81.
12. *The General Laws and Liberties concerning the Inhabitants of the Massachusets* (Cambridge, Mass., 1648), 55.
13. "Cape Cod, September 5, 1854," in Bliss Perry, ed., *The Heart of Emerson's Journals* (Boston and New York, 1926), 264.
14. Thoreau, "The Beach," *Cape Cod*.

a. "Journal of Obediah Turner," quoted in Fred A. Wilson, *Some Annals of Nahant, Massachusetts* (Boston, 1928), 161.
b. *Reports of a Committee of the Linnaean Society of New England Relative to a Large Marine Animal, Supposed to be a Sea-Serpent, Seen near Cape Ann, Massachusetts, in August 1817* (Boston, 1817).

11 Mending the Nets: Living off the Sea

1. Charles Nordhoff, *Whaling and Fishing* (Cincinnati, 1856), 368.
2. John J. Babson, *A History of the Town of Gloucester, Cape Ann . . .* (Gloucester, Mass., 1860), 2.
3. Frank L. Cox, "In Gloucester Harbor," *Century Magazine* 44 (1892):522.
4. Clifton Johnson, *Highways and Byways* (New York, 1915), 157–58.
5. Winfield M. Thompson, "The Passing of the New England Fisherman," *New England Magazine* 19 (Feb. 1896):675.
6. Ibid., 677.
7. George H. Proctor, "An American Fishing Port," *Lippincott's Magazine* 1 (1868):501.
8. L. W. Betts, "Gloucester, the Fishing City," *Outlook* 68 (1901):69.
9. Rudyard Kipling, *Captains Courageous* (London and New York, 1897).
10. Betts, "Gloucester," 65.
11. S. G. W. Benjamin, "Gloucester and Cape Ann," *Harper's New Monthly Magazine* 51 (Sept. 1875):471.
12. Clifton Johnson, *New England and Its Neighbors* (New York, 1902), 197–98.
13. Johnson, *Highways and Byways*, 191–92.
14. Johnson, *New England*, 127.
15. Sarah Orne Jewett, "By the Morning Boat," *The Atlantic Monthly* 66 (Oct. 1890):518.
16. *History of the State of Rhode Island Illustrated from Original Sketches* (Providence, R.I., 1886), 65.
17. Johnson, *Highways and Byways*, 206.
18. Johnson, *New England*, 39.
19. Johnson, *Highways and Byways*, 185–86.
20. Timothy Dwight, *Travels in New England* (1821–1822; reprint, Cambridge, Mass., 1969), 2:358.

a. Commissioner of Narragansett Indians. *State of Rhode Island and Providence Plantations. Third Annual Report of the Commissioner of the Affairs of the Narragansett Indians* (Providence, R.I., 1883).
b. Thomas C. Grattan, *Civilized America*, 2 vols. (London, 1859), 1:50–51.
c. Caroline H. King, *When I Lived in Salem, 1822–1866* (Brattleboro, Vt., 1937), 197.
d. Henry David Thoreau, "The Wellfleet Oysterman," *Cape Cod*.
e. Ibid.
f. Ibid.

12 Along the Bathing Sands: Vacationing

1. Eugene Batchelder, *A Romance of the Sea Serpent* (Cambridge, Mass., 1849), 65.
2. Thomas C. Grattan, *Civilized America*, 2 vols. (London, 1859), 1:46.
3. Ibid.
4. Ibid.
5. Rev. Edward Peterson, *History of Rhode Island* (New York, 1853), 279.
6. Hon. Amelia M. Murray, *Letters from the United States, Cuba and Canada*, 2 vols. (London, 1856), 1:37.
7. George W. Curtis, *Lotus Eating: A Summer Book* (New York, 1852), 168–69.
8. Jonathan Thayer Lincoln, *The City of the Dinner-Pail* (Boston and New York, 1909), 170.
9. Ibid., 180.
10. Gouverneur Morris, "Newport the Maligned," *Everybody's Magazine* 19 (Sept. 1908):322.
11. Ibid.
12. William Dean Howells, "Their Pilgrimage," *Harper's New Monthly Magazine* 73 (1886):116.
13. "The Queen of Aquidneck," *Harper's New Monthly Magazine* 49 (1874):320.
14. Morris, "Newport," 322.
15. E. C. Ackerman, "A Trip to Provincetown" (Boston, 1910).
16. S. G. W. Benjamin, "Gloucester and Cape Ann," *Harper's Monthly* 51 (Sept. 1875):474.

17. *Among the Berkshire and Litchfield Hills, via New York, New Haven and Hartford Railroad* (Boston, 1899), 8.
18. Joseph W. Smith, *Gleanings from the Sea* (Andover, Mass., 1887), 67.
19. Clifton Johnson, *Highways and Byways* (New York, 1915), 207.

a. Timothy Dwight, *Travels in New England* (1821–1822; reprint, Cambridge, Mass., 1969), 2:114–15.
b. Quoted in James T. Flexner, *The World of Winslow Homer, 1836–1910* (New York, n.d.), 164.
c. Lloyd Goodrich, *Winslow Homer* (New York, 1944), 36.
d. Lincoln Steffens, *The Autobiography of Lincoln Steffens* (New York, 1931), 436.
e. Ibid., 437.
f. Ibid., 438.
g. Ibid.
h. Quoted in Pierre Loving, "Eugene O'Neill," *The Bookman* 53 (Aug. 1921): 516.
i. Letter to Stieglitz, 1923, quoted in *Maine and Its Role in American Art,* ed. Gertrud A. Mellon and Elizabeth F. Wilder (New York, 1963), 143.

Bibliography

A "complete" bibliography of works relating to the New England seacoast, or even a list of the works consulted in the preparation of this volume, would far exceed the size of the book in hand. The entries here are the reasonably accessible works that are the best treatment of a subject, or make excellent reading, given a modest interest in the subject, or contain extensive bibliographies on specific topics.

In order to make such a list manageable, titles of all books on specific locales have been omitted unless they can be recommended to a general audience. A list of such works is easily found in the public libraries of those regions; it is also to be found in the excellent Committee for a New England Bibliography series (see that entry). The writer has also omitted obscure works to be found only in scholarly libraries. The bibliography here does, however, contain those valuable sources of information that the average scholar could not be expected to find by means of standard research practices.

This bibliography, combined with the sources cited in the footnotes, will give to the armchair enthusiast ample entertainment and insight, and for those with specialized interests, it will provide a basic foundation of knowledge and offer many avenues for expanding their interests.

General Works

Abbott, Jacob. *American History*. New York and Boston, 1850.

Adams, James Truslow. *Album of American History*. 4 vols. New York, 1944–1948.

———. *The Founding of New England*. Boston, 1921.

———. *New England in the Republic, 1776–1850*. Boston, 1926.

———. *Revolutionary New England, 1691–1776*. Boston, 1923. Adams's books are probably the best histories of the New England region for the general reader.

Albion, Robert G. *Naval and Maritime History: An Annotated Bibliography*. Mystic, Conn., 1972. The standard source.

Albion, Robert G., William A. Baker, and Benjamin W. Labaree. *New England and the Sea*. Middletown, Conn., 1972. The best popular work on the region's maritime trades, with emphasis on offshore activities.

American Guide Series. State guidebooks to interesting and historical sites. First published in the 1930s. Some have been revised and reprinted in the 1970s. Only the modern volume on Maine, unfortunately, approaches the comprehensiveness of the first edition.

Babson, John J. *History of the Town of Gloucester, Cape Ann*. Gloucester, Mass., 1860.

Banks, Ronald F. *A History of Maine. A Collection of Readings on the History of Maine 1600–1976*. Dubuque, Iowa, 1976.

Berrill, Michael. *A Sierra Club Naturalist's Guide to the North Atlantic Coast: Cape Cod to Newfoundland*. San Francisco, 1981. Highly recommended.

Beston, Henry. *White Pine and Blue Water: A State of Maine Reader*. New York, 1950.

Blanchard, Fessenden S. *Long Island Sound*. Princeton, 1958. Cruising guide.

Boating Almanac.

    Vol. 1. *Massachusetts, Maine, New Hampshire*.

    Vol. 2. *Long Island, Connecticut, Rhode Island*.

    Issued annually from Morristown, N.J. Excellent complement to other guides. Reprints nautical charts in convenient-sized (5½ by 9 inches) paperbacks, showing coastline, topography, and roads.

Chapelle, Howard I. *The History of American Sailing Ships*. New York, n.d. Basic study by a recognized expert.

Chase, Mary E., and the Editors of *Look*. *New England*. Boston, 1947.

Clark, Victor S. *History of Manufactures in the United States, 1607–1860*. Washington, D.C., 1916.

[Cobb, Elijah]. *Elijah Cobb, 1768–1848: A Cape Cod Skipper*. New Haven, 1925.

Committee for a New England Bibliography. Bibliographies of New England history:

    Vol. 1. *Massachusetts*. Boston, 1976.

    Vol. 2. *Maine*. Boston, 1977.

    Vol. 3. *New Hampshire*. Boston, 1979.

    In press or preparation: *Vermont, Connecticut, Rhode Island*, and *New England*. When completed, this set will become the most comprehensive bibliography of New England. Entries are by state, county, and town. Exceptionally useful for more obscure but interesting sources, such as magazine articles of the nineteenth and twentieth centuries.

Crofut, Florence S. *Guide to the History and Historical Sites of Connecticut*. 2 vols. New Haven, 1937.

Crosby, Everett U. *Nantucket in Print*. Nantucket, 1946. Readings and bibliography.

Cutler, Carl C. *Mystic: The Story of a Small New England Seaport*. Mystic, Conn., 1945.

"Diggs, Jeremiah." [Josef Berger]. *Cape Cod Pilot . . . by Jeremiah Diggs*. Provincetown, Mass., 1937.Doane, Doris. *Exploring Old Cape Cod*. Chatham, Mass., 1968.

Drake, Samuel A. *Nooks and Corners of the New England Coast*. New York, 1875. The best nineteenth-century general historical tour of the coast.

———. *The Pine Tree Coast*. Boston, 1891. Companion volume to *Nooks and Corners*.

Dunbar, Seymour. *A History of Travel in America*. New York, 1915. Still the best comprehensive study.

Duncan, Robert F. *A Cruising Guide to the New England Coast*. New York, 1937. Many later editions.

Dwight, Timothy. *Travels in New England and New York*. New Haven, 1821–1822. Reprint (4 vols.). Cambridge, Mass., 1969. The classic tour of New England, with descriptions and pithy observations by this Yale president and Puritan throwback.

Federal Writers' Project. *U.S. One: Maine to Florida*. New York, 1938.

Felt, J. B. *Customs of New England*. Boston, 1853.

Fiske, John. *The Beginning of New England*. Boston, 1898. A basic authority.

———. *New France and New England*. Boston, 1904.

Foley, Daniel J. *Gardening by the Sea*. Radnor, Pa., 1965.

Gibson, John. *Walking the Maine Coast*. Camden, Maine, 1977. Twenty-five hikes.

Handlin, Oscar, et al., *Harvard Guide to American History*. Cambridge, Mass., 1954 (and later revisions). The number one bibliography for the graduate student in history.

Hansen, Marcus L. *The Atlantic Migration, 1607–1860*. Cambridge, Mass., 1940.

Hawthorne, Nathaniel. *Nathaniel Hawthorne: The American Notebooks*. Ed. by Claude M. Simpson. Columbus, Ohio, 1972. Diary and observations, many of which deal with the coastal region.

Higginson, Thomas Wentworth. *Oldport Days*. Boston, 1873. Classic essay on Newport.

Homans, George C., and Samuel Eliot Morison. *Massachusetts on the Sea, 1630–1930*. Boston, 1930. Short but comprehensive overview of maritime trades.

Howe, George. *Mount Hope*. New York, 1959. About Bristol, R.I.

Howe, Henry F. *Salt Rivers of the Massachusetts Shore*. New York, 1951. American Rivers series.

Huntress, Keith. *A Checklist of Shipwreck and Disaster at Sea to 1860*. Ames, Iowa, 1979.

Hutchins, John G. B. *The American Maritime Industries and Public Policy, 1789–1914*. Cambridge, Mass., 1941.

Johnson, Clifton. *Highways and Byways of New England*. New York, 1915.

———. *New England: A Human Interest Geographical Reader*. New York, 1917.

———. *New England and Its Neighbors.* New York, 1902. A native New Englander, Johnson (unlike his contemporaries who came in from elsewhere to examine the region as a curious whole) makes some very enlightening observations on character differences between localities, and upon the changes taking place at the turn of the century. He ranks with Timothy Dwight of a century earlier.

Kimball, Gertrude S. *Pictures of Rhode Island in the Past, 1642–1833.* Providence, R. I., 1900. Extracts from travelers' accounts.

Kittredge, Henry C. *Cape Cod, Its People and Their History.* Boston and New York, 1930. The standard popular history.

Laing, Alexander. *American Heritage History of Seafaring America.* New York, 1974.

Lippincott, Bertram. *Indians, Privateers and High Society: A Rhode Island Sampler.* Philadelphia, 1961.

Livermore, S. T. *History of Block Island.* Hartford, 1877. Reprint. Forge Village, Mass., 1961.

Morison, Samuel Eliot. *The Maritime History of Massachusetts, 1783–1860.* Boston, 1921. Rev. ed., 1941. The recognized authority.

National Register of Historic Places, 1972. Washington, D.C., 1972 (and later supplements). Lists sites throughout the country which have been designated "historic."

Palfrey, John G. *History of New England.* 5 vols. Boston, 1865–1890. A comprehensive source.

Payne, Rolce R. *An Illustrated and Annotated Guide to New England Gardens Open to the Public.* Boston, 1979.

Pearson, Hayden S. *Sea Flavor.* New York, 1948. Vivid essays on shore life, both human and natural.

Peterson, Rev. Edward. *History of Rhode Island.* New York, 1853.

Rich, Louise Dickinson. *The Coast of Maine: An Informal History and Guide.* New York, 1962. The first book for those falling in love with the Maine coast.

Roberts, Kenneth. *Trending into Maine.* Boston, 1938. Essays by a native son. N. C. Wyeth illustrations.

Rowe, William H. *The Maritime History of Maine.* New York, 1948. The standard authority.

Russell, Howard. *A Long Deep Furrow: Three Centuries of Farming in America.* Hanover, N.H., 1976.

Saltonstall, William G. *Ports of Piscataqua.* Cambridge, Mass., 1941.

Snow, Edward Rowe. Books on lighthouses, wrecks, storms, legends, etc. New York, ca. 1949–1965.

Sprout, Harold and Margaret. *The Rise of American Naval Power, 1776–1918.* Princeton, 1946.

Strother, D. H. "A Summer in New England," *Harper's Monthly Magazine,* 21 (1860): 1, 442, 745.

Sullivan, James. *History of the District of Maine.* Boston, 1795.

Tedone, David, ed., *A History of Connecticut's Coast.* Hartford, 1982.

Thaxter, Celia. *Among the Isles of Shoals.* Boston, 1901. An Edwardian classic.

Townsend, Charles H. *The Early History of Long Island Sound and Its Approaches.* New Haven, 1894.

Tree, Christina. *How New England Happened.* Boston, 1976.

Tuckerman, Henry T. *America and Her Commentators: With a Critical Sketch of Travel in the United States.* New York, 1864. A classic source, bibliography, and anthology.

U. S. Coast and Geodetic Survey: Carlisle P. Patterson, Superintendent. *Atlantic Coast Pilot.*
Vol. 1. Eastport to Boston. Washington, D.C., 1879.
Vol. 2. Boston Bay to New York. Washington, D.C., 1878.

Verrill, A. Hyatt. *Along New England Shores.* New York, 1936. Excellent and readable.

Warden, Herbert W. *In Praise of Sailors: A Nautical Anthology of Art, Poetry, and Prose.* New York, 1978.

Weeden, William B. *Economic and Social History of New England, 1620–1789.* Boston, 1891. Encyclopedic, and the recognized cornerstone.

Whitehill, Walter M. *Boston: A Topographical History.* Cambridge, Mass., 1963.

Winsor, Justin, ed. *The Memorial History of Boston . . . 1638–1880.* 4 vols. Boston, 1880. An extensive work with essays on various subjects.

———. *Narrative and Critical History of America.* Boston and New York, 1889. A mammoth study written by experts on each era. Especially useful for its reproductions of old maps and for interrelating activities of the precolonial era.

Wroth, Lawrence C., ed., "The Colonial Scene, 1602–1800," *The Proceedings of the American Antiquarian Society* (Apr. 1950): 53. Worcester. A list of works used in an exhibition, with introductory essay and annotated catalogue.

Yeadon, David. *Hidden Corners of New England.* New York, 1976.

Chapter 1

Arnold, Augusta F. *The Sea-Beach at Ebb Tide.* New York, 1901. Reprint, New York, 1968. Naturalist's guide, Bar Harbor locale.

Beston, Henry. *The Outermost House: A Year of Life on the Great Beach of Cape Cod.* New York, 1928. A naturalist's classic.

Billings, M. P. *Bedrock Geology.* Vol. 2 of *Geology of New Hampshire.* Concord, N.H., 1956.

Bloom, Arthur L. *Late Pleistocene Changes in Sea Level in Southwestern Maine.* Augusta, Maine, 1960.

———, and Ellis, Charles W., Jr. *Postglacial Stratigraphy and Morphology of Coastal Connecticut.* Hartford, 1965.

Brigham, Albert P. *Geographic Influences in American History.* Chautauqua Home Reading Series. New York, 1903.

"Connecticut's Coastal Marshes: A Vanishing Resource," *Connecticut Arboretum Bulletin* 12 (Feb. 1961).

Crosby, Irving B. *Boston through the Ages.* Boston, 1928.

Denys, Nicolas. *Description géographique et historique des costes de l'Amérique septentrionale.* 2 vols. Paris, 1672. Reprint, *The Description and Natural History of the Coasts of North America . . . ,* trans. and ed. by William F. Ganong. Toronto, 1908. Primarily Acadia, but some Maine and much on early cod fishing.

Emery, K. O. *A Coastal Pond.* New York, 1969. Site on Cape Cod.

Farb, Peter, *Face of North America.* New York, 1963.

Fenneman, N. M. *Physiography of Eastern United States.* New York, 1938.

Flint, Richard F. *Glacial Geology of Connecticut.* Hartford, 1930.

Goldthwait, J. W., *Surficial Geology*. Vol. 1 of *Geology of New Hampshire*. Concord, N.H., 1951.

Goodsell, Daniel A. *Nature and Character at Granite Bay*. New York, 1901. Concerns Branford, Conn.

Hay, John. *The Great Beach*. New York, 1963. Outer Cape Cod.

——, and Peter Farb. *The Atlantic Shore: Human and Natural History from Long Island to Labrador*. New York, 1966. Naturalists' study.

Hussey, Arthur M., II. *Bibliography of Maine Geology, 1672–1972*. Augusta, Maine, 1974.

Jewett, Amos E. *The Tidal Marshes of Rowley and Vicinity*. Rowley, Mass., 1949.

Johnson, Douglas W. *The New England–Acadian Shoreline*. New York, 1925. The cornerstone study of the coast north of Cape Cod.

Jorgensen, Neil. *A Guide to New England's Landscape*. Barre, Mass., 1971. The modern popular classic on New England geology.

Ketchum, Bostwick, ed. *The Water's Edge: Critical Problems of the Coastal Zone. Coastal Zone Workshop, Woods Hole, Mass.* Cambridge, Mass., 1972.

Knight, J. Brookes. "A Salt Marsh Study," *American Journal of Science* 28 (Sept. 1934): 161. About Branford, Conn.

Larson, Graham, and Byron Stone, eds. *Late Wisconsinan Glaciation in New England*. N.p., 1982. A symposium.

Leopold, A. S. *A Sand County Almanac*. Cambridge, 1966.

Ludlum, David M. *Early American Hurricanes, 1492–1870*. Boston, 1963. Excellent, both as historical reader and chronological guide. Bibliography.

——. *The New England Weather Book*. Boston, 1976. Informative popular work.

Ogburn, Charlton B. *The Winter Beach*. New York, 1966.

Oldale, R. N., and Elazar Uchupi. *The Glaciated Shelf off the Northeastern United States* (U.S.G.S. Prof. Paper 700-B). Washington, D.C., 1970.

Perley, Sidney. *Historic Storms of New England*. Salem, 1891.

Schafer, J. P. "The Ice Age in Rhode Island," *Bulletin of the Audubon Society of Rhode Island* 15, no. 5 (Dec. 1954–Jan. 1955): 55.

Schlee, John. *The Atlantic Continental Shelf and Slope of the United States . . . Northeast Part*. Washington, D.C., 1973.

Shaler, Nathaniel S. *Sea and Land*. New York, 1894. Observations by a geologist who walked the whole Atlantic shore.

Sharp, Henry S. *The Physical History of the Connecticut Shoreline*. Hartford, 1929.

Strahler, A. N. *A Geologist's View of Cape Cod*. Garden City, N.Y., 1966.

Thompson, Betty F. *The Changing Face of New England*. New York, 1958. Still a popular classic.

Townsend, Charles W. *Beach Grass*. Boston, 1923.

——. *Sand Dunes and Salt Marshes*. Boston, 1913. Both are interesting works on the Ipswich, Mass., region by a naturalist-historian.

Uchupi, Elazar. *Maps Showing Relation of Land and Submarine Topography, Nova Scotia to Florida* (U.S.G.S. Misc. Geo. Investigations Maps I-451). Washington, D.C., 1965. Also in *Atlantic Continental Shelf and Slope of the United States . . . Physiography* (U.S.G.S. Prof. Paper 529-C). Washington, D.C., 1968.

University of Massachusetts Coastal Research Group. *Coastal Environments of Northeastern Massachusetts and New Hampshire*. Amherst, Mass., 1969.

Chapter 2

Barratt, Joseph. *The Indian of New England*. Middletown, Conn., 1851.

Beck, Horace P. *The American Indian as Sea-Fighter in Colonial Times*. Mystic, Conn., 1959.

Commissioner of Narragansett Indians. *State of Rhode Island and Providence Plantations. Third Annual Report of Commission on the Affairs of the Narragansett Indians . . .* Providence, R.I., 1883.

DeForest, John. *History of the Indians of Connecticut . . . to 1850*. Hartford, 1852.

Dorr, Henry C. "The Narragansetts," *Collections of the Rhode Island Historical Society* 7 (1885): 135.

Gookin, Daniel. "Historical Collections of the Indians in New England, 1792," *Massachusetts Historical Collections* 1 (1806). Reprint. Spencer, Mass., 1970.

Johnson, Frederick, ed. *Man in North Eastern North America*. Andover, Mass., 1946. Studies by the Peabody Foundation for Archaeology, some very enlightening with regard to American Indian psychology.

Leland, Charles G. *The Algonquin Legends of New England*. Boston, 1898.

Martin, Catherine. *The Wampanoags in the 17th Century*. Occasional Papers in Old Colony Studies, No. 2 (Dec. 1970). Focuses on Plymouth.

Russell, Howard S. *Indian New England before the Mayflower*. Hanover, N.H., 1980. Indians as revealed by early explorers. The most complete work on the period.

Salisbury, Neal. *The Indians of New England: A Critical Bibliography*. Bloomington, Ind., 1982.

Snow, Dean R. *The Archaeology of New England*. New York, 1980. Comprehensive and definitive.

Trigger, Bruce G. *Handbook of the North American Indians*. Vol. 15, *The Northeast*. Washington, D.C., 1979. Part of the Smithsonian's monumental and definitive survey.

Tunis, Edward. *Indians*. New York, 1959. Popular book with historically accurate sketches by the author/artist.

Wilbur, C. Keith. *The New England Indians*. Chester, Conn., 1978. Popular work.

Williams, Roger. *A Key into the Language of America*. London, 1643. Reprint, Providence, R.I., 1936.

Chapter 3

Askowith, Hyman. "Early Explorations of the New England Coast," *The New England Magazine* 28, no. 1 (Mar. 1903): 19.

Cummings, W. P., R. A. Skelton, and D. B. Quinn. *The Discovery of North America*. New York, 1971. Comprehensive study by *American Heritage*.

DeCosta, B. F. *Ancient Norumbega . . . Voyages . . . 1579–1580*. Albany, N.Y., 1890.

Grant, W. L., ed. *Voyages of Samuel de Champlain, 1604–1618.* New York, 1907.

Hakluyt, Richard. *A Discourse Concerning Western Planting* (1584) Reprinted in *Documentary History of the State of Maine,* vol. 2. Cambridge, Mass., 1877.

———. *Principal Navigations, Voyages, and Discoveries of the English Nation . . .* 12 vols. Reprint, Glasgow, 1903–1905. Compilation of all the explorers' accounts to 1600 by a contemporary.

Harrissee, Henry. *Discovery of North America.* London, 1892. Extensive survey and reproduction of pre-1536 maps.

Howe, Henry F. *Prologue to New England.* New York, 1943. The best popular work on the period.

Morison, Samuel Eliot. *The European Discovery of America: The Northern Voyages* A.D. *500–1600.* New York, 1971. The old accounts as seen through the eyes of a historian and an experienced sailor.

Purchas, Samuel. *Hakluytus Postumus, or Purchas His Pilgrims.* 4 vols. Reprint, Glasgow, 1905–1907. Continuation of Hakluyt's project by a contemporary.

Quinn, David B. *North America from the Earliest Discoveries to First Settlements: The Norse Voyages to 1612.* New York, 1977.

Skelton, R. A. *The European Image and Mapping of America.* A.D. *1000–1600.* Minneapolis, 1964.

Smith, John. *A Description of New England.* London, 1616. Many reprints.

Winship, George P. *Sailors' Narratives of Voyages along the New England Coast, 1524–1624.* Boston, 1905. A comprehensive anthology.

Wroth, Lawrence C. *The Voyages of Giovanni da Verrazano, 1524–1528.* New Haven and London, 1970.

Chapter 4

Bradford, William. *Of Plymouth Plantation 1620–1647.* This account of Plymouth's early years did not appear in print until the original manuscript was discovered in England in 1855 and published the next year. Since then, it has been reprinted under various titles. The author made use of the following edition: Davis, William T., ed., *Original Narratives of Early American History: Bradford's History of Plymouth Plantation 1606–1646.* New York, 1908.

Heath, Dwight B., ed. *A Journal of the Pilgrims at Plymouth. Mourt's Relation . . . 1622.* Reprint. New York, 1963.

James, Sydney V., ed. *Three Visitors to Early Plymouth.* Plymouth, Mass., 1963. Compilation of accounts ca. 1622–1628 by John Pory, Emmanuel Altham, and Isaack de Rasieres.

Jameson, J. Franklin. *Narratives of the New Netherlands, 1609–1664.* New York, 1909. An anthology.

Levermore, Charles H. *Forerunners and Competitors of the Pilgrims and Puritans.* 3 vols. Brooklyn, N.Y., 1912.

Morison, Samuel Eliot. *The Story of the Old Colony of Plymouth, 1620–1692.* New York, 1956.

Rutman, Darrett. *Husbandmen of Plymouth: Farms and Villages in the Old Colony, 1620–1692.* Boston, 1967.

Shurtleff, Harold R. *The Log Cabin Myth.* Cambridge, Mass., 1939. About early homes and their construction.

Smith, Capt. John. *Advertisements for the Unexperienced Planters of New-England, or Any Where.* London, 1631. Reprint, Boston, 1865.

Chapter 5

Baldwin, J. F. "Feudalism in Maine," *The New England Quarterly* 5 (1932): 352.

Banks, Charles E. *The Planters of the Commonwealth: A Study of the Emigrants and Immigration of Colonial Times . . . Their English Homes and the Places of Their Settlement in Massachusetts 1620–1640.* Boston, 1930. Shows the division of West Country and East Country English into separate sections of colonial New England.

Bliss, William R. *Colonial Times in Buzzard's Bay.* Boston, 1889.

The Book of the General Laws and Liberties Concerning the Inhabitants of the Massachusets. Cambridge, Mass., 1648. Reprint, Cambridge, Mass., 1929.

Chatterton, Edward K. *English Seamen and the Colonization of America.* London, 1930.

Clark, Charles E. *The Eastern Frontier: The Settlement of Northern New England 1610–1763.* New York, 1970.

Dow, George F. *Everyday Life in the Massachusetts Bay Colony.* Boston, 1935.

Gray, John C. "Remarks on New England Agriculture," *Essays Agricultural and Literary.* Boston, 1856.

Hough, Franklin B. *Papers Relative to Pemaquid.* Albany, N.Y., 1856. Excerpts from colonial documents.

Jenesse, John S. *The Isles of Shoals.* Boston, 1873. The unexpurgated history of the Isles.

Josselyn, John. *An Account of Two Voyages to New England.* London, 1675. Reprinted in *Massachusetts Historical Collections,* 3d ser., vol. 3 (1833): 211.

Kittredge, George Lyman. *Witchcraft in Old and New England.* New York, 1928. Reprint, New York, 1956.

Leach, Douglas E. *The Northern Colonial Frontier, 1607–1763.* New York, 1966.

McElroy, John W. "Seafaring in Seventeenth-Century New England," *The New England Quarterly* 8, no. 3 (Sept. 1935): 331.

McManis, Douglas R. *Colonial New England: A Historical Geography.* New York, 1975. An excellent overview.

Mather, Cotton. *The Fishermans Calling: A Brief Essay to Serve the Great Interests of Religion among our Fisher-men.* Boston, 1712. Sermon.

Mathews, Lois K. *The Expansion of New England.* Boston, 1909. About movements of the New England population.

Morton, Nathaniel. *New England's Memorial.* Cambridge, Mass., 1669. Reprint, New York, 1937.

Pond, William. "Letter, William Pond to Son, the First Winter in the Bay Colony," *Massachusetts Historical Society Proceedings,* 2nd ser., vol. 8 (1894): 471.

Sewall, Rufus K. *Ancient Dominions of Maine.* Bath, Maine, 1859.

Sylvester, Herbert M. *Indian Wars of New England.* 3 vols. Boston, 1910. *A True Relation of the Estate of New-England as it was presented to His Matie.* (From three copies of a manuscript written about 1634 found in the British Museum, and transcribed by Henry F. Waters, A.M. With notes by Charles F. Banks, M.D., 1886). Boston. Reprinted from the *New England Historical and Genealogical Register* (Jan. 1886).

Vaughan, Alden T. *New England Frontier: Puritans and Indians, 1620–1675.* Boston, 1965.

Wood, William. *New England's Prospect.* London, 1634.

Chapter 6

Albion, Robert G. *Forests and Sea Power: The Timber Problem of the Royal Navy.* Cambridge, Mass., 1926.

Arnold, Samuel Greene. *History of the State of Rhode Island and Providence Plantations . . . 1636–1790.* Providence, R.I., 1860.

Bartlett, J. R. "Pirates at Block Island," *Historical Magazine,* 2nd ser., vol. 7 (1870).

Bliss, William R. *Quaint Nantucket.* Boston, 1896.

Bridenbaugh, Carl. *Fat Mutton and Liberty of Conscience: Society in Rhode Island, 1636–1690.* Providence, R.I., 1974.

——. *Cities in the Wilderness . . . 1625–1742.* New York, 1955. The classic work on the colonial cities.

Bushnell, Edmund. *The Compleat Ship-Wright . . .* 8th ed. London, 1716. This edition was addresssed specifically to shipbuilders of Virginia and New England.

Child, Sir Joshua. *A New Discourse on Trade.* London, 1694.

Dow, George F., and John H. Edmonds. *Pirates of the New England Coast, 1630–1730.* Salem, 1923.

Drake, Samuel G. *The History and Antiquities of the City of Boston, 1630–1770.* 2 vols. Boston, 1854, 1856.

Gardner, William E. *The Coffin Saga.* Cambridge, Mass., 1949.

——. *Three Bricks and Three Brothers.* Boston, 1945.

Goldenberg, Joseph A. *Shipbuilding in Colonial America.* Charlottesville, Va., 1976.

Hamilton, Alexander. *Gentleman's Progress: The Itinerarium of Dr. Alexander Hamilton, 1744,* ed. Carl Bridenbaugh. Chapel Hill, N.C., 1948. Diary of an urbane southern physician's tour north. Visited Connecticut, Rhode Island, Massachusetts, towns in New Hampshire and Maine.

Jones, Rufus M. *The Quakers in the American Colonies.* London, 1911.

Mather, Cotton. *Magnalia Christi Americana . . .* London, 1702.

Mitchell, John. *The Present State of Great Britain and North America.* London, 1767.

Molloy, Charles. *De jure maritimo et navali; or, A Treatise of Affaires Maritime and of Commerce.* London, 1676. Maritime law. Interesting information on pirates and wreckers.

Starbuck, Alexander. *History of the American Whale Fishery . . . to 1876.* Washington, D.C., 1876.

Weeden, William B. *Early Rhode Island.* New York, 1910.

Winship, George P., ed. *Boston in 1682 and 1699.* Providence, R.I., 1905. Reprint of two uncomplimentary colonial reports.

Winthrop, John. *The History of New England, 1630–1649.* Edited by James Savage. 2 vols. Boston, 1853. Journal of the governor of the Massachusetts Bay Colony (1629–1640).

Chapter 7

Anonymous. "Smuggling in Maine During the War of 1812," *Bangor Historical Magazine* 3, no. 11 (May 1888): 201.

Bernard, John. *Retrospections of America, 1797–1811.* New York, 1887.

Brown, Ralph H. *Mirror for Americans.* New York, 1943.

Cousins, Frank, and Phil Riley. *Wood Carver of Salem: Samuel McIntyre, His Life and Work.* Boston, 1916.

Dexter, Timothy. *A Pickle for the Knowing Ones: Or, Plain Truths in a Homespun Dress.* Newburyport, Mass., 1802.

Forbes, John D. "Boston Smuggling, 1807–1815," *The American Neptune* 10, no. 2 (Apr. 1950): 144.

Hingham, Robin D. S. "The Port of Boston and the Embargo of 1807–1809," *The American Neptune* 16, no. 3 (July 1956): 189.

Hulton, Anne. *Letters of a Loyalist Lady . . .* Cambridge, Mass., 1927.

Kendall, Edward A. *Travels through the Northern Part of the United States in . . . 1807–8.* 3 vols. New York, 1809.

Kilby, W. H. *Eastport and Passamaquoddy.* Eastport, Maine, 1888. Reprints some scarce early nineteenth-century histories.

McColley, Robert, ed. *Federalists, Republicans, and Foreign Entanglements, 1789–1815.* Englewood Cliffs, N.J., 1969. An anthology.

Manning, Lt. E. "Letters from Eastport, 1814," *Bangor Historical Magazine* 3 (1888): 200.

Marquand, John P. *Federalist Newburyport. Or Can Historical Fiction Remove a Fly from Amber?* Newcomen Society. Princeton, 1952. Marquand is the author of two books on Timothy Dexter and novels about Massachusetts aristocrats.

Mather, Frederick G. *The Refugees of 1776 from Long Island to Connecticut.* Albany, N.Y., 1913.

Phillips, James D. *Salem and the Indies.* Boston, 1947.

——. *Salem in the Eighteenth Century.* Boston, 1937.

——. *Salem in the Seventeenth Century.* Boston, 1933.

"Putnam, Eleanor" [Harriet L. Bates]. *Old Salem.* Edited by Arlo Bates. Boston and New York, 1886.

Simpkins, John. "A Topographical Description of Brewster in the County of Barnstable, January, 1806," *Massachusetts Historical Collections* 10 (1809): 74.

Vaughan, Alden T., ed. *Chronicles of the American Revolution.* New York, 1965.

Verrill, A. Hyatt. *Smugglers and Smuggling.* New York, 1924.

Chapter 8

Aldrich, Thomas Bailey. *An Old Town by the Sea.* Boston, 1893. Childhood memories of Portsmouth, N.H.

——. *The Story of a Bad Boy.* Boston, 1870.

Anonymous. *Selections from the Court Reports originally published in the Boston Morning Post, from 1834 to 1837. Arranged and revised by the Reporter of the Post.* Boston, 1837. Sailors, Irish, Blacks, dandies, and Brahmins—as they appeared before His Honor the judge on the morning after.

Ashley, Clifford W. *The Yankee Whaler.* New York, 1942. A definitive classic. Also includes otherwise unknown artwork of whaling life and industry.

Batchelder, Eugene. *A Romance of the Sea Serpent.* Cambridge, Mass., 1849. Burlesque verse.

Baxter, Sylvester. "Howells's Boston," *The New England Magazine,* n.s., vol. 9, no. 2 (Oct. 1893): 129. Essay with excerpts from many works by William Dean Howells.

Church, Albert C. "The Padanarum Salt Works," *The New England Magazine* 16, no. 6 (Dec. 1909): 489.

Cummings, R. O. *American Ice Harvests . . . 1800–1918.* Berkeley, Calif., 1949.

Everson, Jennie G. *Tidewater Ice Industry of the Kennebec River.* Freeport, Maine, 1970. Maine ice industry.

Grattan, Thomas C. *Civilized America.* 2 vols. London, 1859. Journal of a British consul in Boston.

Hall, Henry. *The Ice Industry of the United States,* [10th Census, 1880]. Washington, D.C., 1888.

Hohman, Elmo P. *The American Whaleman: A Study of Life and Labor in the Whaling Industry.* New York, 1928. An excellent study of whaling's darker side.

Huevelmans, Bernard. *In the Wake of the Sea Serpents.* New York, 1968. Exhaustive work. Extensive bibliography, chronology of sightings, etc.

"Martingale, Hawser" [John S. Sleeper]. *Tales of the Ocean, and Essays for the Forecastle: containing Matters and Incidents Humorous, Pathetic, Romantic, and Sentimental . . .* Boston, 1842. Collected articles by a Boston newspaperman.

Melville, Herman. *Moby Dick.* New York, 1851. The best of the modern editions is that published by Random House in 1930 with illustrations by Rockwell Kent, which was reissued in 1982.

Nordhoff, Charles. *The Merchant Vessel.* Cincinnati, 1856. Contains portions on Land Sharks.

Stackpole, Edouard A. *The Sea Hunters. The New England Whalemen During Two Centuries, 1635–1835.* Philadelphia, 1953.

Tocque, Philip. *A Peep at Uncle Sam's Farm.* Boston, 1851. Contains a portion on Boston's ice trade.

Cogswell, Rev. Jonathan. "A Topographical and Historical Sketch of Saco, County of York, District of Maine, August, 1815," *Massachusetts Historical Collections,* 2nd ser., vol. 4 (1816): 184.

Currier, John J. *Historical Sketch of Shipbuilding on the Merrimack River.* Newburyport, Mass., 1877.

Eskew, Garnett L. *Cradle of Ships.* New York, 1958. About the Bath Iron Works.

Fairfield, Roy P. *Sands, Spindles and Steeples.* Portland, Maine. 1956. History of Saco, Maine.

Hall, Henry. *Report on the Ship-Building Industry of the United States.* Washington, D.C., 1884.

Hansen, Marcus. "The Second Colonization of New England," *The New England Quarterly* 2 (1929): 539. About nineteenth-century Irish immigrants.

Kelly, Roy W., and Frederick J. Allen. *The Shipbuilding Industry.* Boston, 1918.

Kirkland, Edward C. *Men, Cities and Transportation . . . New England . . . 1820–1900.* Cambridge, Mass., 1948.

Lincoln, Jonathan Thayer. *The City of the Dinner-Pail.* Boston and New York, 1909. About Fall River, with some portions of Newport.

Lubbock, Alfred B. *The Down Easters.* Boston, 1929. Maine cargo vessels after 1860.

McKay, Richard C. *Some Famous Ships and Their Builder, Donald McKay.* New York, 1928.

Massachusetts Bureau of Statistics and Labor. *Maine. 1st and 2nd Annual Reports of Maine Department of Industrial Statistics, 1873–1883.* Boston, 1883.

Rich, George A. "The Cotton Industry in New England," *The New England Magazine,* n.s., vol. 3 (1890): 167.

Snow, Ralph L. "Percy and Small Shipyard," *Maine History News* 9 (Apr. 1974): 11.

Thompson, Margaret J. *Captain Nathaniel Lord Thompson of Kennebunkport, Maine, and the Ships He Built, 1811–1889.* Boston, 1937.

Wasson, George S. *Sailing Days on the Penobscot.* Salem, 1932.

Wells, Walter. *The Waterpower of Maine.* Augusta, Maine, 1869.

Whitman, William. *The Future of Cotton Manufacturing in New Bedford.* New Bedford, Mass., 1907.

Yorke, Dane. *The Men and Times of Pepperell.* [Pepperell, Maine], 1945.

Young, T. M. *The American Cotton Industry: A Study of Work and Workers contributed to the* Manchester Guardian. New York, 1903. A British reporter's tour of American mills.

Chapter 9

Baker, William A. *A Maritime History of Bath, Maine, and the Kennebec River Region.* 2 vols. Bath, Maine, 1973. The complete modern study.

Bishop, J. Leander. *History of American Manufactures from 1608 to 1860.* Philadelphia, 1864. The classic reference.

Burgy, J. Herbert. *The New England Cotton Textile Industry: A Study in Industrial Geography.* Baltimore, Md., 1932.

Cheney, Robert. "Industries Allied to Shipbuilding in Newburyport," *The American Neptune* 17, no. 2 (Apr. 1967): 114.

Clark, Arthur H. *The Clipper Ship Era.* New York, 1910.

Chapter 10

Arthur, Stanley M. "The Old Boston Post Road," *Scribner's Magazine* 44 (Nov. 1908): 512. Steamers in Long Island Sound before 1850.

Berry, Robert E. *Yankee Stargazer: The Life of Nathaniel Bowditch.* New York. 1941.

Campbell, John F. *History and Bibliography of* The New American Practical Navigator *and* The American Coast Pilot. Salem, 1964.

Dayton, Fred E. *Steamboat Days.* New York, 1939.

Gardner, Arthur H. *Wrecks around Nantucket.* Nantucket, 1915.

Hamilton, Thomas. *Men and Manners in America.* Philadelphia, 1833.

Holland, Francis R., Jr. *America's Lighthouses: Their Illustrated History since 1716.* Brattleboro, Vt., 1972.

Howe, Mark A. DeWolfe. *The Humane Society of Massachusetts, 1785–1916.* Boston, 1918. Lifesaving stations.

Johnson, William W. "Lifesaving Service of the United States," *The New England Magazine* 8 (1890): 134.

Kittredge, Henry C. *Mooncussers of Cape Cod.* Boston, 1937.

Kobbé, Gustav. "Heroes of Peace: Volunteer Life-Savers," *The Century Magazine* 58, no. 2 (June 1899): 210.

Lewis, E. R. *Seacoast Fortifications of the United States: An Introductory History.* Washington, D.C., 1970.

McAdam, Roger W. *The Old Fall River Line.* Brattleboro, Vt., 1937. McAdam wrote other volumes on New England steamboats as well.

MacKinnon, Capt. L. B., R.N. *Atlantic and Transatlantic Sketches Afloat and Ashore.* New York, 1852. He inspected navy yards.

Morrison, John H. *History of American Steam Navigation.* New York, 1903. Reprint, New York, 1958. Comprehensive work on steamboats and nineteenth-century navigational aids.

Munroe, Kirk. "From Light to Light," *Scribner's Magazine* 20, no. 4 (Oct. 1896): 460. A voyage on the vessel restocking the Atlantic coast lighthouses.

Nordhoff, Charles. "Lighthouses of the United States," *Harper's New Monthly Magazine* 48 (Mar. 1874): 134.

Parker, Lt. W. J. L. *The Great Coal Schooners of New England, 1870–1909.* Mystic, Conn., 1948.

Quinn, William P. *Shipwrecks around Cape Cod.* Orleans, Mass., 1973.

———. *Shipwrecks around New England.* Orleans, Mass., 1979.

"The Shipwrecked Coaster," *The Token and Atlantic Souvenir: An Offering for Christmas and New Year.* Boston, 1833. An eyewitness account of a wreck off Sandwich, Massachusetts.

Snow, Edgar R. *Famous Lighthouses of New England.* Boston, 1945.

Society of Naval Architects and Marine Engineers. *Historical Transactions 1893–1943.* New York, 1945. Essays by the designers of navy yards, large vessels, and yachts. Excellent source of information.

Sterling, Robert T. *Lighthouses of the Maine Coast and the Men Who Keep Them.* Brattleboro, Vt., 1935.

Wisser, Maj. John P. *The Tactics of Coastal Defense.* Kansas City, Mo., 1918. Extensive bibliography.

Wraight, A. J., and E. B. Roberts. *The Coast and Geodetic Survey 1807–1956: 150 Years of History.* New York, 1957.

Wroth, Lawrence C. *The Way of a Ship . . . Literature of Navigation Science.* Portland, Maine, 1937.

Chapter 11

Beers, J. B. and Co. *Map of the State of Connecticut.* New York, 1886. Marks out oyster beds in Long Island Sound.

Benjamin, S. G. W. "Gloucester and Cape Ann," *Harper's Monthly Magazine* 51, no. 204 (Sept. 1875): 465.

Bishop, W. H. "Fish and Men on the Maine Islands," *Harper's Monthly Magazine* 61 (Aug. 1880): 336. A well-written and illustrated account of a tour.

Chapman, Edward M. *New England Village Life.* Cambridge, Mass., 1937. Classic essays on the rustic life of the early twentieth-century Connecticut shore.

Crosby, Katherine. *Blue-Water Men and Other Cape Codders.* New York, 1946.

"Diggs, Jeremiah" [Josef Berger]. *In Great Waters. The Story of the Portuguese Fishermen . . .* New York, 1941.

Dodge, Ernest. *Morning Was Starlight: My Maine Boyhood.* Chester, Conn., 1980.

Farrow, Capt. John P. *The Romantic Story of David Robertson, among the Islands, off and on the Coast of Maine.* Belfast, Maine, 1898. A nineteenth-century Maine fisherman.

Goode, George B. [U. S. Commission of Fish and Fisheries.] *The Fisheries and Fishery Industry of the United States,* 2 vols. Washington, D.C., 1887. A treasury of information. One volume is entirely composed of plates—a fascinating collection of shore illustrations.

Innis, H. A. *The Cod Fisheries.* New Haven, 1940.

Kipling, Rudyard. *Captains Courageous.* London, New York, 1897. Various reprints.

Kochiss, John M. *Oystering from New York to Boston.* Middletown, Conn., 1974. The comprehensive work on the subject.

McFarland, Raymond. *A History of New England Fisheries.* New York, 1911. The basic text.

———. *The Masts of Gloucester: Recollections of a Fisherman.* New York, 1937.

Nordhoff, Charles. *Whaling and Fishing.* Cincinnati, 1856. A vividly written work.

Pierce, Wesley G. *Going Fishin' . . .* Salem, 1934.

Proctor, George H. "An American Fishing Port," *Lippincott's Magazine* 1 (1868): 497. Gloucester.

Prudden, T. M. *About Lobsters.* Rev. ed. Freeport, Maine, 1973. The standard text on the subject. Full bibliography.

Rich, George A. "The New England Fisheries," *The New England Magazine,* n. s., vol. 10, no. 2 (Apr. 1894).

Smith, Joseph W. *Gleanings from the Sea.* Andover, Mass., 1887. About Biddeford Pool, Maine.

Thompson, Winfield M. "The Passing of the New England Fisherman," *The New England Magazine* 19 (Feb. 1896): 675.

Wallace, John. *Village Down East.* Brattleboro, Vt., 1943. Concerns Lincolnville, Maine.

Wasson, George S. *Cap'n Simeon's Store.* Boston, 1903. Maine fishermen.

Chapter 12

Alexander, Lewis M. "The Impact of Tourism on the Economy of Cape Cod, Massachusetts," *Economic Geography* 29 (1953): 320. Era from 1920 to 1950.

Amory, Cleveland. *The Last Resorts*. New York, 1948. Dated but fascinating.

Bliss, William R. *September Days on Nantucket*. Boston, 1902.

Botsford, Amelia H. "Ropes of Sand," *The New England Magazine*, n.s., vol. 24, no. 1 (Mar. 1901): 3. Revegetating the outer Cape Cod.

Brigham, Albert P. *Cape Cod and the Old Colony*. New York, 1920.

———. "Cape Cod and the Old Colony," *The Geographical Review* 10, no. 1 (July 1920): 7.

Burling, Francis P. *The Birth of the Cape Cod National Seashore*. Plymouth, Mass., 1978.

Carter, Robert. *A Summer Cruise on the Coast of New England*. Boston, 1864. Reprint, Somersworth, N.H., 1977. A classic account.

Commonwealth of Massachusetts, Department of Labor and Industries. *Population and Resources of Cape Cod*. Boston, 1922.

Crosby, Everett U. *Nantucket's Changing Prosperity, Future Probabilities*. Nantucket, 1939. Reprinted in Crosby's *95% Perfect*. Nantucket, 1953.

Curtis, George W. *Lotus Eating*. New York, 1852. Tour of Nahant, Newport, and other summer resorts.

Faught, Millard. *Falmouth, Massachusetts: Problems of a Resort Community*. New York, 1945. Excellent analytical account.

McCue, James. *Joe Lincoln of Cape Cod*. Silver Lake, Mass., 1949. The story of the Cape's most famous chronicler.

Mitchell, Edward Valentine. *Maine Summer*. New York, 1939.

Moffett, Ross. *Art in Narrow Streets, the First Thirty-Three Years of the Provincetown Art Association*. Falmouth, Mass., 1964.

Morris, Gouverneur. "Newport the Maligned," *Everybody's Magazine* (Sept. 1908): 311.

Murray, Hon. Amelia M. *Letters from the United States, Cuba and Canada*. 2 vols. London, 1856.

O'Gorman, James F. *This Other Gloucester*. Boston, 1976. Artists.

Seckler, Dorothy G. *Provincetown Painters, 1890s–1970s*. Syracuse, 1977.

Some Account of the Vampires of Onset, Massachusetts. Boston, New England News Co., 1892. Debunking a spiritualist camp.

Tarbell, Arthur W. *Cape Cod Ahoy!* Boston, 1932.

———. *I Retire to Cape Cod*. New York, 1944.

Van Rensselaer, Mrs. John K. *Newport: Our Social Capital*. Philadelphia, 1905.

Waite, Otis F. R. *Guide Book for the Eastern Coast of New England*. Boston, 1871.

Wilder, Elizabeth F., ed. *Maine and Its Role in American Art*. New York, 1963.

Warner, Charles Dudley. *Their Pilgrimage*. New York, 1887. A tour of "watering spots," including Newport and Bar Harbor.

Warner, Frances L. *Pilgrim Trails*. Boston, 1921. Tourism ca. 1920.

Wright, John K. "A Method of Mapping Densities of Population: with Cape Cod as an Example," *The Geographical Review* 26 (1936): 103.

Chapter 13

Ackerman, Edward A. *New England's Fishing Industry*. Chicago, 1941.

Allen, Everett S. *A Wind to Shake the World: The Story of the 1938 Hurricane*. Boston, 1976.

American Geographical Society of New York. *New England's Prospect*. New York, 1933.

Barnes, Robert H. *United States Submarines*. New Haven, 1944.

Boeri, David. *Tell It Good-Bye, Kiddo*. Camden, Maine, 1976. Requiem for the fishing industry.

Bowdoin College, Center for Resource Studies. *A Symposium: The Maine Coast, Prospects and Perspectives*. Brunswick, Maine, 1967. How to keep tourism and still not destroy the region.

Carse, Robert. *Rum Row*. New York, 1959. Prohibition rumrunning.

Chase, Mary Ellen. *Fishing Fleets of New England*. Boston, 1961.

Corbett, S. *The Sea Fox*. New York, 1956. A Cape Cod rumrunner.

Federal Writers' Project. *New England Hurricane*. Boston, 1938. See also the many local picture books of hurricane damage.

Kinnard, William N., Jr., ed. *The New England Region: Problems of a Mature Economy*. Storrs, Conn., 1968.

Morris, Richard K. *John P. Holland*. Annapolis, Md., 1966.

Rosenfeld, Morris. *The Story of American Yachting*. New York, 1958.

Spectorsky, A. C. *The Exurbanites*. Philadelphia and New York, 1955. The classic study of New York City's elite commuter towns, including those of Fairfield County.

Thompson, Ellery. *Draggerman's Haul: The Personal History of a Connecticut Fishing Captain*. New York, 1950.

U.S. Government, Office of Coastal Zone Management: The federal overseer of individual state Coastal Area Management Programs. Consult each state's "CAM" office and its publications for latest evaluation of coastal ecology and future goals.

Waters, Harold. *Smugglers of Spirits*. New York, 1971. Coast Guard vs. rumrunners.

Books with illustrations pertaining to the New England shore

(In addition to those works already listed)

Anonymous. *Pirates' Own Book*. Portland, Maine 1855. Reprint, Salem, Mass., 1924.

Arr, E. H. *New England Bygones*. Philadelphia, 1883. The greatly illustrated third edition.

Barber, John W. *The History and Antiquities of New England.* Hartford, 1856.

Berchen, William. *Maine.* Boston, 1973.

Bunting, William. *Portrait of a Port: Boston, 1852–1914.* Cambridge, Mass., 1971. The photographs of Nathaniel Stebbins.

Brewington, M. V. and Dorothy. *The Marine Paintings and Drawings in the Peabody Museum.* Salem, 1968.

Bryant, William C. *Picturesque America.* 2 vols. New York, 1872.

Chamberlain, Samuel. *Ever New England, The New England Scene,* and many other books of photographs taken between 1930s and 1960s.

Church, Albert C. *American Fishermen.* New York, 1940. Vessels.

———. *Whale Ships and Whaling.* New York, 1938.

Crosby, Everett U. *Eastman Johnson at Nantucket.* Nantucket, 1944.

Czestochowski, Joseph. *94 Prints by Childe Hassam.* New York, 1970.

Davidson, Marshall B. *The American Heritage History of the Artists' America.* New York, 1973.

Dietz, Lew. *Night Train at Wiscasset Station.* Garden City, N.Y., 1977. Photographs by Kosti Ruohomaa.

Dow, George F., and John Robinson. *The Sailing Ships of New England, 1607–1907.* 3 vols. Salem, Mass., 1922–1928.

Gardner, Albert T. E. *Winslow Homer.* New York, 1961.

Gleason, Herbert W. *Thoreau's Cape Cod.* Princeton, 1974. Photographs taken ca. 1900–1920.

Hamilton, Sinclair. *Early American Book Illustrators and Wood Engravings, 1670–1870.* Princeton, 1958.

Howells, John M. *Architectural Heritage of the Merrimack.* New York, 1941.

———. *Architectural Heritage of the Piscataqua.* New York, 1937.

Johnson, Merle, comp. *Howard Pyle's Book of the American Spirit.* New York, 1923.

M. & M. Karolik Collection of American Paintings, 1815 to 1865. Cambridge, Mass., 1949. Paintings in the Museum of Fine Arts, Boston.

M. & M. Karolik Collection of American Watercolors and Drawings, 1800–1875. 2 vols. Boston, 1962.

Lancaster, Clay. *Nantucket in the Nineteenth Century.* New York, 1979.

Meyerowitz, Joel. *Cape Light.* Boston, 1978.

Norton, Bettina A. *Edwin Whitfield: Nineteenth-Century North American Scenery.* Barre, Mass., 1977.

Porter, Eliot. *Summer Island: Penobscot Country.* San Francisco, 1966.

Reilly, Elizabeth C. *A Dictionary of Colonial American Printers' Ornaments and Illustrations.* Worcester, Mass., 1975.

Rinhart, Floyd and Marion. *Summertime: Photographs of Americans at Play, 1850–1900.* New York, 1978.

Springfield Museum of Fine Arts. *John Sloan: The Gloucester Years.* Springfield, Mass., 1980.

Stark, James. *Antique Views of ye Towne of Boston.* Boston, 1901.

Stebbins, Theodore E., Jr. *Martin Johnson Heade.* College Park, Md., 1969.

Thaxter, Celia L. *An Island Garden.* Boston, 1894. Illustrations in color by Childe Hassam.

Thoreau, Henry D. *Cape Cod: With Illustrations from Sketches in Colors by Amelia M. Watson.* 2 vols. Boston and New York, 1899. The most beautiful of the illustrated editions of *Cape Cod.*

Tice, George. *Seacoast Maine: People and Places.* New York, 1973.

University of Connecticut, William Benton Museum of Art. *Connecticut and American Impressionism: A Cooperative Exhibition.* Storrs, Conn., 1980.

White, C. R. *By the Sea.* Portland, Maine, 1889.

Whitehill, Walter M. *Massachusetts.* New York, 1976.

———. *Prints, Maps and Drawings, 1677–1822: A Massachusetts Historical Society Picture Book.* Boston, 1957.

Williams, Hermann W., Jr. *Mirror to the American Past: A Survey of American Genre Painting, 1750–1900.* Boston, 1973.

Wilmerding, John. *American Light: The Luminist Movement, 1850–1875.* New York, 1980. The most complete study of these painters, most of whom worked along the New England shore. Excellent bibliography arranged alphabetically by artist.

———. *A History of American Marine Painting.* Boston, 1968.

Worth, Lawrence C., and Marian W. Adams. *American Woodcuts and Engravings.* Providence, R.I., 1940.

The New England shore in literature

There have been innumerable writers whose works have vividly evoked the character of this region. The following is a list of the more readily available volumes. For the enthusiast, also recommended are the many now-forgotten nineteenth-century authors such as Benjamin Barker, Alice Brown, Hezekiah Butterworth, Sylvanus Cobb, John W. DeForest, Jeanette Hart, Joseph Holt Ingraham, Charles P. Ilsley, Elijah Kellogg, John Neal, Maria Pool, Martha Russell, Seba Smith, Alonzo Tripp, Augusta Watson, Esther Wheeler, and Catherine Williams.

Anonymous. *Afloat and Ashore, or, A Sailor's Life.* Boston, 1848.

Averill, Charles E. *The Pirates of Cape Ann; or, The Freebooter's Foe.* Boston, 1848.

Beck, Horace P. *The Folklore of Maine.* Philadelphia and New York, 1957. Both history and fiction.

Botkin, B. A., ed. *A Treasury of New England Folklore.* New York, 1947.

Brooks, Noah. *Tales of the Maine Coast.* New York, 1894.

Chase, Mary Ellen. *Silas Crockett.* New York, 1935. Social history of eastern coastal Maine, based on actual records.

Drake, Samuel A. *A Book of New England Legends and Folk Lore.* Boston, 1884.

Elliot, Maude H. *A Newport Aquarelle.* Boston, 1883.

Forbes, Esther. *The Running of the Tide.* Boston, 1948. Salem ca. 1800.

Garside, Edward B. *Cranberry Red.* Boston, 1938.

Greene, Sarah P. [McLean]. *Cape Cod Folks: A Novel.* Boston, 1881.

Hale, Edward Everett. *Christmas in Narragansett.* New York, 1884.

Harrison, Constance. *Bar Harbor Days.* New York, 1887.

Hart, Joseph C. *Miriam Coffin: or, the Whale Fisherman: a Tale.* New York, 1834. Nantucket's "Aunt" Keziah Coffin.

Hawthorne, Nathaniel. *The House of Seven Gables.* Boston, 1851.

———. *The Scarlet Letter.* Boston, 1850. See also his short stories.

Hazard, Thomas R. *The Jonny-Cake Letters . . . by Shepherd Tom.* Providence, Later reprinted in the now-standard illustrated edition: Hazard, Rowland Gibson, ed., *The Jonny Cake Papers of "Shepherd Tom," . . . by Thomas Robinson Hazard.* Boston, 1915. The classic stories from Rhode Island's South County.

Higginson, Thomas Wentworth. *Malbone: An Oldport Romance.* Boston, 1869. Newport locale.

———, ed. *Thalatta: A Book for the Sea-Side.* Boston, 1853. Collected poems about oceans and shores.

Howells, William Dean *A Woman's Reason. A Novel.* Boston, 1883. One of Howells's many novels about Victorian Boston.

Jewett, Sarah Orne. *The Country of the Pointed Firs and Other Stories.* 1896. Various reprints. A Maine coast classic.

Lincoln, Joseph C. *Cape Cod Yesterdays.* Reprint (with illustrations). Silver Lake, Mass., 1946. Lincoln was Cape Cod's most illustrious chronicler. He wrote dozens of novels about Cape life, active ca. 1900–1940.

Nordhoff, Charles. *Cape Cod and All along Shore.* New York, 1868.

Reynolds, J. *Peter Gott, the Cape Ann Fisherman.* Boston, 1856. Highly recommended.

Roberts, Kenneth. *Arundel, Northwest Passage,* and other novels.

Sigourney, Lydia H. *Sketch of Connecticut, Forty Years Since.* Hartford, 1824. Norwich and other shore locales.

Silliman, Augustus E. *A Gallop among American Scenery.* New York, 1843.

Stoddard, Elizabeth D. B. *The Morgessons.* New York, 1862. Salem ca. 1830.

Stowe, Harriet Beecher. "A Student's Sea Story," *The Atlantic Monthly* 43, no. 255 (Jan. 1879): 100. Passage on a coaster from Maine to Boston.

———. *The Pearl of Orr's Island.* Boston, 1852. A classic.

Trillin, Calvin. *Runestruck.* Boston, 1977. Two gas-jockeys discover a Viking runestone in a New England town. The characters and humor are all too accurate.

"Triton, Willie" [Alonzo Tripp]. *The Fisher Boy.* Boston, 1856. Commercial fishing.

Untermeyer, Louis, ed. *An Anthology of New England Poets.* New York, 1948.

Vonnegurt, Kurt, Jr. *Welcome to the Monkey House.* New York, 1970. A collection of his early short stories. Many reflect the Cape Cod locale where he lived at this time.

Watson, Augusta. *The Old Harbor Town.* New York, 1892. New London locale.

Sources of Illustrations

All illustrations not cited here are photographs taken by the author. Illustrations reproduced courtesy of the following sources:

Boston Anthenaeum: D. C. Fabrionus (1864), 14; 23; 51; Certificate of Enlistment with copper engraving by T. Johnston (1765), 60; Photograph by F .Cousins from *Salem Book* (1908), 93; 96; 110; 115; 117 (both ills.); 118; 143; 167 (both ills.); 168. Bronson Museum, Massachusetts Archaeological Society, Attleboro, Mass.: 14. Connecticut Historical Society: 83; 85; 133; Lithograph by D. W. Kellogg & Co., published by Morgan & Ferre, 139; 140; 163; Photograph by R. S. Delamater, 177. The Connecticut River Foundation: (W. F. R. photo), 98. Currier Gallery of Art, Manchester, N.H.: 10–11. Everson, Eleanor L., Dresden, Maine: 103. Fogg Art Museum, Harvard University: Anonymous gift, 153. Harborview Restaurant, Stonington Conn.: Photograph by Frank J. Raymond, 188. Houghton Library, Harvard University: 17; 25. Library of Congress: 61; 78; 91; 120–121; Courtesy Architect of the Capitol, 147. Maine Maritime Museum: 128–29; Photograph by J. C. Higgins, 130; Photograph by J. C. Higgins, 131. Marine Museum, Fall River, Mass.: 141. Metropolitan Museum of Art: Gift of George A. Hearn, 1909 (09.72.6), 52; Gift of Mrs. Harold G. Henderson, 1976 (1976.106.1), 143. Museum of Art, Rhode Island School of Design: Gift of Mr. Robert Winthrop, 18. Museum of Fine Arts, Boston, Mass.: M. and M. Karolik Collection, 41; M. and M. Karolik Collection, 43. Mystic Seaport Museum, Inc., Mystic, Conn.: 126; W. H. Tripp Collection, 123; Photograph by Charles Cushing, 154; Hudson Collection, 157; 163. Nantucket Historical Association: 70; Photograph by Josiah Freeman, 74; 75; 146. New-York Historical Society, New York, N.Y.: Bella C. Landauer Collection, 138. New York Public Library: Spencer Collection, Astor, Lenox and Tilden Foundations, 80–81. Norton Gallery and School of Art, West Palm Beach, Fla.: Photograph by Lee Brian, 151. Ocean House Hotel, Watch Hill, R.I.: (W. F. R. photo), 176. Old Dartmouth Historical Society, New Bedford, Mass.: 24; 107. Peabody Museum of Salem, Mass.: Photograph by M. W. Sexton, 88–89. Pioneer Village, Salem, Mass.: Photograph by Paul. J. Weber, 35. Plimoth Plantation, Plymouth, Mass.: (W. F. R. photo), 32; (W. F. R. photo), 34; (W. F. R. photo), color. Portland Camera Club: Photograph by J. H. Samson, copyright Portland Camera Club, 137. Preservation Society of Newport County: (W. F. R. photo), 169. Seamen's Bethel and Mariners' Home, New Bedford, Mass.: 106. Shelburne Museum, Shelburne, Vt.: 125. Submarine Force Library and Museum, Groton, Conn.: 134. U.S. Naval Academy Museum, Annapolis, Md.: Photograph by Robert Scott Wiles, 102. Yale University Art Gallery: Bequest of Christian A. Zabriskie, 160–61. Yale University Library: Benjamin Franklin Collection, 112.

Illustration sources:

Ashley, Clifford W., *The Yankee Whaler* (1926): 71. Ashton, John, *The Devil in Britain and America* (1896): 47. *Ballou's Pictorial* (1855): 173. Barber, John W., *Historical Collections . . . Massachusetts* (1841): 165. Barber, John W., *The History and Antiquities of New England* (1840): 45. Blaney, Henry R., *Old Boston* (1896): 155. *The Book of Commerce by Land and Sea* (1837): 27; 97. Burke, Edmund, *An Impartial History of The War in America* (1782): 83. De Bry, Theodore, *Collectiones peregrinationum in Indiam Orientalem et Indiam Occidentale* (1634): 21. Des Barres, Joseph F. W., *American Neptune* (1784): 56–57. *Domestic History of the Learned Seals* (1860): 167. Drake, Samuel Adams, *New England Legends and Folklore* (1884): 12. *The Echo—with Other Poems* (1807): 108. Female Society . . . for Relief of British Negro Slaves, *Report* (1835): 68. Fiske, John, *The Beginnings of New England* (1898): 58. Folsom, George, *History of Saco and Biddeford* (1830): 117. Fox, Ebenezor, *The Adventures of Ebenezor Fox* (1838): 84. *Gleason's Pictorial* (1852): 178. Goode, George B., *The Fisheries and Fish Industry of the United States* (1887): 73; 107; 152; 156; 159; 162. Greene, Welcome A., *The Providence Plantations* (1886): 7. *Harper's Monthly*: (1860), 111; (1874), 53; (1882), 181; (1895), 135. *Harper's Weekly*: (18), 145. Howe, M. A. De Wolfe, *The Humane Society of Massachusetts* (1918): 148. Mathews, L. K. (after), *The Expansion of New England* (1909): 49. *Naval Chronicle*, vol. 32 (1814): 86. Nutting, Wallace, *Connecticut Beautiful* (1923): 39. *Port Folio* (1811): 76–77. Schlee, John (after), *The Atlantic Continental Shelf* (1973):

4. Sleeper, John S., *Tales of the Ocean* (1842): 110. Smith, John, *A Description of New England* (1616): 28. Thaxter, Celia, *An Island Garden* (1894): 182 (location of original artwork unknown). *Transactions of the American Philosophical Society* (1786): 51. Trumbull, John, *McFingal* (1795): 85. Van Rensselaer, Mrs. J. K., *Newport, Our Social Capital* (1905): 171. White, George S., *Memoir of Samuel Slater* (1836): 115. Winsor, Justin, *Memorial History of Boston* (1880–81): 57. Wood, William, *New England's Prospect* (1634): 36. *Yankee Notions:* (1856), 170; (1857), 172.

Index

Abnaki Indians, 22, 23, 48–49
Acadia National Park (Maine), 6, 189
Acushnet River, 104
Adams, Charles Francis, his *Founding of New England*, 56
Adams, John, 82
Agamenticus. *See* York
Aldrich, Thomas Bailey, 136, 164
Algonquian Indians, 13, 15
American Coast Pilot, The, 140–141
American Lighthouse Service, 142
America's Cup Race, 173
Ames, Nathaniel, 164
Androscoggin basin (Maine), 127
Androscoggin River, 126, 127
Anglicans, 33, 47
Appledore Island, New Hampshire, 182
Aptuxcet Trading Post (Bourne, Massachusetts), 113
"Archaic" Indians, 13
Arnold, Benedict, 86
Artists, 181–183
Ashley, Clifford, his *Stove Boat*, 106
Ashley, Edward, 45
Atlantic (steamship), 138
Atlantic Neptune (Des Barres), 56–57, 140–141
Atlas (square-rigger ship), 133
Augusta, Maine, ix, 116

Bachelder, J. B., 118
Back Bay (Boston, Massachusetts), 13
Bacon, Delia, 164
Bailey's Beach (Newport, Rhode Island), 172
"Banks, The," 154, 155. *See also* Georges Bank, Grand Banks, etc.
Barber, John Warner, 163
Bar Harbor, Maine, 169
Barnstable, Massachusetts, 44
Bath, Maine, 99
    shipbuilding in, 127–135
Bath Iron Works (Bath, Maine), 134
Beaches, 172, 177, 178–181, 186
Beacon Hill (Boston, Massachusetts), 81
"Beacon Rock" (Rhode Island), 62–63
Bega, 23
Belle of Oregon (ship), 130
Bellows, George, 183
Belmont, Augustus, 149
Bendall, Edward, 134
Benjamin, Asher, 131
Berkeley, Bishop, 64–65
Biard, Père Pierre, 13
Biddeford, Maine, 116, 118, 119
Biddeford Pool (Maine), 26, 175
Bierstadt, Albert, his *Gosnold at Cuttyhunk*, 24
Blacks, 108
    See also Slave trading

Blaeu, Willem Janszoon, 15
Blaxton, William, 33
Block, Adriaen, 25, 28
Block Island (Rhode Island), 12, 21, 67, 69, 99, 149, 175
Blue Hill, Maine, 189
Blunt, Edmund, 140–141, 142
Blunt, George William, 141, 142
Boston, Massachusetts, 25, 36, 42, 68, 81, 88, 110, 147, 187
    Alexander Hamilton on, 78
    business in, 50, 57–60
    colonial, 56–61
    foreign trade by, 88–89, 101
    ice trade in, 102, 103
    Indians in, 13, 15, 19
    manufacturing in, 116
    occupation of, 82–83
    shipbuilding in, 125–126
    tourism in, 166, 167
Boston Aquarial Gardens, 167
Boston Basin, 6
Boston Fish Pier, 154
Boston Harbor, 12, 19, 28, 29, 33, 42, 96, 102, 125, 173
Boston Light, 144
Bourne, Massachusetts, 113
Boxer (Royal Navy brig), 99
Bradford, William, 67
Bradstreet, Anne, 164
Branford, Connecticut, 67
Breakwater (Newport, Rhode Island), 170
Bridgeport, Connecticut, 134, 136
Bristol, Rhode Island, 68, 114
Brown, Moses, 114–115
Browns Banks, 8, 20
Brunswick, Maine, 116
Bucksport, Maine, 147
Bull, Dixy, 47
Bushnell, David, 98, 134
Bushnell, Edmund, 60
Buzzards Bay (Massachusetts), 7, 24, 104, 113, 122, 175, 186, 188
Byram, Connecticut, 184

Cabot, John, 20
Cadillac Mountain (Maine), 6
Cambridge, Massachusetts, 87, 102
Camden, Maine, 135
Camden Hills (Maine), 6
Campbell, Augusta Watson, 187
Campobello Island, 67, 96
Cape Ann, Massachusetts, 6, 9, 19, 34, 143, 150, 174, 189
Cape Cod, Massachusetts, 2, 6, 8, 20, 30, 85, 99, 102, 148, 186
    colonial, 69–79
    cranberry picking on, 161–162
    fishing on, 24, 25, 158, 163
    navigation off, 140, 142
    saltworks on, 112–113
    tourism on, 175–183
Cape Cod Bay, 6, 33, 34, 178
Cape Cod Canal, 122, 149

Cape Cod Folks (Greene), 164
Cape Cod National Seashore, 178
Cape Elizabeth, Maine, 34
Captains Courageous (Kipling), 156
Casino (Newport, Rhode Island), 172
Castine, Maine, 45, 86, 100, 102
Castle Island, 12
Cedar Swamp Brook, 25
Champlain, Samuel de, 16, 17, 19, 25
Chancellor Livingston (steamship), 137
Charles River (Massachusetts), 116
Chatham, Massachusetts, 25, 53, 146
Church, Frederic, 125
Churches, 65, 155
Church of Our Lady of the Good Voyage (Gloucester, Massachusetts), 155
"City of Palaces" (New Bedford, Massachusetts), 104
City of Worcester (steamship), 140
Clarke, James Freeman, 166
Clermont (steamship), 136
Cliff Walk (Newport, Rhode Island), 169
Clipper ships, 127
Coastal Plain, 6
Coasters Island (Rhode Island), 168
Coasting trade, 42
Cobb, Elijah, 87
Cobb, Sylvanus, 164
Coffin, Keziah, 79
Cohasset, Massachusetts, 142, 148
Connecticut:
    coast of, 9, 184–186, 188
    colonization of, 37–44
    fishing in, 158, 163
    Indians in, 15, 37, 39, 41–43
    shipbuilding in, 125, 134
    tourism in, 174–175, 176–177
Connecticut River, ix, 15, 41, 60, 125
Connecticut River Foundation, 98
Cooper, James Fenimore, 66
Cos Cob, Connecticut, 182–183
Cranberry picking, 161–163
Crocker Park (Marblehead, Massachusetts), 54
Cuffee, Paul, 108
Currier, Nathaniel:
    his *Flying Cloud*, 127
    his *Lexington*, 139
Currier and Ives, 139
Custom House (Salem, Massachusetts), 94, 101
Cutting, James Ambrose, 167
Cuttyhunk Island (Massachusetts), 24

Dakotah (ship), 133
Damariscotta, Maine, 16, 26
Damariscove, Maine, 26, 28, 34
Darien, Connecticut, 184
Dartmouth, Massachusetts, 104
Dauphine, La (ship), 21
Deer Isle, Maine, 189
Demuth, Charles, 183
Des Barres, Joseph-Frédéric Vallet, 56–57, 140–141
Dexter, Timothy, 91

McIntire Garrison House (York, Maine), 46
MacKay, Donald, 102, 127
Madison, Connecticut, 38–39
Magnalia Christi Americana (Mather), 30
Maine:
  coast of, 6, 189
  colonization of, 44–50
  exploration of, 22–24, 26–29
  fishing in, 157, 158, 161, 164–165
  ice trade in, 103
  Indians in, 15, 16, 17, 19, 22–24, 29, 45, 48–49, 159
  lighthouses in, 144–145
  manufacturing in, 116–119
  in Revolutionary War, 86
  shipbuilding in, 126–135
  tourism in, 169, 173, 175
  in War of 1812, 99–100
Malbone, Godfrey, 66
Manufacturing, 114–135
Marblehead, Massachusetts, 84, 87
  settlement of, 50, 53–55
Marble House (Newport, Rhode Island), 170–171
Marin, John, 183
Marquand, John P., 91
Martha's Vineyard, Massachusetts, 2, 4, 8, 24, 28, 69, 76, 159, 175, 179
Mason, John, 44
Massachusetts:
  coast of, 6, 8, 186–189
  colonization of, 30–35, 50, 53–55
  exploration of, 30–35, 50, 53–55
  fishing in, 150–158
  Indians in, 13, 14, 15, 24, 25, 29, 32, 72, 159
  lighthouses in, 142, 144
  manufacturing in, 116, 119–124
  resorts in, 166–168, 175–183
  saltworks in, 112–113
  shipbuilding in, 59, 60, 125–126
  whaling in, 69, 71–73, 102, 104–111
Massachusetts Bay, 6, 124, 143
  settlement of, 33–36
Massachusetts Bay Colony, 12, 56
Massachusetts Humane Society, 147
Mather, Cotton, 30, 50, 61, 62
Mather, Cotton, House (Boston, Massachusetts), 155, 164
Mathews, L. K., 49
Mayflower, 32, 72
Mayflower II, 30–31
Melville, Herman, ix, 102, 104, 105, 106, 108, 109, 111
Menemsha Indians, 159
Merrimac River (Massachusetts), 91, 125
Metcalf, Willard, 182
Middleton, Rhode Island, 62–63
Milford Haven, Massachusetts, 30
Milford Point, Connecticut, 163
Millennial Grove Camp Meeting Grounds (Massachusetts), 178

Mills, 115–124
Minot's Ledge (Massachusetts), 142, 144
Mitchell, Maria, 77
Moby Dick (Melville), ix, 102, 104, 105, 106, 108, 111
Monhegan Island (Maine), 26, 34, 157
Mooncussing, 145–146
Morgan, E. D., 63
Morison, Samuel Eliot, 103
Mount Desert Island (Maine), 26, 189
Museums, 93, 134, 148, 168
Mystic River (Connecticut), 60

Nahant, Massachusetts, 143, 159, 166–167
Nahant Hotel (Nahant, Massachusetts), 166, 168
Nantasket, Massachusetts, 50
Nantucket, Massachusetts, 2, 4, 8, 101, 104, 111, 170, 184
  colonial, 69–79
Nantucket Shoals, 8, 30, 142
Nantucket Sound, 25, 175, 178
Napatree Point (Westerly, Rhode Island), 188
Narragansett Bay (Rhode Island), 7, 16, 21, 23, 36, 41, 60, 62, 119, 122, 125, 140, 186
Narragansett Indians, 159
Narragansett Pier, 174
National Oceanic and Atmospheric Administration, 142
National Ocean Survey, 142
Nauset Indians, 25
Nautilus (submarine), 98, 134
Naval War College Museum (Rhode Island), 168
Navigational aids, 140–144
Neal, John, 164
Neck River (Connecticut), 38–39
Nena A. Rowland (oyster sloop), 162
New American Practical Navigator, 141
New Bedford, Massachusetts, 43, 75, 76, 186, 188
  manufacturing in, 119, 122–124
  whaling in, 102, 104–111
Newburyport, Massachusetts, 60, 88, 91, 101, 119
New Hampshire:
  colonization of, 50, 51–53
  Indians in, 15
New Haven, Connecticut, 163
New Haven Colony, 43
New London, Connecticut, 42, 67, 68, 73, 86, 98, 99, 140, 147, 187
New London Ship and Engine Company (Groton, Connecticut), 134
Newport, Rhode Island, 21, 86, 115, 145
  colonial, 62–69
  tourism in, 168–173
Newport Asylum, 168
Newport Bridge, 186
Newport Harbor, 62–63, 145, 186

Niantic Indians, 18
Ninigret II, 18
North River (Massachusetts), 60
Norumbega, 22–24
Norwich, Connecticut, 98, 116, 139
Nyack, Connecticut, 39

Oak Bluffs Camp Meeting Grounds (Martha's Vineyard, Massachusetts), 179
Ocean House (Newport, Rhode Island), 168–169, 176–177
Oldham, John, 42
Old Harbor Lifesaving Station (Cape Cod, Massachusetts), 148
Old Lyme, Connecticut, 7, 78, 125, 182
Old Post Road (Connecticut), 184
Old Saybrook, Connecticut, 67, 98
Old Town Mill (New London, Connecticut), 187
O'Neill, Eugene, 183
Otis, Joseph, 80
Oyster fishing, 163

Padanaram, Massachusetts, 113
Page House (Bath, Maine), 131
Palatine (ship), 12
Palatine Light, 12
Palmetto (whale ship), 121
Passamaquoddy Bay (Maine), 96
Passamaquoddy Indians, 159
Pawtucket Falls, Rhode Island, 115
Peabody Museum (Salem, Massachusetts), 93
Pelletier, David, 17
Pemaquid, Maine, 28, 34, 55
  settlement of, 45–50
Pemaquid Harbor, 48
Pemaquid Point, 26
Penniman, Captain Edward, House (Eastham, Massachusetts), 132
Penobscot Bay (Maine), 6, 20, 22, 23, 29, 86, 189
Penobscot Indians, 159
Penobscot River (Maine), 6, 126
Pepperell Manufacturing Company, 119
Pequot Indians, 42, 159
Pilgrim Hall (Plymouth, Massachusetts), 142
Pilgrim Memorial Monument (Provincetown, Massachusetts), 8
Pilgrims, 30–35
Pirates, 66, 67, 87
Piscataqua basin (New Hampshire), 60, 123
Piscataqua settlements, 44
Pittston, Maine, 103
Pleasant Bay (Cape Cod, Massachusetts), 142
Plimouth Plantation (Massachusetts), 32, 34
Plunger (submarine), 134
Plymouth, Massachusetts, 6, 25, 60, 69, 112, 142
  setttlement of, 32–36

Androscoggin River

Augusta

Pittsto

Wisc

Bath

Brunswick

Casco Bay

OR ISI

Saco River

Portland

Saco

Cape Elizabeth

Old Orchard Beach

Biddeford

Piscataqua River

York

Great Bay

Portsmouth

ISLES OF SHOALS

Hampton

Salisbury

Newburyport

Lawrence

Ipswich

Rockport

Lowell

Essex

Gloucester

Beverly Farms

Salem

Massachusetts Bay

Marblehead

Cambridge

Nahant

Waltham

Boston

Nantasket

Weymouth

Minot's Ledge

Cohasset

Marshfield

Provincetown

CAPE COD

Plymouth

PLYMOUTH BAY

Truro

Wellfleet

NAT

SEA

Pawtucket

Dighton

CAPE COD CANAL

Eas

Hartford

Providence

Onset

Sandwich

Orle

Bristol

Fall River

Fairhaven

Bourne

Brewster

Barnstable

Middletown

Narragansett Bay

New Bedford

Falmouth

Chat

Portsmouth

Dartmouth

Buzzards Bay

Hyannis

MON ISLAND

Norwich

Kingston

ELIZABETH ISLANDS

Woods Hole

NANTUCKET SOUND

New London

Groton

Galilee

Newport

CUTTYHUNK ISLAND

Oak Bluffs

New Haven

Stony Creek

Old Saybrook

Old Lyme

Mystic

Point Judith

VINEYARD SOUND

Edgartown

Milford

Guilford

Westbrook

Watch Hill

Menemsha Pond

Nantucket

Bridgeport

Stonington

BLOCK ISLAND SOUND

MARTHA'S VINEYARD

Siasc

Westport

NANTUCKET ISLAN

Darien

LONG ISLAND SOUND

BLOCK ISLAND

Cos Cob

Stamford

Greenwich

New York

Connecticut River

d'ART STUDIO